CARSON

Carson

The Man Who Divided Ireland

Geoffrey Lewis

Hambledon and London

London and New York

Hambledon and London

102 Gloucester Avenue, London NW1 8HX

175 Fifth Avenue
New York, NY 10010
USA

First Published 2005

ISBN 1 85285 454 5

A description of this book is available from the
British Library and from the Library of Congress.

Typeset by Carnegie Publishing, Lancaster,
and printed in Great Britain by Cambridge University Press.

Distributed in the United States and Canada
exclusively by Palgrave Macmillan,
A division of St Martin's Press.

Contents

Illustrations

Text Illustrations

Illustration Acknowledgements

The author and publishers are grateful to the following for their kind permission to reproduce illustrations: the Estate of Sir Max Beerbohm, by permission of Berlin Associates, p. 158; the *Belfast Telegraph*, pl. 20; the Carson Family, pls 2–4, 6, 14 and 19; Getty Images, pl. 1; Tessa Hawkes, pls 10, 17, 18, 21 and 22; the House of Lords Record Office, pls 12 and 13; the Linen Hall Library, Belfast, pls 11, 15 and 25; the National Portrait Gallery, pls 8, 9, 23 and 24; and the Ulster Museum, Belfast, pl. 16.

Introduction

The difficulty with Irish history is to know where to begin. Whatever point is chosen, some antecedent outrage or disaster looms out of the past, demanding to be first understood. But the creation of the movement called Unionism was different. The exact moment of its birth can be identified. It was 8 April 1886. On that afternoon Mr Gladstone went down to the House to introduce his Government of Ireland Bill, known to history as the first Home Rule Bill. He was then seventy-six. Fortunately for posterity an eye-witness has left a picture of the Grand Old Man at that moment.

> He then looked an old man of wondrous energy and endurance. The once resonant voice had become husky and was not always distinctly heard; the oratory sank and rose with a sort of cadence, like the wind. Only those who heard him for the first time would be aware that he spoke with a decidedly provincial accent, derived, I believe from Lancashire. But what struck me and has continued to strike me ever since, is his impassioned gesture. When excited in speech, he swings [his arms] round with a sweep, as that of a scimitar, and yet the movement is both graceful and appropriate. The poetic and romantic passages in his speeches are extremely fine.[1]

After pondering long Gladstone had convinced himself that Ireland must have its own Parliament. Whether his decision was born of a humane desire to satisfy Irish aspirations, or out of tactical advantage, does not matter here. Whatever its origins, it broke his own Liberal Party in pieces and set in train a course of events whose violent impact is still being felt.

Edward Carson was then in his early thirties, a young barrister in Dublin just beginning to make his way with a wife and three small children. Gladstone's initiative permanently changed the direction of his life. 'I have never had the slightest doubt', he wrote to a friend within two years of his death, 'that it would have been impossible to have made any lasting settlement in Ireland after the G. O. M. had adopted the Home Rule policy ... In my long experience of the government of the country, I have always felt certain that the parties of disorder would in the long run come to the top.'[2]

It was to preserve the Union, and to fight against anarchy in his own country, that Edward Carson devoted his life. But for that he would never have entered public life. He would have stayed at the Bar. The shifts of politics, the undiscriminating appetite for office, the ultimate dishonesty of the trade were all abhorrent to him. But the imperative which kept him in politics in spite of all was the maintenance of the Union.

To Carson and those of like mind the Union meant the whole of Ireland as an integral part of the United Kingdom. The division of Ireland was in no one's mind. What was this Union for which Carson was ready to sacrifice everything? The Act of Union of 1801 had merged the Westminster and Dublin Parliaments into a single legislature for the United Kingdom of Britain and Ireland. Over time the reasons for maintaining it changed. The Younger Pitt had brought it in to fortify the state against the threat of revolution and Napoleonic aggression. Its immediate occasion was the Irish rebellion of 1798, which the French had actively supported. In the House of Commons Pitt described Ireland as 'the point in which that enemy thinks us the most assailable'.

The Union was opposed by many of the landed Anglo-Irish Protestants, who did not want change. They were against the transfer of power to London, and they did not like the methods employed by Pitt and his henchman Castlereagh of bribes of office and peerages. Colonel Napier, an Ulsterman, found it hard to decide on which side right lay; but he was sure about some of the unwanted effects which would follow from Union. 'The obsequious Unionists', he wrote in 1799, 'modestly insinuate that a Kingdom derives consequence from having its legislative powers transferred to another country and accumulates wealth from 130 of its richest subjects with their long sequel of Pimps and Parasites, transporting themselves to pursue the trade of Parliament in a distant capital.'[3]

On the other hand, many Roman Catholics hoped that the Union would bring about the conciliation and regeneration of Ireland. They looked forward to their emancipation. Since the end of the seventeenth century they had been under disabilities. They could not hold office in central or local government, and they could not sit in Parliament. But these humiliations were not removed by the Union. The Irish government continued to sit in Dublin Castle to remind people that the English Protestant was still Ascendant. The Catholics were disappointed and the Protestants came to see that the Union would fortify their position. It was not until 1829 that Daniel O'Connell rallied massive popular support and convinced London that Catholic emancipation must be granted. O'Connell wanted to go on and repeal the Union. Irish opinion became sharply polarised. The new Orange Order, rabidly sectarian and established to keep holy the memory of the Dutch Calvinist William III, who had established the supremacy in the British islands of the True Protestant Religion, vehemently supported the

Union. On the other side of the divide, Catholic Ireland lay powerless and resentful in spite of emancipation.

The potato famine of 1845–46 decimated the Irish people, leaving in its train terrible distress, with its accompaniment of agrarian violence. There was wholesale emigration to the United States and the Colonies. The population of eight million in 1841 was reduced by a quarter by hunger and emigration. For more than twenty years after the famine nothing was done to improve the life and fortune of the Irish peasant farmer. His landlord often lived in England and acted through an agent. The landlord could rack-rent and evict the tenant at will. While the poor farmers who remained in Ireland could do little that was lawful to help themselves, their emigrant kinsmen became wealthy and influential in the United States. After the end of the American Civil War in 1865, these American Irish formed the Fenian Movement, whose ruling principle was hatred of England and whose policy was Irish separatism. Their methods were criminal and their money and violence soon made themselves uncomfortably felt by the authorities.

Gladstone was the first English statesman to feel that for Ireland to be ruled indefinitely by an alien minority was an affront to the dignity and manhood of its people. His Land Act of 1870 was the first in a long series whose object was to achieve, little by little, fair rents and security of tenure for the Irish tenantry. But, when it came to Home Rule, his hand was forced. In 1880 the leadership of the Irish Party in the House of Commons passed to Charles Stewart Parnell. This strange figure was born into an Irish Protestant landowning family, but he pursued his objective of a separate Parliament for Ireland with a cold and indifferent hatred for Liberals and Tories alike. By inflexible discipline and the ruthless subversion of parliamentary procedures, he achieved a position with his eighty votes in which he could bring the business of Westminster government to a standstill. The Liberals and Conservatives had either to agree between themselves on a policy for Ireland, or one of them had to make peace with Parnell. Eventually Gladstone came to terms.

Gladstone's Bill proposed a separate Irish Parliament to sit in Dublin. The Irish Members who had sat in Westminster since the beginning of the century were to sit there no longer. The effect of the Bill was to repeal the Union of Britain and Ireland. But in doing so, it proposed only a modest transfer of power to Dublin. There was no question of Ireland leaving the Empire, or of its rejecting the ultimate authority of Westminster. Nonetheless, the Bill aroused fierce opposition. It failed to pass its second reading. An alliance of Conservatives and the new Liberal Unionists voted it down and quickly came to power under Lord Salisbury.

The Bill had aroused visceral fears in the Unionist mind. To give way to the call for Home Rule, Unionists felt, would be to set foot on a downward slope at the bottom of which lay complete independence. In Carson's words, there could be 'no permanent resting place between complete union and total separation'. If separated, Ireland would become a foreign, probably hostile, neighbour along Britain's western coast. In any case, Unionists believed that it was in Ireland's interests to remain within the United Kingdom. With good government and the transfer of land into the ownership of those who worked it, the demand for self-determination would, they hoped, fade away. But if it separated, Ireland would descend into the chaos which had threatened for centuries. In the last resort it was a choice between order and anarchy.

The defence of the Union was also a matter of imperial necessity. If Ireland were to have its own Parliament, a centrifugal force would be felt throughout the Empire. The dream of England as a great hub of trade and finance, tutor to the world in the art of government, would be undone. The country's unrivalled prestige would crumble. Ireland lay at the heart of the imperial structure. If the centre cracked, the rest must break into pieces.

Then there was Ulster. In the counties of the north east, but nowhere else in Ireland, Protestants, mainly Presbyterians, were in a majority. To be forced under the Popish authority of a Dublin government was a nightmare that haunted them. It was far from being a matter of religious belief only. To the Protestant Ulsterman Irish nationalism was a dark conspiracy. Its objects were murder and outrage. It was maintained by ignorance and fuelled by the idolatrous superstition of its priesthood. These gothic images did not vanish in the light of morning. Safety for the Protestants of the north could lie only in remaining part of the United Kingdom, and from the time of Gladstone's Bill they were prepared to fight for it.

Ulster was the 'Orange Card' which Gladstone could not trump, and which Lord Randolph Churchill played when he went to Belfast in 1886. 'Ulster will fight,' he said, 'and Ulster will be right.' His object was simply to dish Home Rule – and Gladstone with it. Carson was later to play the card for all it was worth, trying to save the Union. But neither Gladstone nor Parnell took Ulster seriously. They did not reckon with its blocking power. Gladstone's agreement with Parnell that the new Ireland should include Protestant Ulster flew in the face of racial, religious and political facts. Neither accepted that there were two nations in Ireland, differing from each other not only in religion but in almost every other conceivable way. Neither foresaw that Ulster was the battleground of the future into which all the odium of centuries would spill its poison.

It was as if Ulster had been foreordained for Edward Carson. A Dubliner and a member of the Church of Ireland himself, the Presbyterians of the north were the people with whom he came to feel most akin and whose qualities he came most to admire. Their cause became his cause. It was in Ulster that all his hopes and fears, and ultimate failure, were to be.

There are many people I have to thank for help and encouragement. I have been fortunate to have the friendly cooperation of members of the Carson family. Heather Carson, Edward Carson's daughter-in-law, and her son, Rory, have given their help without stint and most hospitably. They have made available the private correspondence between Edward Carson and Ruby Frewen, who became his second wife, which more than any other source throws light on his private life. Mrs Sally Greenwell, Edward Carson's granddaughter, and Mrs Paddy West, his sister Bella's granddaughter, have also given generous help.

My publishers, Tony Morris and Martin Sheppard, have both been infectiously enthusiastic throughout. The archivists at the Public Record Offices in Belfast and London, the House of Lords Record Office, the British Library, the Bodleian Library and the Churchill Archives Centre were consistently resourceful and courteous; but I must mention particularly the staff of the Public Record Office in Belfast who made my research easier in countless ways, often beyond the call of duty.

I also thank Maureen Dibble for her help in researching sources in Belfast, and Tessa Hawkes for providing pictures of the Ulster Crisis from her family home in Limavady; Bruce Batten of BBC Northern Ireland; and Tony Stewart, the doyen of Ulster historians, for his unfailing generosity and encouragement to me to venture into the dangerous shoals of Irish history. His books have been an inspiration and *The Narrow Ground* is a source that I have returned to again and again.

Dublin

Edward Henry Carson was born on 9 February 1854 in Dublin. His first home was at 4 Harcourt Street on the corner of St Stephen's Green, which was then a private garden. The house is no longer there, having been replaced by a glass and steel protuberance serving as a hotel lobby and stuck like a thumb on the end of the elegant Georgian street.

His father, also Edward Henry, was an architect and civil engineer. The local professional journal described him as having enjoyed a 'tolerably fair practice', but it need not have been so faint in its praise.[1] The elder Carson designed a long line of public buildings and substantial houses and eventually became Vice-President of the Royal Institute of Irish Architects. He was an enterprising businessman. While engaged in developments in the southern suburbs of the city, he built a sewer along the length of the Marlborough Road at his own expense. He was an unsuccessful candidate for the post of Dublin City Architect, but became a member of the city corporation in 1877, sitting as a 'Liberal Conservative', a label designed to confuse. In his obituary notice in 1881, the *Irish Builder* reported, perhaps pointedly, that the funeral was attended by personal friends and family, 'but alas! The architectural and engineering professions were almost entirely unrepresented'.

The story that the Carsons were descended from an Italian family of architects and designers called 'Carsoni', although colourful, is fiction.[2] The elder Carson was in fact the second of three sons of William Carson of Dumfriesshire, a chip and straw hat merchant who set up business in Dublin. He is supposed to have specialised in Leghorn or Tuscany hats (made of a fine straw plait) which were then popular for children.[3] Carson is in any case a well known Scots-Ulster name. William Carson's other two sons never married and became clergymen of the Church of Ireland. Edward Carson the elder is said to have remained a Presbyterian all his life, a circumstance that may have had significance for his son's upbringing. Nevertheless, his son Edward, the subject of this book, was baptised at five weeks in the Anglican church of St Peter's, Aungier Street, which his father had remodelled architecturally.

The architect had an eye for the main chance. He married well. His bride was Isabella Lambert of Castle Lambert, County Galway. He went there to redesign a stable block and successfully courted the daughter of the house. Her family was directly descended from John Lambert, one of Cromwell's Major-Generals. They were well-founded members of the Anglo-Irish Ascendancy, hunting their own pack and living high. The younger Edward Carson loved going to the far west to stay with them in his school and university holidays, riding, going to the fairs in the district, playing hurling with the local team. Eventually, as could have been predicted, he was captivated by the high spirits and fearless riding of Katie Lambert, one of his cousins, and fell in love with her. His home life would have been very different if he had married her, but she became the wife of a soldier instead and died young in childbirth.

The 'middle nation' of the Anglo-Irish, of whom the Lamberts were good examples, were aware of their social and intellectual attainments, which could rise on occasion to brilliance and gave them a sense of superiority. They lived in the great houses and were landowners on a large scale. There was a gulf between them and their peasant tenants. Their culture was English and they depended on the English remaining in Dublin Castle. The Castle was the apex of the social pyramid and the seat of government, which was colonial in all but name. Although the Anglo-Irish were long established in Ireland, they could never feel secure, for they were alien occupiers and in the long run doomed. Carson was once taunted with this insecurity by an opponent: 'He has no country – he has a caste.'[4]

Isabella Lambert was the seventh daughter of Peter Lambert and Eleanor Seymour of Ballymore Castle, member of another Ascendancy family. Her picture shows a substantial and confident figure. The bust and bustle are what you notice first, then an expression which could move easily into disdain. She bore the architect six children. Edward was the second and reputed to be his father's favourite. His elder brother, William, became a solicitor, but his passion for horses and hunting distracted him from his practice. His younger brother, Walter, became a medical officer in the army. The eldest girl, Ellen, married a soldier who became a Resident Magistrate. The sister to whom Edward was closest, Isabella, married a Mr St George Robinson, Crown Solicitor in Sligo. It is tempting to believe that it was from the Lamberts that Edward Carson acquired his social poise, and from his father his affinity with Presbyterianism. According to Edward Marjoribanks, his first biographer, he was initiated into the Orange Order at the age of nineteen,[5] but this cannot now be verified.

It was a united family and a happy childhood, but it passed under the shadow of the Famine in which a million had died only a few years before Edward Carson was born. The magnificent public buildings of the capital presided over a city whose sprawling slums were filled with poor. How much of this entered the consciousness of the rising middle-class family in Harcourt Street?

The architectural practice was carried on at home. The elder Carson had his office in a room at the back for himself, his pupils and his clerks. Edward was frequently there and seemed to have a natural gift for architectural drawing, but his father had other ideas for him. 'I was *put* to the Bar', said his son. No. 4 soon became too small for all this and the growing family. They moved up the street to the more substantial no. 25. This house still stands in its high, flat-fronted Georgian terrace, one of the many which give Dublin its grandeur and its sense of space.

In another fine house at the corner of Merrion Square lived Sir William Wilde, the internationally famous eye and ear surgeon, medical historian and archaeologist. His wife Jane, an iconoclastic poet much given to para-dox, affected the name Speranza. Their younger son, Oscar Fingal O'Flahertie Wills Wilde ('Is not that grand, misty and Ossianic?' asked Sper-anza of a friend), inherited his wit from his mother and his freebooting style from his father, who, in Regency manner, had three illegitimate children to balance the three born in lawful wedlock. Both Sir William and his wife were Irish Nationalists. Oscar Wilde was born a few months later than Edward Carson. They are said to have played on the shore together as small boys.[6] But they were poles apart.

The young Edward went to school first at a little primary school in Harcourt Street, and then to board at Arlington House, Portarlington, in Queen's County. The school took sons of Protestant professional gentle-men, was presided over by the Rev. Dr F. H. Wall, and had a good reputation. Edward was not a scholar but Dr Wall took to him, and they went together on walking holidays to Wales and Switzerland. He made some lifelong friends at Arlington: William Ridgeway, who became Professor of Archaeology at Cambridge, and James Shannon, who was later to have an outstanding but short-lived career at the Bar.

Edward took the entrance examination for Trinity College in 1871 and was given a place to read Classics. Dr Wall wanted him to sit for a scholarship. He was awarded an exhibition. But after five years' toil at the civilisations of Greece and Rome, he emerged with an ordinary pass degree. He was to all appearances a plodder and showed little sign of real promise. Around him were many who were more able by far: Shannon and Ridgeway from his schooldays, Charles O'Connor who was to become Master of the Rolls on the Irish bench, James Campbell, later the first President of the Senate of the Irish Free State; Oscar Wilde, too, already an aesthete of meteoric and man-nered brilliance. Wilde despised most of his contemporaries and their obsession with sport. 'If they had any souls', he said, 'they diverted them with coarse *amours* among barmaids and women of the streets.'[7]

None of these strictures applied to Carson but he and Wilde could have had nothing in common. Wilde later claimed that he and Carson were friends and used to walk about arm in arm. Carson, a serious-minded, fastidious young man, denied the friendship, saying that he disapproved of Wilde's 'flippant' approach to life. Neither he nor Wilde liked or respected the other. Carson liked Oscar's brother Willie – as clever as Oscar and a notorious womaniser – no better.

Edward Carson was happy among Trinity's graceful buildings in the heart of the city. Although open to Catholics, it was almost entirely Protestant. It was a stronghold of Unionism and when Carson first sat as one of its two Members at Westminster in 1892, he fitted its politics perfectly. He was happy too with the friendships of the years he was there. Most of these flowered in the College Historical Society, whose origins went back to Edmund Burke and whose membership was a thing of prestige. It was the oldest debating society in Ireland, and its members at one time or another had included Henry Grattan, Wolfe Tone, W. E. H. Lecky, and Isaac Butt, the Irish Nationalist leader who is credited with first coining the term 'Home Rule'. It was here that Carson first worked at public speaking, learning how to marshal his arguments logically, and to seek out the weaknesses in his opponent's position.

The minute books survive and the copperplate hands are as clear now as they were when the records were first written.[8] They show that Edward Carson, William Ridgeway and Oscar Wilde all became members in December 1873. In the session before that (1872/3), the Auditor (the senior officer of the society with disciplinary powers over members and the other officers) was one Abraham Stoker. 'Bram', the future author of *Dracula*, was larger than life in every way. He was a giant of a man and a legendary athlete. His forceful rule as Auditor is evident from the minutes.

Carson was slow to find his feet and did not speak for two years after he became a member. But in the session for 1876/7 he was elected Librarian and in the following session he stood for Auditor. He was second in a three-cornered fight, the winner being Charles O'Connor, a strong candidate and the then Treasurer.

The debates were chaired not by the Auditor but by distinguished outsiders, Carson among them in later years, and were on historical or political topics. Some motions were debated again and again in successive sessions. Among these were 'That the social and political disabilities of women should be removed', 'That an hereditary chamber endowed with legislative powers is essential to the welfare of the nation', 'That Pitt's Irish policy was worthy of a wise and upright statesman', and 'That the French Revolution was more beneficial than injurious in its results'. Carson spoke in favour of all these. He spoke against the motion 'That the system of land tenure in Ireland needs reformation'.

His earlier biographers have suggested that Carson had liberal, even radical tendencies at this time of his life, and that the reports of debates in the Historical Society demonstrate this. The case hardly seems to be made out. It would be fairer to describe the evidence of the minute books as showing pragmatism, a quality which certainly marked his later career. Why would he speak in favour of retaining the oppressive Irish law of landlord and tenant? And Pitt's Irish policy was something of a curate's egg. The Union was neither liberal nor radical, but Pitt wanted to bring Catholic Emancipation with it by gradual degrees. It was not his fault that George III had stood in the way. Perhaps it is just as likely that the debates were exercises in public speaking as that they showed anything of the speakers' political tendencies.

There is no record that Oscar Wilde ever spoke in a debate in the Historical Society. He may have thought it demeaning to join in discussion with people who took themselves so seriously. In any case, after winning a succession of prizes, he left for Oxford without degree or regret. The redoubtable Rev. J. P. Mahaffy, Professor of Ancient History and Wilde's tutor, was not discountenanced. 'You're not quite clever enough for us here, Oscar. Better run up to Oxford.'[9] Edward Carson looked back differently at his time at Trinity: 'I have no more pleasant recollection in my life', he said just after his eightieth birthday, 'than my career in Trinity College, Dublin, and especially in the College Historical Society.'[10]

In Edward Carson's time the preparation of an Irish barrister for admission to the mysteries was more picturesque than rigorous. Book learning came a poor second to practical experience. The pupil followed his master about, in court and in conference, watching how he behaved, picking up tips and trying his hand at his master's written work. He came to accept the pomp and circumstance as natural, and to see that the companionship of his profession was more important than what divided barristers – even religion or politics. Not all barristers were then Protestant graduates of Trinity, although most were. Catholic Nationalists were entering in increasing numbers. Eight out of the sixteen judges in the High Court bench at the time of Carson's call were Catholics.[11] But for all its gradual opening to the other side of the politico-religious divide, the profession was resolutely single sex and it would have been unthinkable for a woman to have attempted to enter it.

There was a difference between the London and Dublin Bars. In London the tradition was to remain neutral in politics. You left your prejudices in the robing room before going into court. In Ireland law and politics were fused to a degree that would have been frowned on in London at any time. This was because so much of Irish legislation had an avowedly political purpose, especially in land law and criminal law. The changes in landlord and tenant law wrung from England reflected attempts at conciliating Ireland. The periodic Coercion Acts were the instruments by which the government handed out stiff doses of medicine to a recalcitrant subject people. It was expected by all that advocates would associate themselves with one side or the other. Carson became notably successful in his appearances for tenants after Gladstone's Irish Land Act of 1881 had brought a lot of business to the Bar. And many barristers like Tim Healy, Carson's frequent opponent, thought nothing of making outright political speeches in court. This agreed well with the Irish attitude to litigation as entertainment. So long as he had a good run in court, the litigant did not mind losing too much. As the journalist and writer James O'Connor said, 'Ireland, too, is full of people who would rather lose a case gaily – with the salt rubbed into the sore spots of an opponent's carcass – than win it soberly and sombrely'. Healy was not seldom briefed with the object of discomfiting the opposition, regarded as an end in itself. 'I thought I told you that T. M. Healy MP was my counsel', wrote one of his clients. 'I hope to pour plenty of boiling water into that nest of wasps in the Kildare St Club.'[12]

Carson never used the state of the country as an argument for securing a conviction, even at the height of the land war. In due course, however, Carson was anathematised as a 'Castle Hack': that was inevitable as he went up and down the country prosecuting under Balfour's Coercion Act of 1887. But Carson did not make political speeches in court and did not play to the political gallery.

After completing his arts degree course, Carson did a year at Trinity reading law and then continued his studies at the King's Inns, which although a plural noun is usually treated as singular. Like its counterparts in London, the Dublin Inn was responsible for the education of its student members, and was supposed to provide them with the social side of their professional life. But in Dublin the Inn did not provide much in the way of social life. This was because the headquarters of the Irish Bar for all purposes except teaching was not in the King's Inns but in the library of the Four Courts. Moreover, as if it were a mark of servitude of the Irish nation, Bar students had to join one of the London Inns and 'eat dinners' there. Servile or no, this had the advantage of bringing the student into touch with London legal life and with some of the judges and senior advocates there.

Carson made the journey by boat to eat his dinners in Middle Temple Hall four times. In 1877 he took his final examination at the King's Inns. He was proposed for his call by Serjeant Armstrong, a great advocate of the day and, as a serjeant-at-law, in rank one of the most senior barristers. The unfortunate Armstrong had earlier lost his reason while travelling by the packet boat from Dublin to Holyhead, and it was fortunate that when he proposed Carson for admission he was having a lucid interval. Carson had by then submitted his 'Memorial' to the tautologically named 'The Right Honorable and Honorable the Benchers of the Honorable Society of the King's Inns'. By this document he declared that he had not been, nor ever would become, while he practised at the Bar, an attorney or solicitor or parliamentary agent – presumably the sin of sins. The novitiates then gathered in the Lord Chancellor's court where the Lord Chancellor bowed to each in turn and asked the mystifying question, 'Do you move?' Each in turn would bow back and the ceremony was over.

Carson was admitted in the Easter Term of 1877. In a little over two years he was married and in another two years he had two children. In a life almost devoid of romance, at least until he met his second wife, it was a romantic episode. When he married he had almost no income and £50 in the bank. His father was appalled by his son's recklessness.

The impoverished young man had had to give up all thought of Katie Lambert, the cousin who had challenged his spirit during the Galway holidays. Her father would not hear of her marrying a barrister who was just starting and could not tell where the next fee was coming from. James Shannon was his best friend and they spent a lot of time together. During the summer vacation, when the courts had risen, the two often went to the sea near Dublin and hired a boat for an hour or two. One day, during the summer of 1879, he caught sight of a slim fair girl on the shore. He was attracted immediately and asked Shannon if he knew her. He did, and told Carson that she was Annette Kirwan, and that she lived with her widower father, a retired County Inspector in the Police. But at first he refused to introduce his friend. Eventually, under the threat that Carson would introduce himself if his friend would not oblige, he did so. Did Shannon think perhaps that it would be an unsuitable match? Nothing more is known about the incident, but in any case the two fell violently in love. They met as often as they could and by the end of the summer they were engaged. Carson was then twenty-five and living at home. His father had made it clear that he could not support him after he qualified as a barrister. Annette had no money to bring to the marriage. 'Who is she?', asked the elder Carson, 'I have never heard of her.' 'Well, that is quite likely', said his son. It was an inauspicious beginning. According to Carson's second wife, who must have had it from him, the elder Carson went round to see Mr Kirwan and 'words passed between them'.[13] The discontent father, who had not long to live, did not forgive his son for his improvidence. But the son was not deterred. When his mind was settled, nothing ever did deflect him.

The marriage took place on 19 December 1879 at Monkstown Parish Church and the bridegroom's former schoolmaster, the Rev. Frank Wall, officiated. His father did not attend. The couple spent their honeymoon over the Christmas holidays in London and ran through Carson's £50. Nevertheless, they were deliriously happy. Annette's adopted uncle, a retired Resident Magistrate, made room for them in his house in Herbert Place in Dublin. She was soon pregnant and they decided to take a chance and rent a small house in the same street. Within two years of marriage, they had two children, William Henry, known always as Harry, and Aileen. Work was beginning to trickle in until the trickle became a stream.

As a newly admitted barrister, Carson had no chambers in which to set himself up, so he went at once to the 'Four Courts', where the Bar congregated. It was a fine Georgian court house, unhappily destroyed in the Irish Civil War in 1922, which housed the four civil courts of Queen's Bench, Exchequer, Common Pleas and Chancery. The library in the Four Courts where the Bar worked, lived, moved and had its professional being had no counterpart in England.

The barristers sat, wigged, robed and packed in together like children in a poor school. They sat on benches at long tables or, if they were sufficiently senior, at a large round one in front of the fire, and they chattered incessantly. 'Library boys', some very old indeed, tottered about fetching and carrying the books that were needed by learned counsel. Anyone having business with a barrister, most likely a solicitor seeking an opinion for his client, gave the name of the barrister he wished to consult to a warrant officer type at the door, called 'the Crier', who then bellowed the name of the fortunate one. He and the solicitor would confer in one of the alcoves between the book stacks. If a barrister left the library, he gave the Crier a note of where he could be found. The library was a noisy place. The parade-ground tones of the Crier mingled with the hubbub of legal debate, gossip and scandal. It would take some time before a new barrister could learn to work against the din.[14] This was not the sepulchral silence of the libraries of the London Inns. It was Dublin where talk is all, and where the library was thought of as the best club in the city. When it closed in the evening, work continued in the barrister's home. His papers and books were carried there by a 'bag woman' and returned by her to the library in the morning. These were Dickensian ladies whose habits and asides on life and law ought to have been recorded. But they did not long survive Carson's entry into the profession. They were replaced soon by horse-drawn vans known as the 'legal express'.

Tim Healy's nephew, Maurice, thought that more solid work was done than would have been possible under the chambers system in London – which may be doubted; and that the habit of working close together in the library during the day and then over a bottle of wine in the evening at home 'assumed a more sociable aspect than could easily be found in the Temple' – a more convincing point.[15] Carson did the usual six months' pupillage and then some law tutoring to keep body and soul together. As there were no chambers and no clerks, there was no one to steer business in the way of the young hopefuls. But the newspaper accounts of trials were important advertisements for the Bar. In the days before radio and television, the great state trials, actions for breach of promise and other cases with an element of titillation provided the public with its entertainment. The progress of cases was followed avidly and discussed in the street and around dinner tables. The first chapter of Trollope's novel *The Kellys and the O'Kellys* describes the state trial of Daniel O'Connell and others for conspiracy and involvement in the Repeal (Home Rule) movement and shows how public excitement was whipped up by a big trial. Naturally barristers played to this gallery.

Carson did not begin to practise as soon as he was called to the Bar. His father had made clear to him that he could not support him further, so he went into partnership with a solicitor as law tutors – or 'grinders', as they were known. Eventually, he started his practice in 1878, and he naturally took whatever cases were offered to him. The fees were small, sometimes as low as one guinea (the equivalent now of about £50) on a brief to appear in court. One solicitor recalled that in the early eighties he had heard Carson make great jury speeches on briefs marked at two guineas. 'He is killing at the money!'[16] Although his father was unwilling or unable to help the young barrister financially through the difficult early years, he did introduce at least one case to his son, in which a builder was suing his customer and in which the elder Carson had acted as architect.[17]

Carson did not build his practice as quickly as some of his more brilliant contemporaries like James Shannon or James Campbell, whom he had known from the College Historical Society. His style as it developed was different from theirs and perhaps from most Irish advocates. Most observers rated Campbell, for instance, much above Carson in the early years. Campbell was flamboyant, hectoring, excitable, and a superb improviser. Trusting 'to his magnetic contact with the witness to guide his most daring excursions', he was a touch artist of the courts and had the panache which was bound to be admired in Ireland. Carson by contrast, said Maurice Healy, was quiet, sarcastic and imperturbable. He delivered his shafts without show and in the beguiling Dublin lilt which later became his trademark in London. He 'scored his points because he had read and re-read his brief'.[18] Here lay a difference between the forensic methods of England and Ireland. Here also lay a reason why Carson succeeded so quickly in London. The English view is that the secret of a successful cross-examination is absolute mastery of the case: no amount of theatre can take its place. The Irish would never accept that as an immutable rule.

Carson's method allowed him to be succinct. In one breach of promise case the disappointed lady brought an action to recover presents which her inconstant *fiancé* had seen fit to take away again. Carson represented her when he was quite green. In his cross-examination of the man, he asked simply, 'Why don't you give the lady back her presents?' The man began to bite his hat and could not answer. Eventually he said, appealing to the bench for protection, 'I think that's a very leading question'.[19]

In another, later case, he embarked on the difficult art of re-examination. This is the opportunity an advocate has to ask some concluding questions of his own witness after cross-examination by his opponent. If the cross-examination has been destructive it is a perilous business to try to repair the damage, and it might only serve to make matters worse to put the rattled witness through further questioning. The case was one in which a husband had been defamed by allegations that he was an adventurer who had been living on his wife's fortune. The cross-examination of the wife took her through the household finances in unrelenting and embarrassing detail. When his turn came to re-examine, Carson rose, slowly unwinding his long body, and turned his melancholy face towards the lady. In a weary tone, as if the whole affair were painful to him, he asked the lady whether she was in love with her husband. 'I was', she said. 'Is there any one of these things, about which my friend has asked you, which you regret?' 'No.' 'If the opportunity arose again today, would you be proud and happy to do it all again?' 'I would', she said with feeling. Those three questions, to all of which there could only be one answer, were decisive of the case.[20]

Carson was not above a bit of theatre. In common with most of his colleagues he liked to make use of the superlative and the exaggerated. In 1889 he prosecuted William O'Brien, the firebrand Nationalist MP and journalist (not for the first or last time), in Tralee. Tim Healy defended. Healy had defended O'Brien earlier at Mitchelstown in 1887. Before the trial at Mitchelstown, Healy, who was conducting a public campaign against the magistracy, had announced to the world that his client was to go before 'this brace of gibbering Castle hacks who would settle everything beforehand'.[21] Now at Tralee, in his biographer's phrase, he conjured a 'a comedy of provocation calculated to reduce the proceedings to politically charged farce'. His opening submission was that the presiding magistrate was not a proper person to hear the case since he had previously convicted a man for cheering the defendant. Carson responded that a bolder or more insulting application had never been heard in a court of justice. Expressions of that kind were later to be heard from him in the House of Commons. But he bore Healy no ill will and helped him as much as he could when Healy came to practise in London.[22]

The early years of Carson's marriage were golden. He had joined the Leinster circuit and was beginning to travel the south east to the assize towns of Kildare, Wicklow, Wexford, Carlow and Tipperary. His friend James Shannon had already begun to practise there and Carson enjoyed the companionship of the circuit mess. Shannon was the son of a solicitor and was soon busy. He made a faster start than Carson, but that did not interfere with the friendship. As at Trinity, it took Carson time before he showed his calibre. Shannon was an attractive character and enjoyed excellent health. Carson, by contrast, had to give up sport while at Trinity and was pursued all his life by poor health. An obsessive hypochondria preyed on his mind and made matters much worse. It was an irony that it was Shannon who, within a few years of his call, was suddenly struck down by diphtheria and died, without leaving the reputation that he deserved; and that Carson, with his only modest promise and vulnerable physique, lived on into his eighties and international fame.

Shannon's young wife begged Carson not to see her husband for fear of catching the disease. But Carson insisted. Inevitably he caught it. Annette nursed him with devotion and saw him through. A year or two later, Carson was found to have gall stones. An operation was then considered very risky but he undertook it, and again was ministered to by his wife and recovered quickly. These were years when the young couple were deeply in love and it was as much a satisfaction as it was natural for Annette to care for her husband. Life, however, was never as light-hearted as it was when James Shannon was alive. Nor was Carson's marriage to mellow into the sympathetic companionship which it promised. His career was shortly to be changed, and with it his life.

2

Home Rule

While the political world was being turned inside out by Gladstone's conversion to Home Rule, Edward Carson was preoccupied with building his legal practice. But he was far from indifferent to the fate of Ireland. His attachment to the Union was deeply coloured by his admiration for England. He was proud of being an Irishman but could hardly conceive of an Ireland separated from the mainland of the other island. He was a member of a group of Dublin Liberals who felt shocked and betrayed by Gladstone's desertion of the Union. In November 1885, in the approach to the general election, he attended a Liberal meeting and spoke. He was a Liberal voter, he said, who came to ask Liberals to vote Tory. But the efforts of the Unionists among the Liberals to prevent a Gladstone victory at the polls were in vain. With a block of eighty Irish votes at his disposal, the Grand Old Man was elected with a clear mandate to bring in Home Rule.

The violence of the Tory reaction knew no bounds. Britain had embarked on a great imperial adventure in Africa and the Far East. Gladstone was putting it all at hazard. He was a half-mad old man who had set in train forces which could dismember the Empire and threaten even the sanctity of private property. While the debates on the Bill were going on, Lord Salisbury, the Tory leader, made a speech in St James's Hall on the theme that the Irish were not ready for self-government. He allowed a racist tone to be heard. 'You would not confide free representative institutions to Hottentots, for instance', he remarked. Home Rulers did not wait to hear him say that he rated the Irish well above savages.[1]

In 1886, Carson knew next to nothing of the northern province of Ulster. Amidst the furore created by Gladstone's sudden conversion, few indeed realised its importance. Even then 'Ulster' was a term which was loosely used. It is now often employed to denote the focus of resistance to Home Rule or, more recently, as a synonym for Northern Ireland. But the ancient province was and is neither. It consists of nine counties: Antrim, Down, Londonderry (formerly Coleraine), Armagh, Fermanagh, Tyrone, Cavan, Monaghan and Donegal. Only in the first four, at most, was there a Protestant majority; and the last three were never part of the partitioned Northern Ireland.

Ulster has always been different. It was inaccessible and the people of the hilly and thickly wooded terrain held out longest against the early incursions of the English. There was a great Gaelic rebellion there at the end of the reign of Elizabeth I. It was not finally put down until after the Queen's death, when the rebel Earls, Hugh O'Neill of Tyrone, Rory O'Donnell of Tyrconnel and Cúconnacht Maguire of Fermanagh, were put to flight. Elizabeth's successor, James I, seized the Earls' lands and took the opportunity to put a permanent end to Ulster insurrection. He planted the province with English and Scots settlers of Protestant persuasion. The plantation, however, did not extend to the counties of Antrim, Down and Monaghan, where the Scots were already well settled by the beginning of the seventeenth century. Antrim and Down, looking across the narrow channel to Scotland, acquired a distinctive Scottish character, adhering to the Calvinism and the inflexible moral precepts of Knox. The Calvinist Presbyterians who settled in the north east were thrifty, hard-working, dourly resolute. They worshipped a different God from their Roman Catholic neighbours and were utterly unlike those Merry Andrews with whom, according to Liberal statesmen, they formed a single nation. The divide was a racial one.

The constitutional settlement at the end of the seventeenth century placed William III, a Dutch Calvinist, on the throne. Catholic James II, dethroned in England, continued to resist in Ireland until in 1690 he was defeated at the crossing of the River Boyne, near Drogheda, where the Jacobites unsuccessfully attempted to bar William's progress southwards towards Dublin. The memory of the battle is held dear by the Protestants of Ireland, and with good reason. For it completed Cromwell's work and secured for centuries afterwards that Ireland should be ruled from London by English Protestants, whose viceroy and agents in Ireland formed the Ascendancy. In England the settlement removed religion from politics once and for all. Never again would the government at Westminster be troubled by religious scruple. It was not so in Ireland. The division between Catholic and Protestant continued to haunt Irish life.

By 1911 the province of Ulster had a population of one and a quarter million, which had not changed much during the nineteenth century. It was about equally divided between Catholics and Protestants. The Protestants were concentrated in the counties of Antrim, Armagh, Down and Londonderry, and in the cities of Belfast and Londonderry. In Fermanagh and Tyrone the numbers of Protestants and Catholics were nearly equal. Cavan, Donegal and Monaghan had Catholic majorities. If there were to be a partition along a sectarian line it would have to be drawn around the north-east corner of the island. This enclave was as atypical in economic character as it was in religious belief. It had a prosperous farming community whose tenants, by Ulster Custom, had better security of tenure than elsewhere in Ireland. More importantly, it became a thriving industrial base. The foundation was the spinning, bleaching, weaving and finishing of linen cloth. These activities had been carried on in Ireland since at least the seventeenth century; but it was not until the second half of the nineteenth that linen in the north east boomed and became the biggest industrial enterprise in Ireland. The expansion of linen stimulated the manufacture of machinery in Belfast, first for linen spinning, then more generally, and then shipbuilding. By 1910 Harland and Wolff had in Belfast the largest shipyard in the world and employed 12,000 men.

Belfast was itself an anomaly. Economically, it was almost an extension of industrial England. In an agrarian island it was the only industrial city. Michael Collins, the Irish Nationalist insurrectionary, remarked that it had become merely an inferior Lancashire. 'Who would visit Belfast or Lisburn or Lurgan to see the Irish people at home?' he asked. 'That is the unhappy fate of the North East. It is neither Irish nor English.'[2] Like Lancashire, Belfast boomed in the nineteenth century. The 1891 census showed that for the first time it had overtaken Dublin and become the most populous city in Ireland. Its grimy red brick gave it the look of the black north of England, and it faced across the Irish Sea to the mainland, the source of its prosperity. It was natural that Protestant Belfast should identify its success with the Union. It was the capital of another Ireland.

But it was not simply a Protestant city. There was a large minority of Catholics, attracted into the city by its demand for labour, who were divided from the Protestants by street plan and by class. There were no middle-class Catholics. Below a layer of wealthy Protestant professionals and businessmen, the Catholics formed an urban proletariat living cheek by jowl with working-class Protestants. The sectarian line between the Falls and the neighbouring Shankill had been drawn by the time Gladstone introduced the first Home Rule Bill in 1886.

Gladstone gave little time to the problem of the Protestant majority in the north east of Ulster. All he said, when he introduced his Bill, was that he could not allow the Protestant minority in Ulster to rule the question at large for Ireland, but they should have their wishes considered to 'the utmost practicable extent'. There were, he said, a number of possible ways of dealing with the problem, and, if any proposals were laid on the table, they would be looked at favourably. But he put none forward.[3]

Such insouciance was surprising. Lord Randolph Churchill's celebrated descent on Belfast in February 1886 was warning enough. A huge, excited crowd assembled to hear him speak at the Ulster Hall. He urged the Loyalists to defend themselves and make England listen, for the Empire depended on their success. His flamboyant oratory became part of the northern mythology, and he coined the phrase which was to be its watchword: 'Ulster will fight and Ulster will be right.' But Lord Randolph's pyrotechnics did not impress the Tories, let alone the Home Rulers. He was not trusted anywhere, even in Belfast. And he returned the compliment by complaining to Lord Salisbury that 'those foul Ulster Tories have always ruined our party'.[4] The Liberals thought it all Orange bluster anyway.

In that they were mistaken, as they were to be again. It was not bluster. Lord Randolph had lit a fire, or more accurately, added fuel to one that was already alight. For the origins of northern resistance to Home Rule lay in the crisis of 1886. A quarter of a century later, Carson and his chief lieutenant, James Craig, organised an armed militia to protect Protestant Ulster against the threat of 'Rome Rule'. The foundations for what they did were laid down in 1886. The formation of the Ulster Unionist Party dates from then.[5] The Grand Orange Lodge of Ireland decided to support the embryo party. All Protestant clergy were made honorary members. The Rev. Dr Kane, a particularly militant member, called for an appeal to Germany if England turned a deaf ear.[6] Between the first and second readings of the Home Rule Bill, the *Belfast News-Letter* advocated armed resistance and carried advertisements for rifles and for drilling instructors. The paper called for an association of all Loyalists and a Solemn League and Covenant.[7] And when there were difficulties between the Conservatives and the Orange Institution, the Rev. Dr Hanna, another fighting man of the cloth, demanded a new organisation and a Moses or a Joshua to lead it.[8]

Drilling was going on in country districts. The Orange Order hoped to raise a body of volunteers 100,000 strong. At the beginning of May the *Pall Mall Gazette* argued in its editorial that it would be necessary for force to be used if Home Rule were to be made to stick in the north. The article was headed ominously 'Are We Ready to Bombard Belfast?' It followed this up on 31 May by giving details of an army of volunteers of 38,000, with a further reserve of 28,000. The numbers may have been wishful thinking, but there was certainly a substantial body of men ready to try conclusions with any government attempting to enforce Home Rule.

Anyone who studies these developments in Ulster can see how precisely they prefigure what happened a quarter of a century later. None was invented by Edward Carson or James Craig – not the well-drilled army of volunteers, nor the threat of force, nor the Solemn League and Covenant, nor the thought of an appeal to Germany if Britain proved a broken reed. But then, in the years of the Ulster Crisis of 1912–14, the movement had its Moses and its Joshua.

The crisis of 1886 was soon over. Gladstone's Bill was killed by Joseph

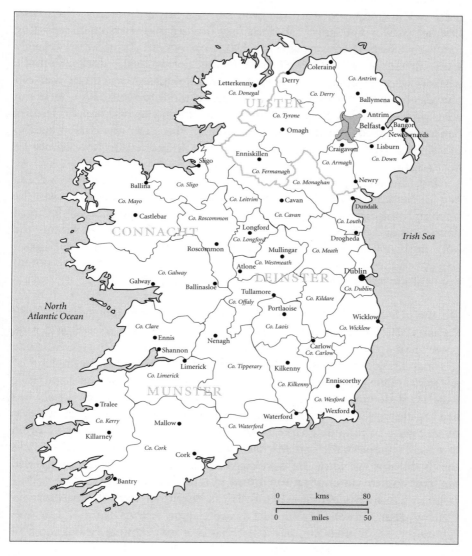

Ireland

Chamberlain's stab and the defection of the other Liberal Unionists when
the vote on second reading on 8 June was lost by thirty votes. Ninety Liberals voted against their leader and joined in uneasy alliance with the Tories.
The old Liberal Party was permanently riven. Dublin remained quiet and
there was nothing to disturb the even tenor of Edward Carson's home life.
But Belfast was not quiet. Inflammatory oratory and newspaper reporting
had their effect. There was also much unemployment and distress. An ugly
sectarian temper rose. On 5 June there was rioting in the docks. Catholic
workers were set upon by their Protestant colleagues. A seventeen-year-old
boy was forced into the sea and drowned. In the following days a mob ran
wild around Shankill Road and Sandy Row, killing several people. Disturbances continued into the summer, although the crisis was over. This too
presaged a dark future. The names of Shankill and Sandy Row would be
heard again.

Gladstone had tried to bring about a revolution in Ireland and in so doing
had opened Pandora's box. One of the spirits which flew out was the
uncompromising militancy of Ulster, which was to prove one of the most
dangerous and difficult for any statesman to deal with. As in the legend, the
only spirit remaining in the box was hope. Among other unintended consequences, the old prophet had brought about the birth of a new and potent
political movement in Ulster.

On the defeat of his Home Rule Bill Mr Gladstone immediately dissolved
Parliament. The new Unionist alliance won the ensuing election and took
power under the Marquess of Salisbury. The new Prime Minister's attitude
to Ireland was that it was an affliction or punishment visited on England by
an inscrutable providence. His policy was not to try any new initiative
('incessant doctoring and meddling' was his description of new ideas) but
to keep things simple: what this most intractable of problems required was
twenty years of resolute government. Lord Londonderry was sent to Dublin
as Lord Lieutenant with Sir Michael Hicks Beach as Chief Secretary. Hicks
Beach did not last long. He developed an eye condition which threatened
his sight and in March 1887 was forced to retire. He was replaced by Arthur
Balfour, Salisbury's nephew. Before Hicks Beach left Ireland, his Attorney-
General, John Gibson, appointed Edward Carson Crown Counsel. Carson's
reputation as an advocate, particularly as a cross-examiner, was known to
the Castle, and he was now entrusted with much of the burden of restoring
order and respect for the law. There was a mountain to climb. Agrarian
crime was the worst problem. The Irish felt profoundly that the land should
belong to those who worked it and lived on it, and that the landlords, many
of whom were remote, contributed nothing except the title that birth had

conferred. Parnell and his lieutenants were encouraging tenants to refuse to pay rent, and to ostracise those who did or those who were willing to take the place of evicted tenants. War was declared against landlordism. Parnell accepted the Presidency of the Land League, the focal point of the campaign. William O'Brien, the proprietor of the radical newspaper, *United Ireland*, published a 'Plan of Campaign'. Under the plan, tenants would offer their landlords what they considered a fair rent. On its being refused, the tenants would pay the fair rent into a fund to help their fellow-tenants who were evicted. These tactics were backed up by boycott, arson and brutal, sometimes senseless, murder. It was only five years since an earlier Chief Secretary, Lord Frederick Cavendish, whose wife was Gladstone's niece, and his Under-Secretary had been murdered while walking in Phoenix Park.

The new Lord Lieutenant and his wife proved to be influential figures in Edward Carson's life; the new Chief Secretary changed its direction permanently. Charles Vane-Tempest-Stewart, the sixth Marquess of Londonderry, was thirty-three when he became Viceroy of Ireland. His family had been in County Down since the plantation of Ulster at the beginning of the seventeenth century. They had been political magnates in the province since the eighteenth. The first Marquess was Viscount Castlereagh, who was chiefly responsible for steering the Act of Union through the Irish Parliament, and was later Foreign Secretary. The family typified the Ascendancy in Ulster. Unlike their peers in the south and west, they stood up to be counted when the crisis came and the Union was in danger. They led the resistance to Home Rule and gave it social respectability, if not political credibility.

Although they were much of an age, the relationship between the sixth Marquess and Carson was that of patron and protégé. That relationship was then common enough, as it had been throughout the nineteenth century. Gladstone, for example, had had for patron the Duke of Newcastle, who, when Gladstone was only twenty-two, found a constituency for him and paid half his election expenses.[9] Londonderry and his wife helped Carson steadily in his career in countless ways, not least socially. By their patronage of Carson, the Londonderrys recruited a forceful prosecutor to serve the interests of the Tory government which had placed them in Dublin Castle. As events unfolded, their protégé demonstrated a passion and an ability which made him the leader of the resistance to Home Rule in the north, where the Londonderrys' interests lay. The friendly relationship turned out to be extraordinarily fruitful to both sides.

Londonderry was well adapted to the ceremonial parts of his viceregal job. He had a strong sense of duty. He shared the family addiction to racing and was described by *Vanity Fair* as 'socially a good fellow', 'a very fine host who "does" his guests royally'.[10] His rather mournful expression hid a modest and generous spirit. He was to give unvarying loyalty to Carson, a man who at first was his official subordinate. Londonderry was a friendly and popular man, with none of his wife's *hauteur*.

His wife, Lady Theresa Chetwynd Talbot, usually called Nellie, was twice the man her husband was. She was ambitious and had a masculine mind. She raced, hunted and sailed single-handed. She interested herself in politics and power and sought to intervene – although with what effect is debatable. There are many descriptions of this remarkable woman. When she died in 1919 Colonel Repington wrote that she was a *grande dame* of a period which was passing: 'one of the most striking and dominating feminine personalities of our time. She was unsurpassed as a hostess, clear-headed, witty, and large-hearted, with unrivalled experience of men and things social and political ...'[11] Her friend Lady Fingall called her the staunchest of friends, adding that 'she was deeply interested in the love affairs of her friends and very disappointed if they did not take advantage of the opportunities she put in their way. She used to say of herself: "I am a pirate. All is fair in love and war". And woe betide anyone who crossed her in either of these.'

The Lord Lieutenant's daily round was one of considerable state. He lived with his family at the Castle during the Season, which began after Christmas and ended with a ball on St Patrick's Night when debutantes were presented to him and he kissed each in turn on both cheeks. For the rest of the year he and his family lived in a handsome house in Phoenix Park. There were constant receptions and dances. The Londonderrys were in their element. According to E. F. Benson in *As We Were*, Theresa Londonderry enjoyed standing at the head of the stairs while a big party was in progress 'with the "family fender", as she called that nice diamond crown gleaming on her most comely head, and hugging the fact that this was her house'.[12]

The Carsons were soon invited to a reception. It was the beginning of a lifelong friendship between Edward Carson and both Londonderrys. His friendship with Theresa Londonderry was of a type which could hardly develop today. Although he was two years the older, he became her protégé and she his confidante. She did everything she could, and it was much, to further his career. He became an *habitué* first at the viceregal homes, then later at Londonderry House, the foremost Tory *salon* in London, and the other great houses of the Londonderry family, Mount Stewart on Strangford Lough near Belfast and Wynyard Park in County Durham. Theresa Londonderry and Edward Carson kept up a regular correspondence. It is a thousand pities that, with very few exceptions, only his letters to her survive. This was a friendship between pirates, she by her own admission, he by the description given him in 1916 by the American Ambassador to London as 'that Ulster Pirate'. Because it was a blameless friendship between man and woman, without sexual charge or even undertone, Carson's friendship with the Marquess was untrammelled. Edward Carson found that he could move easily in these elevated regions. But, unfortunately, Annette Carson was a casualty. She was not comfortable in the Castle or the other great houses. Nor could she be at her ease with Lady Londonderry, who did not number mercy among her virtues. It was inevitable that Annette should feel pangs of jealousy and fear.

Arthur Balfour arrived in Dublin to take up his duties as Chief Secretary at the beginning of March 1887. His reception from the Nationalists varied from the incredulous to the derisive. *Freeman's Journal* laughed aloud. 'This young gentleman has three qualifications for the post', its editorial ran on 7 March. 'He is the nephew of Lord Salisbury; he has no reputation for statesmanship to injure; and he knows nothing of Ireland.' On the same day the paper's London correspondent described in self-indulgent prose how the new chief executive of the country was wont to lie along the Treasury Bench in an attitude of muscular collapse. 'It seems like breaking a butterfly to extend Mr Balfour on the rack of Irish politics. He is an elegant, fragile creature, a prey to aristocratic languor.' The Nationalist press and its readership enjoyed themselves, but Lord Salisbury knew what he was doing. Arthur Balfour was to become the ablest and toughest Irish proconsul of modern times. 'Niminy Piminy' would soon become 'Bloody Balfour'.

Balfour's first job was to get the new Crimes Bill on the statute book. The Bill had the Prime Minister's approval. Salisbury wrote to his nephew on 19 March 1887: 'A very good Bill – if men's minds were in a temper to take good Bills'.[13] The Bill would empower the Lord Lieutenant to 'proclaim' a district to bring it under the new powers, one of which was to move a jury trial to another part of the country to be tried by a 'special jury' – that is, one with a convenient property qualification. Any association which was considered 'dangerous' could also be 'proclaimed' and suppressed. Offences such as conspiracy, intimidation and participation in riots and unlawful assemblies could be tried by two Resident Magistrates without a jury. (This last was the tribunal derided by Tim Healy as a pair of gibbering Castle hacks who fixed everything up beforehand.) The new law was a powerful tool. As it made its way through Parliament, it was subjected to every filibustering tactic known to those experts in obstruction, Parnell and his troops. It had to be guillotined twice and passed into law in July.

It was not enough, however, to have the law in place. It would have to be enforced. Balfour would need resolute lawyers for this. Amidst the complacency and feebleness of the Castle officials, the worst of all was in the Law Room. 'It is borne in on me', Salisbury wrote to his nephew, 'as I suppose it is on most people – that you have the stupidest lot of lawyers in Ireland any government was ever cursed with'.[14] The Crown lawyers did not like risk and balked at important prosecutions. A notable exception, however, was Peter O'Brien, who was appointed Solicitor-General in 1887 and Attorney-General in the following year. He was a forceful character who acquired a reputation for securing 'safe' juries and so earned the sobriquet of 'Peter the Packer'. O'Brien was a Roman Catholic and was later a distinguished chief justice. In Balfour's view, the judges were cowardly and corrupt. Whenever John Dillon, William O'Brien or other prominent Nationalists appealed against sentence the judges granted bail, knowing perfectly well that the offences would be repeated in short order.[15]

There were difficulties too about prosecuting the Nationalist press and moving against the priesthood. Balfour was advised by his Under-Secretary, Sir Joseph Ridgeway, that he had collected evidence against seditious Catholic priests, also that a Protestant parson had made a very violent speech in County Clare. Ridgeway considered that it would be politic to prosecute parson and priest simultaneously.[16] The symmetry appealed to Balfour. The more so as the problems of prosecuting the priest were serious. He was a ubiquitous figure (in fact and fiction) who did not draw a line between matters spiritual and temporal. His knowledge of his flock and his influence over it could hardly be exaggerated. Yet his prosecution raised again the spectre of state-sponsored religious persecution.

This depressing horizon was changed dramatically by Carson and by the spark struck at Mitchelstown. Carson was appointed Counsel to the Attorney-General in 1887. He was then thirty-three and he rapidly became the outstanding government prosecutor and thoroughly earned the sobriquet 'Coercion Carson'. It was the incident at Mitchelstown that convinced Balfour that in Carson he had the strong man he needed.

On 9 September 1887, William O'Brien and John Mandeville were charged with making inflammatory speeches. Both were Nationalist MPs. O'Brien was an extraordinary character: a political organiser and mob orator, agitator, writer and proprietor and editor of *United Ireland*, a militant journal given to garish prose and cartoons which could only have been conceived in Ireland. In one issue it described the police, the bailiffs, and all who did the Chief Secretary's bidding as having 'lusted for slaughter with a eunuchized imagination'.[17]

Carson prosecuted the case, the first prosecution under the new Crimes Act. A large crowd gathered in the square at Mitchelstown, County Cork, for a meeting called by the Land League, and to see one of the most celebrated Nationalists challenge the Act. Many were armed with heavy blackthorns and some were mounted. Although O'Brien failed to appear, other MPs, who included John Dillon and the radical Henry Labouchere, joined the crowd. All his life Labouchere had been a rebel against authority and orthodoxy. He had many friends among the Irish Nationalists and was in sympathy with the Home Rule movement. Carson applied for and was granted a warrant for O'Brien's arrest. The proceedings were then adjourned. He came out of court into the square. The mood of the crowd was sullen. Carson walked through them, showing no fear. He was asked whether a warrant had been issued and answered yes. There was still no jeering or disturbance. He then walked up to the castle above the town and so did not see the violence in the square which followed.

When the speeches began the magistrate, who was present in the square, ordered a path to be cleared through the crowd so that a police reporter could take a note of what was being said. The fragile temper of the armed mob erupted. They refused to make way, cursing and attacking the police with their clubs. The police were hugely outnumbered and withdrew to their barracks. Confusion and panic followed, the police opened fire on the advancing mob, killing two and wounding several others. The incident acquired instant notoriety. Labouchere, who with Dillon had done nothing to damp down the anger of the mob but rather incited them, accused the police of acting like wild beasts; and Gladstone made 'Remember Mitchelstown!' a rallying cry in the Land War.

Carson saw a man lying dead outside the police barracks and observed that the police drawn up across the square, although calm, 'presented a very battered appearance'. 'The conduct of the "Members" ', he reported to the Attorney-General the next day, 'was very bad, they kept walking up to everybody engaged with the police asking for their names and their rank and attempting to interfere.' He was given a good account of the actual disturbance, which he did not see himself, by the carman who drove him to Mitchelstown. It showed how ready for violence the mob was. The carman told Carson that about 150 'mounted peasantry' rode down on the police and trampled them underfoot. 'I am informed by some of the police', wrote Carson, 'that the day before the riots Leahy [presumably a policeman] who had been so much injured when ordering goods in Mitchelstown said he would call for them next day and was told, well you will get them "if you are alive", and as he was specially set upon it looks as if he was marked.'[18]

Carson thought that the affair had been badly muddled, and that the behaviour of the Irish Nationalist and Liberal politicians who had stoked up the fire and condoned it afterwards was inexcusable. The police had failed to pass their first test under the new Act, but Balfour refused to accept any blame on their part. He continued to back them in the subsequent enquiry, as did Carson when he gave evidence to the enquiry. But, as Carson told Balfour's niece and biographer, Blanche Dugdale, many years afterwards: 'It

was Mitchelstown that made us certain we had a man at last ... Balfour
never admitted anything. He simply backed his own people up.'

The warrants for the arrest of O'Brien and Mandeville were quickly exe-
cuted and the two MPs were incarcerated in Cork gaol. They stood their trial
at Mitchelstown two weeks later in an atmosphere of high theatre. Cheering
crowds lined the road leading to the courthouse and girls presented bou-
quets to the accused. O'Brien, who had not seen Carson before, described
him as a 'liverish young man with the complexion of one fed on vinegar and
with features as inexpressive as a jagged hatchet'. After a highly coloured
trial during which Carson and the defence counsel, Tim Harrington, also a
Nationalist MP and later Lord Mayor of Dublin, traded personal insults, the
defendants were convicted and sentenced to three months' imprisonment.[19]

Carson also prosecuted the traveller, politician and poet Wilfrid Scawen
Blunt. 'I was delighted to see you had run Wilfrid Blunt in', wrote Lord
Salisbury to Arthur Balfour.[20] It was no wonder that Salisbury enjoyed
Blunt's discomfiture, for Blunt considered Empire to be synonymous with
exploitation, and he warmly espoused the cause of Home Rule. In October
1887 he went to County Galway to hold a public meeting and exhort the
tenants of Lord Clanricarde, a notably vicious landlord, to resist eviction,
and to promote the Plan of Campaign. He was charged under the Crimes
Act, convicted and sentenced to two weeks' imprisonment. In his recollec-
tions of the trial, Blunt wrote: 'The case against me was conducted by
Atkinson and Carson, two of the Castle bloodhounds, who for high pay did
the evil agrarian work in those days for the government ... It was a gloomy
role they played, especially Carson's, and I used to feel almost pity for the
man ...'[21] Carson would not have wanted Blunt's pity. He was making a
name for himself in these prosecutions. His successes were well known to
Balfour, who told his niece, Blanche Dugdale:

> I made Carson in a way. I made Carson and Carson made me. I've told you how
> no one had courage. Everybody right up to the top was trembling ... Carson had
> nerve however. I sent him all over the place, prosecuting, getting convictions. We
> worked together.[22]

Carson spent three years engaged on this work. The opposition was turbulent. At any moment a case might erupt into violence. He went about in
danger of his life. But the experience opened a window on the wider world.
'I was only a provincial country lawyer', he said, 'and, till I saw Arthur Balfour, I had never guessed that such an animal could exist.'[23] The association
grew into friendship, and Balfour made Carson understand that he might
have ambitions which, for the good of himself and his country, lay beyond
the Irish county court bench, even beyond Ireland.

3

London

When Arthur Balfour first came to Dublin in March 1887 few men gave him credit for strength of any sort. They were deceived by his style of the gifted amateur. Now that he had proved that he could fight fire with fire, they were deceived again. 'Bloody Balfour' was not a Gauleiter. His policy was to conciliate Ireland, but not until order was restored. He did not conciliate in order to win favour with the Nationalists. It was not opportunism but policy. It was futile, he thought, to try to govern by alternate kicks and ha'pence. He did, however, believe that it would be possible to kill Home Rule by kindness. If order were restored and life became tolerable – or better – for the tenant farmers, the nonsense that was Irish Nationalism would evaporate.

Balfour's views on Irish Nationalism were typical of Unionist attitudes. They were certainly shared by Edward Carson while he was enforcing Balfour's coercion law. The Unionist denied that Ireland had a separate national heritage. The reasons for discontent were old agrarian wrongs, inflicted by England, and the sectarian differences between Catholic and Protestant, which also reflected social differences. These had allowed Irish aspirations to take on an anti-British colour. The tint could be removed by careful improvement of the tenant farmer's situation and by the relief of destitution. But if it were allowed to remain it might lead to complete separation from England. As for Gladstonian Home Rule, this was, in Balfour's own phrase, a 'rotten hybrid' which could not provide a complete answer to the Irish question. As Carson said, there was no resting place between Union and Irish independence. It was either one thing or the other. The Unionist had that master of paradox, George Bernard Shaw, on his side when he wrote in the preface to *John Bull's Other Island*: 'There is indeed no greater curse to a nation than a nationalist movement, which is only the symptom of a suppressed natural function.'

Balfour's successive land reforms of 1887, 1888 and 1891 were concerned to give security of tenure to tenants through fair rents, and to make it easier for tenants to buy their holdings with government help. By the last of these Acts Balfour tackled the problem of regenerating depressed areas. In the autumn of 1890 the Chief Secretary went to the west to see for himself the heart-breaking conditions in Donegal and Connemara. He took with him George Wyndham, an ambitious and visionary Tory reformer, who was later to carry the policy of conciliation to its furthest point. Wyndham described the scene to a poet friend: 'a maze of rocks and walls; a lace-work of sea indentations, islets and promontories. The sea on one hand, the bog and mountain on the other and between a fringe on which humanity is huddled to exist by *seaweed* ... the place is a beautiful, stagnant desolation'.[1]

By 1889 it appeared that coercion had done its work. Ireland was quieter. Even the Pope had been persuaded to condemn the Plan of Campaign, boycotting and other activities which interfered with the sanctity of contract.[2] Balfour had earlier been providing the Vatican, through the Duke of Norfolk, with ammunition about seditious priests.[3]

There is no surviving correspondence to show what Carson thought privately about Balfour's attempts to improve the lot of the peasant farmers, but there is nothing to show that he was against the policy. His feeling that the continuing process of strengthening the position of tenants at the expense of landlords had gone too far was not to break surface until 1896, and then there were other factors at work to affect his mind. Up to 1889, he was concerned with enforcing the law. His saturnine face, sarcastic destruction of hostile witnesses and utter determination had become the very personification of coercion. Ireland having become quieter by the summer of that year, however, there was less court work needed to enforce the Crimes Act. He ceased to be a prosecutor for the Crown and 'took silk' – that is he became Queen's Counsel in Ireland – the youngest in the country at thirty-five. According to the ancient forms, he could now sit in the front row in court and handle the more serious cases himself, civil as well as criminal.

It could only have been a relief to Annette. Her husband would no longer be in constant danger and could spend more time at home with their children, Harry, born in 1880, Aileen in 1881 and Gladys in 1885. Another boy, Walter, followed in 1890. They now lived in comfort in Merrion Square, and had a seaside house at Dalkey as well, where they spent the summer. The shadow of London, although growing closer, had not yet darkened the happiness of the family.

Carson continued to be devoted to Balfour. He told Blanche Dugdale in 1928 that 'the ha'pence were very well done too'. 'You've heard of Balfour's "famine"', he asked her. 'That was the fund he raised, and the arrangements he made when the potato crop failed. "Thanks be to Mary and all the Saints and to Bloody Balfour, ould Ireland will be saved yet", as one old woman said at that time – and she was right.'[4] Such interviews with elderly men looking back through a rosy retrospect and without the encumbrance of contemporary notes should always be treated with caution. But there can be no doubt about Carson's opinion that Balfour never again rose to the heights he attained during his time in Ireland, nor of Balfour's continued admiration for Carson's abilities.

The Chief Secretary now intervened decisively in Carson's career. He was concerned lest his protégé might progress in the normal way from Queen's Counsel to the Irish Bench. He wanted Carson instead to become a law officer, as soon as a vacancy arose, with a seat in Parliament. Then he could be brought into the centre of things in London. It looked as if this might be possible at the end of 1889, when it was thought that the Irish Attorney-General, Serjeant Madden, would become a judge and vacate his seat for Trinity College, Dublin.

Balfour wrote Carson a circumlocutory letter to say that it appeared 'not improbable that changes are likely to occur in the legal appointments connected with the government'. This also gave him an opportunity to let him know how greatly his services had been valued. Although he could not pledge the government, 'so far as I am able to form an opinion upon the matter it would not be possible for me or for my successor in Office to find any one in the ranks of the Irish Bar more fitted than yourself to hold the post of Law Officer of the Crown and with greater advantage to the public service'.[5]

Carson agreed to let his name go forward as a candidate for the Trinity seat. In doing so he was conscious that, if successful, he would be the first Liberal (although a Liberal Unionist) to sit for the Ultra-Conservative University. But he had to fortify him another letter from the Chief Secretary written in May 1890. Balfour did not know 'whether he had any right or title to interfere directly or indirectly in the question now pending with regard to the representation of Trinity College', but said that Carson had his good wishes for success. He continued more plainly, 'I regard your presence in the House of Commons ... as not merely a matter of convenience to the Government but one little short of absolute necessity'.[6] There could be no mistaking that last encouragement. Balfour wrote the next day to the Rev. James Rountree at Trinity, apparently without regard to any right or title to do so, saying that he believed Mr Carson to be a most able and excellent man of whom any constituency might be proud.[7]

But it was all put off because the Attorney-General decided to wait for his preferment until the next general election. By the time that came in July 1892, the Nationalists had been divided and gravely weakened by the fall of Parnell. Parnell had been living in an adulterous relationship with Katherine O'Shea. Her husband, Captain William O'Shea, a Home Ruler MP, was not so much complaisant as complicit, hoping for political advantage for himself out of the liaison. Both husband and wife had acted as intermediaries in the complex manoeuvres which preceded Gladstone's first Home Rule Bill of 1886. In 1889, the will of an aunt of Kitty O'Shea disappointed the captain's expectations, and he publicly exposed his wife's adultery in a petition for divorce. Parnell had not understood what Gladstone and the Irish bishops would do if and when they learned of his adultery. They ruined him. He was hounded out of public life. He married Kitty O'Shea as soon as her divorce became absolute, but was dead within six months.

In the election the Unionists did well in Ireland, but in Britain there was a resurgence of support for Gladstone. It would not be long before Home Rule became an issue once more. Madden, the Irish Attorney-General, became a judge and Carson was appointed Solicitor-General. It was therefore with the excellent credential of an Irish Law Officer appointed by the Unionist Government that he contested the vacant seat in the two-Member constituency of Trinity. There were three candidates, the other sitting Member, who was almost bound to be re-elected, Carson and a Colonel Lowry. Carson's Liberal antecedents were against him and made much of by Lowry. But he was given a warm reception when he said that Lowry's views about his Conservatism were hardly relevant when it was approved by Lord Londonderry and Mr Balfour. He came second in the poll by a large margin and was duly elected. Time would show that the University had nothing to fear in the reliability of its representative's politics. He served as its Member for twenty-six years.

When Parliament met on 4 August 1892 for the swearing in ceremony, the Liberals and the Irish Nationalists together commanded a majority. It was clear that the Conservative government would be defeated at once and have to give way to Gladstone. If Carson was to pursue a career in politics, he would be needed in Westminster to give advice to Balfour who, as Leader of the Opposition in the Commons, would be in charge of the campaign to defeat the now inevitable second Home Rule Bill. The probabilities were that this would mean that he would have to try to earn his living at the London Bar and make his home in the metropolis.

These were crucial decisions in his life, but the answers were not in doubt. They were implicit in his having accepted the appointment of Irish Solicitor-General. It is likely that he had already decided to devote his career to Ireland and the Union. His work as a Crown prosecutor had been a proving ground for his political outlook. In and out of court he had become convinced that the Land War was at bottom a political movement, and that the impoverished tenants had been made pawns in a deadly game whose gambits were criminal. The forces of disorder would have to be combated in public life.

He must have hesitated, however, before deciding to give up his now flourishing practice in Dublin, and then trying to build a reputation anew at the more difficult and more competitive London Bar. Moreover, his rank as an Irish QC would not carry the same seniority in London and he would have to start again as a junior. But just before Parliament met he was introduced to Charles Darling, a QC and Conservative MP, in the Carlton Club. Darling was enthusiastic and encouraging. He told Carson that his name was already known in London, that Arthur Balfour thought the world of him, and that he, Darling, would find room for him in his own chambers in the Temple.[8]

The Conservatives were duly defeated on the motion for the Address in August. The censure was moved by a young Liberal barrister whose star was rising. He pronounced the death of the Unionist government in Latin: 'Roma locuta est. Causa finita est'. 'Rome has spoken. The case is over.' His name was Herbert Asquith, of much the same age as Carson, and he was to be Home Secretary in the new administration. Parliament rose and would not reconvene until the end of January, then to face Gladstone's last attempt to give Ireland her own Parliament. Carson went home to wind up his practice and to let his wife know that their life from now on was to be made in London. She could be forgiven for being fearful of the unknown. How could she be expected to appreciate the irony that in order to preserve their Irish way of life, her husband had to move himself and his family to England?

While Edward Carson was preparing to help repel the forthcoming Home Rule Bill, John Morley returned to Dublin as Gladstone's Chief Secretary. Morley at once took steps to repeal those parts of Balfour's Crimes Act which had been most resented by the Irish. He released the so-called 'Gweedore Prisoners' conditionally on their good behaviour, and he set up a commission to consider the claims of the tenants who had been evicted for their part in the Plan of Campaign.

The wretched circumstances in which Inspector Martin of the Royal Irish Constabulary was murdered in Gweedore in 1889 had aroused intense interest in England as well as Ireland, and the resultant case provoked bitter controversy in Parliament. Father McFadden was parish priest in Gweedore, a village in a remote and wild part of Donegal. He regularly incited his parishioners to take part in the Plan of Campaign, although to do so was an offence under the Crimes Act. Having already spent six months in prison, he immediately resumed the offending conduct on his release. A warrant was issued for his rearrest. Unwisely, the police chose to execute the warrant as the priest was leaving church after celebrating Mass, dressed in full canonicals. The inspector who was in charge of a small contingent of police told the priest that he had to arrest him under the Crimes Act. A struggle then ensued between the priest and the inspector. The congregation rushed to help the priest. The inspector drew his sword and retreated, but was quickly battered to death by the crowd. Twenty-three were arrested, of whom ten were charged with murder and manslaughter, and the rest with conspiracy. Carson was led by the Attorney-General for the prosecution, and Tim Healy was junior counsel for the defence. Healy impressed the jury with the argument that a man who drew his sword in these circumstances would be thought by the Donegal peasantry, or indeed anyone at all, to be threatening violent sacrilege. The first prisoner was convicted of manslaughter and sentenced to ten years' penal servitude. The jury disagreed on the guilt of the second prisoner. The prosecution and the defence then agreed that the second prisoner and most of the others should plead guilty to lesser charges, and that the Crown would offer no evidence on the more serious charges. Father McFadden himself pleaded guilty to obstructing the police and was bound over. The others received light sentences.

The Plan of Campaign left many evicted tenants in its train. Morley's commission was set up to help the government decide what should be done about them. They might get back their old tenancies, the course favoured by the government. But if so, on what terms, and what should happen to the tenants who had taken their places? These new tenants were social outcasts and lived in fear of life and limb. The commission had a difficult task. It was not made easier by the conduct of its President, Sir James Mathew. He was a well-regarded English judge of Irish Catholic birth. He had to his credit that he had set up the new Commercial Court in London. He was also John Dillon's father-in-law. But distinguished judge though he was, he still gave good ground for Carson to accuse him of prejudice during the hearings of the commission. The commission sat in Dublin during the autumn of 1892. Carson represented Lord Clanricarde, an unpredictable character whose name was a byword for harsh treatment of his tenants. It was inevitable that Mathew and Carson would clash. Mathew refused to allow Carson to cross-examine witnesses who were to speak for the evicted tenants and who had incited them to take part in the Plan of Campaign. Carson persisted. There were angry words. Mathew told Carson that the commission would not hear him more. Carson gathered up his papers and withdrew. More angry words were to be heard later in the House of Commons.

The House met on 31 January 1893. The Queen's Speech was debated over several days. It promised to be a stormy session. When Colonel Saunderson spoke, the authentic voice of Ulster Presbyterianism was heard for the first time. Saunderson represented North Armagh and was the first leader of the Irish Unionists in the House. An Orangeman, pugilist and boat builder, he was a man of narrow piety. He had given notice the previous August that, even if the Lords and Commons passed the Home Rule Bill, he, speaking in the name of the Ulster Loyalists, would reject it. 'Who are you?' asked an unnamed Member. Saunderson replied that no one had a better right to speak. 'I say, in their name, that we will reject it; and that if you ever try to enact it in Ireland we will crumble it to dust.'[9] Now, in the debate on the Address the following February, he called Father McFadden a murderous ruffian. There was uproar. Amid the din, John Dillon was heard to move that Saunderson be no longer heard. Gladstone and Balfour appealed for dignity. Eventually Saunderson agreed to amend his description of the priest to 'excited politician'.[10] Carson and Saunderson became collaborators.

Before the session began, Balfour asked Carson to come to see him, to inform him of the state of Ireland and to discuss tactics. Balfour told him that, notwithstanding that it was to be Carson's maiden speech, he wanted him to make the main speech on Ireland. He did not want him to mince words, and to include the Gweedore prisoners and the Mathew Commission.[11] Late in the evening on the second day, Carson rose to deliver his speech.[12] If he was nervous, he did not betray it. Nor did he hesitate to adopt the pugnaciously forensic style for which he would become famous. Morley had claimed that crime had decreased in the six months he had been Chief Secretary. Carson attacked his statistics, saying that the recrudescence of crime in Ireland depended largely on the course the political agitators found it convenient to take at a particular moment.

He then proceeded to 'a few observations upon that grotesque performance, the Evicted Tenants Commission', describing it as a 'monstrous pretence' and Mathew's opening statement as scandalous and incompetent. He had not moderated his Dublin hyperbole. He followed by taking the House in detail through his difficulties in getting a fair hearing before the commission. He had wanted to cross-examine tenants and the agitators who spoke for them, but was refused. Surely, he told the House, he was entitled to ask a question of one witness, who happened to be the Member for Galway East, and who had made a speech to the tenantry of one landlord, in which he told them that they ought to throttle the landlord 'until the glass eye fell out of his head'. 'I should like to know,' he said, 'before this House is called upon to vote away public money [on tenant relief], whether it would not be well to inquire why these tenants had not availed themselves of their rights in the Courts. Not one single question on any one of these points was asked while I was there.'

He attacked Morley for releasing the Gweedore prisoners. There was no doubt about their guilt and no miscarriage of justice. In any case, the prisoners had pleaded guilty. On what basis therefore had Morley exercised the prerogative of mercy? Father McFadden had said that he was the law in Gweedore, and that it would take the whole British Army to take him out of it. He had described landlords and policemen as murderers, and they would have vengeance fall on them 'in this world and the next'.

He turned to the forthcoming Home Rule Bill, which had been foreshadowed in the Queen's speech, and took a point which was to become a *leitmotiv* of Unionist argument. The Chief Secretary, he said, 'knows that there is not the slightest chance of the Home Rule Bill becoming law until he and [the Prime Minister] summon sufficient courage to put the issue to the country'.[13] It was a good debating point. But neither then nor later did the Unionists face up to the situation that would arise if the country said 'yes' to Home Rule. In truth their defence was elsewhere, in the apparently immovable obstacle of the House of Lords.

The speech created a sensation. *The Times* devoted an editorial to it. Being committed to the Unionist cause, the Thunderer was delighted with the way in which Mr Carson had 'analyzed with masterly skill the tissue of transcendental and sentimental excuses put forth by ... Mr Morley for the main incidents of the Irish administration during the last few months', and how he had mercilessly stripped off 'the triple integuments of cant in which Mr Morley wraps himself'.[14] Joseph Chamberlain wrote Carson a note the morning after the speech: 'You must allow me to congratulate you warmly on your splendid speech. It was the best debating speech I have heard for a long while in the House of Commons, and for a maiden effort I think it is unprecedented.' This from the destroyer of the first Home Rule Bill was praise indeed, and Chamberlain was ever afterwards one of Carson's heroes.

On 13 February 1893 Gladstone introduced his second Home Rule Bill. He was eighty-three. Once more he summoned a supreme effort and beggared age. But this time he lacked the credential of a unified Irish ally in the House. The Irish Party was fractious and split by the Parnell disaster. As he had in 1886, the old statesman asked for a blessed oblivion of the past. 'If it were my last breath I would entreat you to let the dead bury their dead, and to cast behind you every recollection of bygone evils ...' But it was a moral certainty that the Lords would veto his Bill, even if he were successful in the Commons. Did he think that if the Lords obstructed he could rally his countrymen in a 'People versus Peers' campaign? In the bitterness of failure, he would discover that the British people were bored with Ireland.

The substantive debate on the second reading took place in April. In that debate and in the apparently endless debates during the summer while the Bill was in committee, Gladstone made no concession to Ulster. He called on the Protestants of Ireland to form 'a noble and glorious unity' with the rest of their fellow-countrymen.[15] The plea was as hopeless as it was exalted.

Gladstone never could conceive that Ireland was two nations, not one. It had been said many times in the House,[16] but his mind could not accept it. On the face of it, it was surprising that the Conservatives did not take the cue and play the Orange card. For if they were to call for separate treatment for Ulster, it might wreck the Bill, as Lord Randolph Churchill had hoped in 1886.

Although he spoke frequently and effectively while the Bill was in committee later on, Carson's speech in the second reading debate was strangely ineffective and disappointing after his storming maiden speech. It was not a rallying call to give protection to the 300,000 Loyalist Protestants who would be cast under a Popish Parliament in Dublin if the Bill were passed. All he said was that Ulster people were not easily roused but at the same time they were not easily quieted.[17]

Why did the Opposition not use the Ulster argument? Of course there was no thought of partition at that time, but the value of the point as a wrecking device had been shown, and it could be used again. What was going on behind the Unionist lines was revealed many years later. The Irish Unionists refused to court the risk of partition. In a memorandum which Carson wrote for Andrew Bonar Law in November 1911, he said: 'During the opposition to the Bill in 1893 we frequently discussed this question [separate treatment for Ulster] and Mr Chamberlain I think was always in favour of creating the difficulty for the government, but the Irish members never would agree to it and I don't think it was ever raised as a substantive amendment.'[18] Carson's recollection was correct. The point was never raised.

The Bill was finally carried on its third reading by a majority of thirty in the early hours of 2 September 1893. It was the culmination of a long summer's struggle in the Commons, during which Gladstone had worked without cease and had had to resort to the guillotine more than once. But, less than a week later, the Bill was thrown out neck and crop by the Lords. Lord Salisbury moved its rejection in these words: 'If you allow this atrocious, this mean, this treacherous revolution to pass, you will be untrue to the duty which has descended to you from a splendid ancestry; you will be untrue to your highest traditions; you will be untrue to the trust which has been bequeathed to you from the past; you will be untrue to the empire of England.'[19] The Bill was rejected by 419 to 41.

Gladstone did not resign until the following March but he was a spent force. It was a sad way to end a wondrous career. The cause for which he had laboured tirelessly had been cast aside like a broken toy. The campaign for Home Rule was also spent – for nearly twenty years. Something would have to be done about the House of Lords if it were ever to be carried. Until the Liberal Party was in power and needful again of Irish Nationalist support,

Irish policy would be made by Tory conciliation, a process which Carson came to think could be pushed too far.

In April 1894 the Liberals, now led by Lord Rosebery, brought forward their Bill to deal with the problem of evicted tenants. It was introduced by John Morley and was based on the report of the Mathew Commission. It proposed to reinstate the tenants who had been evicted for taking part in the Plan of Campaign. Morley argued that to do so was essential to the peace of Ireland. Carson made a powerful response which was much admired by his Unionist colleagues. He conceded that the resolution of the problem of evicted tenants meant a great deal to the peace of Ireland, but he warned that public funds should not be used to reward those who had by their own admission taken part in a political campaign.[20]

For him the real offence in Liberal policy was that it promoted lawlessness in the name of peace. 'What the House is called on to do now', he said in the debate on the second reading, 'is to sacrifice the rights of landlords and the rights of the new tenants, not for the purpose of benefiting the tenantry of Ireland, but in order to pay a political debt.'[21] The Bill was passed by the Commons, but inevitably it met the same fate in the Lords that had overtaken the Home Rule Bill – unceremonious dismissal. The debate showed that Carson's real fear about the fate of Ireland was that Nationalist manipulators would bring chaos and disorder to the country.

Edward Carson's private life was changing as radically as his public life. On arriving in London he first took rooms in Bury Street, St James's, leaving his family behind in Dublin. He then moved to a flat near Marble Arch. Annette and the children joined him here and they gave up the house in Merrion Square. Eventually, when he had become established in his practice and in his public life in the first years of the next century, the Carsons took a town house in Rutland Gate and a seaside house in Rottingdean under the South Downs.

Harry, the eldest child, went away to school. He showed no inclination to follow his father in his career in law. Amusing, feckless and wildly extravagant, he gave his parents much anxiety. He went to South Africa to farm and brought back a wife who was called 'the Boer' by the family. He was constantly in debt and a gambler. His father had to bail him out again and again – out of generosity (he was naturally generous with his children) as well as out of fear of publicity. Harry became a taboo subject in the family. Aileen was a beautiful child with Irish charm. Gladys was equally beautiful but suffered from childhood with bad health. Both girls had high spirits and were devoted to their father. Carson hoped that Walter, the youngest child born in 1890, would go into the legal profession. But he joined the Navy instead and made his career there. Although it was at first difficult for Walter to communicate with his father, they later formed a close relationship during the First World War, when Walter won Carson's admiration by serving in the tiny and dangerous two-man submarines.

Carson once described his children to Lady Londonderry as 'a rum lot'. With the exception of Aileen, they probably caused him either anxiety or disappointment. But he was happy in their company and they in his. The notion that he was in some way responsible for any shortcomings they might have had is simplistic and unfair. He was a remote figure who seldom appeared. The children had no idea what their father was doing, as work was never talked about at home. Probably he should have given more of himself to his family. But his weakness as husband and father, judged by today's standards and conventions, has to be put in context. Late Victorian and Edwardian family life was formal almost beyond modern comprehension.

For Annette the move to London was a serious set-back. It was not just a matter of getting used to living in a foreign city. In London, her husband entered the world of high Tory conclave and powerful hostesses quickly and smoothly. She hated it all and could not follow him. She looked back to the professional middle-class Dublin which she knew. The glittering evenings of London society were frightening and alien. In her granddaughter's phrase, she 'did not make the jump'. She became jealous of the way her husband was being lionised. Edward Carson's sister Bella used to stay with them in London and recalled that 'every day letters would come from Lady This and Lady That which used to infuriate Annette ... Edward had his letters sent to the club'.[22] For Annette, Lady Londonderry was the worst. She went to the House of Commons to watch over her protégé from the gallery. She called him 'the Solicitor' and invited him constantly to Londonderry House. Life at home cannot have been the haven it had promised to be in the early years of marriage.

4

Oscar Wilde

Carson's famous cross-examination of Oscar Wilde in the witness-box at the Old Bailey in 1895 did not 'make' him. He already had a formidable name at the London Bar, and far sooner than he had hoped. Within a year of his call in 1893 he was able to satisfy the Lord Chancellor that his London practice was 'heavy' enough to justify his becoming an English Queen's Counsel. By 1895 he was known, at least to the profession, as an advocate of great power. But after the case, the most celebrated of his career, he was a public figure, as instantly recognised as a modern film star. Wilde's friend, Reggie Turner, himself a young barrister, advised Wilde to retain Carson, but it was too late. He had already been retained by his opponent, the Marquess of Queensberry.[1] That was unfortunate for Wilde. Carson would surely have advised him better than Sir Edward Clarke, who appeared for him at the trial.

Since Carson and Wilde had known each other at Trinity College, Dublin, Wilde's career had been dazzling. He had taken a double first and won the coveted Newdigate Poetry Prize at Oxford. On hearing the news of the Newdigate, his mother congratulated him with unintended and chilling irony: 'Well, after all, we have *Genius* – that is something attorneys can't take away.'[2] In London his epigrams were a legend, and he had written poetry, plays and exquisite fantasies whose fame was instant and lasting. His pen flowed as easily as his talk. At the height of the crisis of his struggle with Queensberry, he wrote his masterpiece, *The Importance of Being Earnest*. He was the high priest of the aesthetic movement. Art for art's sake. Beauty was everything and trumped morality. Wilde both proclaimed and practised this philosophy. For this he earned the hatred and ridicule of the guardians of public morals and the puritan mob. W. S. Gilbert ridiculed the movement in *Patience* which, although written in the 1880s, was still being vastly enjoyed at the Savoy Theatre at the time of the trial. *Poseurs* were invited to cultivate 'a sentimental passion of a vegetable fashion', and 'an attachment *à la Plato* for a bashful young potato'.

All this ensured that the trial would have more than the sensational interest due to its subject matter. It pitted the orthodox morality of the day against a butterfly genius who flaunted his art and the style of his life. In court Wilde's antagonist was Carson. He must have seemed to Wilde to represent the attorneys whom his mother despised, and of whom Wilde would write, when it was all over:

> What is loathsome to me is the memory of interminable visits paid by me to the solicitor Humphreys, when in the ghastly glare of a bleak room I would sit with a serious face telling serious lies to a bald man till I really groaned and yawned with ennui. There is where I found myself, right in the centre of Philistia, away from everything that was beautiful or brilliant or wonderful or daring. I had come forward as the champion of respectability in conduct, of puritanism in life, and of morality in art. *Voilà où mènent les mauvais chemins.*[3]

Wilde's prosecution of the Marquess of Queensberry for libel arose out of the attachment between Wilde and the Marquess's son, Lord Alfred Douglas. 'Bosie', as Douglas was known, had been smitten by *The Picture of Dorian Grey* when it was first published in 1891. He demanded to be introduced to the author. There began an affair between the two. Although married, Wilde had begun homosexual practices some years before he met Douglas and did not take care to conceal his inclinations. Bosie was a young man of arresting if effeminate good looks, and a consuming lover and friend. He craved excitement and enjoyed living on the edge. He was also carrying on a war to the knife with his father. He used Wilde as a weapon in his campaign.

The Marquess was a highly unpleasant eccentric whose main interests were horses and dogs. Brute belligerence was his leading characteristic. He had been a champion amateur boxer and had given his name to the Queensberry Rules, which, in an extreme of incongruity, were about fair play in the ring. There may have been some element of fatherly concern in his tireless efforts to separate Wilde from his son, but it is hard to believe that his motives were unmixed. His relations with his son strain belief. The flavour may be gained from one exchange between the two. After seeing Wilde and Douglas lunching together at the Café Royal one day, Queensberry joined them for a while and was temporarily charmed by Wilde. He soon resumed his old feelings, however, and wrote to his son: 'With my own eyes I saw you both in the most loathsome and disgusting relationship as expressed by your manner and expression. Never in my experience have I ever seen such a sight as that in your horrible features.' His son replied by telegram: 'What a funny little man you are.' Wilde thought 'the commonest street-boy' would have been ashamed of the telegram.[4]

Wilde wrote love letters to Bosie in purple poetics and paid money for them when examples came into the hands of professional blackmailers. A copy of one of the letters reached Queensberry. He fell into a frenzy and started to persecute Wilde, threatening that he would thrash them both if he caught Wilde and his son together. He wrote to his son alleging that Wilde's wife was seeking a divorce on the ground of her husband's sodomy. The allegation was a most serious one, and quite untrue. The loyalty and demeanour of Wilde's wife, Constance, were beyond reproach throughout the affair.

Sodomy and other unnatural acts had been punishable by death since the time of Henry VIII at least. Sir William Blackstone, writing between 1765 and 1769 in his *Commentaries on the Law of England*, had said of the punishment for these offences: 'This the voice of nature and reason, and the express law of God, determined to be capital.' This remained the position until 1861, when the punishment was changed to a term of imprisonment. But homo-sexual acts *in private* had been made criminal offences by statute less than a decade earlier than Wilde's trial by the Criminal Law Amendment Act of 1885. Such private acts were not included in the Bill in the form in which it was introduced, but Henry Labouchere, the Radical Member, moved an amendment in committee to include such acts within the range of offences. There was no discussion of the amendment, save for increasing the maxi-mum sentence from one to two years with hard labour. It went through on the nod. In this way the aptly called 'blackmailer's charter' became law.[5]

Wilde consulted Charles Humphreys, a solicitor with much experience of the criminal law but no knowledge of the homosexual underworld. Humphreys advised Wilde to take no action beyond demanding an apology from Queensberry. Queensberry replied predictably, refusing to apologise for anything. Queensberry called on Wilde, accompanied by a prize fighter, and threatened him, but Wilde saw them out with the help of a porter. Wilde said to the porter, 'This is the Marquess of Queensberry, the most infamous brute in London. You are never to allow him to enter my house again.'

Queensberry was not going to rest until the fight had been fought to a finish. Wilde and Douglas went on holiday to Algiers and there they met André Gide. Wilde told Gide that a well-known peer was insulting and taunting him. Gide advised him not to go back to London; the risks were too great. But Wilde would not be persuaded. He returned for the first per-formance of *The Importance of Being Earnest* at the St James's Theatre on 14 February 1895. The Marquess arrived at the theatre with his accomplice the prize fighter, but they were refused admission. They left a grotesque bouquet of vegetables. Queensberry withdrew to consider his next move. It proved to be the crucial one. On 18 February he left a card with the porter at Wilde's club on which he had written: 'To Oscar Wilde posing as somdomite'. In his rage he had misspelt the vital word.

Wilde went back to Humphreys. The solicitor asked Wilde whether there was any truth in Queensberry's allegation. Wilde assured him solemnly that he was innocent. Then you should succeed, said the solicitor. This was the lie that Wilde so regretted – not so much for itself, but because he had thereby joined the hypocrites and pharisees. Humphreys obtained a warrant to arrest Queensberry on a charge of criminal libel. The Marquess was taken to a magistrate's court, formally charged and bailed.

Wilde had intended to consult the celebrated solicitor Sir George Lewis, who had an unrivalled reputation for settling awkward society cases out of court. But by then Queensberry had consulted him. In fact, Lewis withdrew from the case, after a brief appearance at the magistrate's court, and was replaced by Charles Russell. So Wilde was doubly unfortunate: both the solicitor and counsel of his choice had been pre-empted. After the case was over and Queensberry had been acquitted, Wilde again tried to consult Sir George Lewis. 'What is the good of coming to me now?', said Lewis. 'If you had had the sense to bring Lord Queensberry's card to me in the first place, I would have torn it up and thrown it in the fire, and told you not to make a fool of yourself.'[6] He would very probably have taken a more sceptical view than Humphreys of Wilde's claim to innocence, if only because of the notoriety of Wilde's behaviour. Carson too would surely have advised Wilde of the extreme peril of the prosecution. It was an act of folly, a booby trap, as Wilde afterwards bitterly acknowledged in De Profundis. A mixture of quixotry, provocation and importunate prompting by Bosie led him into it.

Charles Russell took the advice of his father, the Lord Chief Justice, and went to Carson's chambers to ask if he would agree to represent Queensberry. Carson's biographer, Edward Marjoribanks, who was himself a barrister, says that he was hesitant about acting against a fellow student of Trinity, Dublin. Carson also thought that the evidence against Wilde was thin, consisting, apart from letters from Wilde to Bosie and Wilde's published writings, only of hearsay or mere gossip. The subject matter of the case was distasteful. He declined to act.[7]

Marjoribanks says that Carson 'never quite held the orthodox view' that, in order to ensure that no one is shut out from the courts, a barrister must take any case offered to him, however much he may dislike the client, unless he is precluded from doing so for some strictly professional reason.[8] Sir John Simon, to similar effect, wrote that Carson picked his cases with special care.[9] However that may be, Russell wanted Carson and did not give up. He busied himself finding evidence that would show that Wilde had not only been posing, as the Marquess had alleged, but, if possible, that he had in fact been indulging in homosexual practices. For, this being a case of criminal libel, Queensberry's defence would have to establish not only that his allegation was true, but also that its publication was in the public interest.

Detectives employed by Russell uncovered evidence. The trail led to a woman prostitute who told them that she attributed a falling off in her trade to unfair competition from Wilde and his like. She led them to a young man called Taylor who was a pimp at the centre of a large homosexual circle. There were links with Wilde. It was probable that he had committed indecencies with one or more youths at hotels.[10] Russell returned to Carson with the information. Carson went to Lord Halsbury, who had been Lord Chancellor in the last Conservative government, and asked him what he should do. Halsbury was a downright old lawyer, terse of utterance and reactionary in standpoint. He told Carson that the great thing was to arrive at justice, and that it was Carson, he believed, who could best do this.[11] Carson put aside any scruple he may have had about acting against Wilde and accepted the brief.

When he heard that Carson had been retained by Queensberry, Wilde is supposed to have gone round telling his friends, perhaps recalling Carson's mediocre performance at Trinity, Dublin, 'I am going to be cross-examined by old Ned Carson'.[12] This is not a likely tale, if only because Wilde had wanted to retain Carson himself. Sir Travers Humphreys, who represented Wilde as a junior in the case, had a first-hand recollection. When he told Wilde that he was to be cross-examined by Carson, Wilde replied: 'No doubt he will perform his task with all the added bitterness of an old friend.'[13]

The evidence against Wilde was now very serious. He and his advisers knew what it was. So did his friends, Frank Harris, George Bernard Shaw and others. They advised him to leave the country and drop the case. It was excellent advice but, egged on by Bosie, he would not take it.[14] 'Everybody wants me to go abroad', said Wilde, 'I have just been abroad. And now I have come home again. One can't keep on going abroad, unless one is a missionary, or, what comes to the same thing, a commercial traveller.'[15]

Wilde's lawyers, Charles Humphreys and Sir Edward Clarke QC, were under a duty to warn him of the extreme peril of proceeding, and to stop him if they could. It is far from clear that they did. So far as is known, they simply asked him whether there was any truth in Queensberry's accusations. If that was all, they did Wilde a grave disservice. His advisers had another warning. On 30 March, just before the trial was due to open, Queensberry filed a plea of justification, that is a plea that the allegation was true – which is a complete defence to libel.[16] The plea alleged not only that Wilde had *posed* as a sodomite, but also that Wilde had solicited and incited a number of named young men to commit acts of sodomy and other gross indecencies, and had in fact committed acts of gross indecency with them. If an advocate as experienced as Carson was willing to put his name to such allegations, it was certain that there was cogent evidence.

The trial opened at the Old Bailey on 3 April 1895 before Mr Justice Henn Collins. The dingy court room with its patina of past tragedy and squalor was packed an hour before the hearing began. Wilde was represented by Sir Edward Clarke QC, Mr Charles Mathews and Mr Travers Humphreys; Queensberry by Carson, Mr Charles Gill and Mr Arthur Gill.[17] After his opening statement, Clarke put Wilde in the box. He asked him whether there was any truth in the accusations impugning Wilde's conduct with named individuals. Wilde replied that there was no truth whatever in any of them.

Just before lunch, Carson began his cross-examination. It continued for the rest of the day and into the following morning. The *Daily Chronicle*'s court reporter gave a picture of Carson in action.

> It was a duel of thrilling interest. Mr Carson's wig throws his white, thin, clever face into sharp relief. When he is angry it assumes the immovability of a death mask. He is deliberate in the extreme but on the other hand, when he has a good point to make, he bursts out with it in irresistible interruption. When he has not the answer he expects, he pauses, he looks at the bar; he looks at the jury; he looks at the spectators. Then he raises his voice in an 'I ask you, Sir, —.' When, on the contrary, he thinks he has scored, he smiles an exceedingly grim smile to his junior, he glances at the judge and he glances at his client. His self-possession is absolute ...[18]

The first part of the questioning was devoted to a selection of Wilde's writings. Carson endeavoured to show that they were immoral, depraved or blasphemous. He seemed cumbersome by comparison with the gadfly he faced. Wilde's impromptu wit flashed. Of one story, 'The Priest and the Acolyte', about a priest who fell in love with the boy who served him at the altar (which as it happened had not been written by Wilde), Carson asked if it were not improper. 'From a literary point of view, I think it highly improper', agreed Wilde. 'I think you are of the opinion, Mr Wilde, that there is no such thing as an immoral book?' 'Yes.' 'Then, I suppose I may I take it that in your opinion the piece was not immoral?' 'Worse, it is badly written' (*laughter*).

Carson turned to *The Picture of Dorian Grey* and referred to a phrase in the book used by the painter Basil Hallward to Dorian Grey: ' "I quite admit that I adored you madly." Have you ever adored a young man, some twenty-one years younger than yourself, madly?' 'No, not madly ... I prefer "loved" – that is higher' ... 'Never mind going higher. Keep down to

the level of your own words.' 'Keep your own words to yourself. Leave
me mine ...' 'I want an answer to this simple question. Have you ever felt
that feeling of adoring madly a beautiful male person many years younger
than yourself?' 'I have never given adoration to anybody except myself'
(*loud laughter*).[19]

There was a good deal of this, all much enjoyed by the public gallery. But
the tone of the examination changed when Carson moved to the relations
between Wilde and the youths he had been consorting with. He admitted
that they had been introduced to him by Taylor, who was a procurer. The
young men were Wilde's guests at London hotels and restaurants, where he
had entertained them. He had dressed up a newsboy in new clothes and
taken him to a hotel in Brighton where they stayed the night. He denied any
improper conduct, but the net was closing on him, as his friends had warned
him. 'What enjoyment was it to you, Mr Wilde, to be dining and entertain-
ing grooms and coachmen?' 'The pleasure of being with those who are
young, bright, happy, careless and amusing.' 'Yes, but – ' 'I don't like the
sensible and don't like the old. I don't like them.'[20]

Then Wilde fell into a trap. Carson referred to a boy of sixteen who
waited at table for Bosie at Oxford. He told Carson that he had never dined
with the boy. 'Did you ever kiss him?' 'Oh, no, never in my life; he was a
peculiarly plain boy.' 'He was what?' 'I said I thought him unfortunately –
his appearance was so very unfortunately – very ugly – I mean. I pitied him
for it.' Carson seized this answer and would not let go. He asked Wilde again
and again whether that was why he had not kissed the boy. Finally, he got
under Wilde's guard. 'Pardon me, you sting me, insult me and try to
unnerve me in every way. At times one says things flippantly when one
should speak more seriously, I admit that, I admit it – I cannot help it. That
is what you are doing to me.'[21]

The damage was done and could not be repaired. Sir Edward Clarke re-
examined Wilde and showed him the letters which had been exchanged
between Queensberry and his son. This was a dangerous gambit. The letters
certainly lit up Queensberry's offensive character, but they were likely to be
thought by the jury to be attempts by a father to rescue his son.

On the afternoon of the second day Carson opened the case for Queensberry. His cross-examination of Wilde has become something of a legend.
It was, however, more workmanlike than brilliant. And it might seem a mystery why, when there was the devastating evidence of the young men and
boys, Carson chose to open with, and devote so much time to Wilde's writings, a subject on which he was at risk of being worsted by his mercurial
opponent. His object became clear when he made his opening speech. This
was a most impressive piece of court oratory, and it was what destroyed

Wilde. One extract will demonstrate its sardonic power. Carson was here drawing the crucial contrast between Wilde's approach to his writings and his art, and his relations with the boys and young men.

> As regards literature his standard was a very high one. His works were not written for the Philistines nor for the illiterate. His works could really only be understood by the artist and he was indifferent as to what the ordinary individual thought of them or how the ordinary individual might be influenced by them ... In relation to his books he was a complete artist. In relation to his books he wrote only in the language of an artist for artists. Gentlemen of the jury, contrast that with the position he takes up as regards these lads. He picks up with Charlie Parker, who was a gentleman's servant and whose brother was a gentleman's servant. He picks up with young Conway, who sold papers on the pier in Worthing, and he picks up with Scarfe ... and when you come to confront him with these curious associates of a man of high art, his case is no longer that he is dealing in regions of art, which no one can understand but himself and the artistic, but his case is that he has such a magnanimous, such a noble, such a democratic soul (*laughter*) that he draws no social distinctions, and it is exactly the same pleasure to him to have a sweeping boy from the street – if he is only interesting – to lunch with him or to dine with him, as the best educated artist or the greatest *littérateur* in the whole kingdom. Gentlemen, I say his position in this respect is absolutely irreconcilable.[22]

The real menace in the speech came on the third morning of the trial. Carson threatened to call, one by one, the pimps and young male prostitutes with whom Wilde had been consorting. He revealed that they were all available to go into the witness-box.

> It will be my painful duty to bring before you these young men one after the other to tell their tale ... let those who are inclined to condemn these men for allowing themselves to be dominated, misled, corrupted by Mr Oscar Wilde, remember the relative positions of the two parties, and remember that they are men who have been more sinned against than sinning.[23]

He drew a lurid picture of the curtained and perfumed den maintained by Taylor the procurer, and of the transactions between Wilde and the young men who had been procured for him.

It was more than Wilde and his counsel were prepared to endure. Before the statement was finished, Clarke pulled at Carson's gown and indicated that he wanted to make a statement. In some emotion, he told the judge that in face of what they had heard, the jury might think that Queensberry was justified in saying that Wilde had been posing as a sodomite. He was throwing in the towel. He offered the compromise of acquitting Queensberry of libel for saying that Wilde, through his writings, had been posing. He wanted to prevent 'an investigation of matters of the most appalling character'. But the judge would have no limitation. It was either guilty or not guilty. The jury were directed to acquit Queensberry.

Wilde had one more brief chance to escape from England. Otherwise, it was inevitable that he would be charged with indecent offences. A prurient, humbugging press and a public with an insatiable appetite for excitement and titillation made sure of that. Again, he failed to take his opportunity. Charles Russell sent all the witness statements to the Director of Public Prosecutions, who decided, with the concurrence of the Law Officers and the Home Secretary, Herbert Asquith, to apply for a warrant for Wilde's arrest. Meanwhile Wilde had gone to the Cadogan Hotel where Bosie was staying. Robert Ross, another friend who was with him, advised Wilde to leave the country immediately. But Wilde was in a state of pathetic indecision. He sat drinking glass after glass of wine waiting for the inevitable. Eventually, two policemen found him in his hotel room and arrested him.[24]

After two trials, in neither of which Carson took part and in the first of which the jury disagreed, Wilde was convicted and sentenced to the maximum of two years' imprisonment with hard labour. He died in Paris in 1900, only five years after the fateful libel action. 'All trials are trials for life,' he wrote in De Profundis, 'just as all sentences are sentences of death ... Society, as we have constituted it, will have no place for me, has none to offer; but Nature, whose sweet rains fall on just and unjust alike, will have clefts in the rocks where I may hide ...'

Immediately after the libel trial, the judge wrote a note to Carson. 'Dear Carson, I never heard a more powerful speech, or a more searching cross-examination. I congratulate you on having escaped the rest of the filth. Yours ever, R. Henn Collins.'[25] Carson's material, the evidence brought to him by Queensberry's private detectives, was overwhelming. In the end it was his mastery of the detail of the case and his absolute ruthlessness in deploying it, particularly in his opening speech, which made his success certain.

He had hesitated before taking the case, but, having decided to act, he was bound professionally to drive it to a successful conclusion if he could. He was well fitted to do so. He was, said Lord Birkenhead, a very straightforward and simple character. 'He did not, I should say, like intrigue or subtlety ...' He saw things black and white and was not a man for half measures. He had no opinion of Wilde's ability and used to say angrily that he was a charlatan.[26] Posterity has taken a different view of Wilde's art.

It is hard to rid oneself of the bad taste the case leaves. Did Carson feel any remorse at being the leader of the pack that hounded Wilde to prison and to death? One would have guessed not, and that he felt he was bound

by professional obligation. But when Wilde was to be prosecuted for indecency offences, Carson is said to have tried to intercede with the
Solicitor-General, Sir Frank Lockwood, suggesting that he leave Wilde alone
as having suffered enough. Lockwood replied that he had no alternative but
to continue what Carson had begun.[27] The story may or may not be true.

The paths of Carson's and Wilde's lives had crossed and recrossed. There
were stories of two more such crossings, but the accounts cannot now be
independently verified. The first occurred some time before Queensberry left
his fateful card at Wilde's club. Carson was crossing the Strand on foot when
he was nearly run down by a fine carriage. It stopped and a flamboyantly
dressed Wilde stepped out. The two recognised each other and exchanged
some friendly words. Wilde invited Carson to dine some day with him at his
home in Tite Street. The invitation was not intended seriously by either, and
was not taken up. If it had been, it is most likely that Carson would have
refused to act against Wilde in the libel action, as he made it a rule never to
act against anyone from whom he had had hospitality.[28]

The second incident occurred, if it took place at all, for it has been widely
disbelieved, in Paris after Wilde had been released from prison. Carson was
walking alone in the street on a wet day. He had started to cross when a
fiacre came up suddenly and forced him to step back quickly to the pave-
ment. In doing so, he knocked someone down. 'I beg your pardon', he said,
and looked at his unintended victim. It was Wilde, living under an assumed
name and dying of syphilis.[29]

5

The End of Unionist Government

The Conservative and Liberal Unionist alliance won a sweeping victory in the election of July 1895. The alliance was now known simply as the Unionist Party, an acknowledgement of how Ireland had forced itself to the centre of English politics. Nevertheless, the country's verdict was that it had had enough of Home Rule. The Union was to all appearances secure. The massive and comforting figure of Lord Salisbury again presided over the country's destiny, ready to banish all forms of nonsense with his sardonic wit. Salisbury's views about the Irish were unchanged, that is to say contemptuous. He thought there was something in the Irish atmosphere that sent people mad; and, of Sir James Mathew's performance in the Evicted Tenants' Commission, he complained to Lord Halsbury that the sight of the shillelagh and the whiskey of his youth had been too much for him. 'He gave a wild hurroo and became a Galway boy again.'[1] Arthur Balfour's brother Gerald went to Dublin as Chief Secretary with the intention of killing Home Rule by kindness, a policy in which his brother concurred, even if their uncle did not.

At this moment everything seemed to be set fair for Edward Carson. He cut a tall elegant figure in court and in society, and he was a lion of the Tory hostesses. He had shown what a formidable debater he could be in the Commons. He was relied upon for Irish advice by the party hierarchy, and was on the best of terms with Arthur Balfour, known with good reason to readers of *Punch* as 'Prince Arthur'. Every detail of the Oscar Wilde trial had been followed by a public hungry for sensation. No newsboy or dinner table was ignorant of Carson's star role in it. He was now acknowledged as one of the leaders of the Bar.

A year after the Wilde trial, Carson was briefed for the defence in a great state trial arising out of the celebrated Jameson Raid. His principal client was the protagonist, Leander Starr Jameson, known to the press as 'Dr Jim'. Jameson was a buccaneer of a stamp peculiar to late Victorian imperialism. In 1878 he went to Kimberley as a twenty-four year old to practise medicine with a seemingly distinguished professional career ahead of him. The town was then little more than a diamond-mining camp. Its outstanding figure was Cecil John Rhodes, a man of the same age as Jameson, and of the same traits of character, but writ large. Rhodes persuaded the doctor to give up medicine and join him in the realisation of his dream to expand British civilisation northwards from the Cape to the great lakes, and on to Cairo. Jameson's imagination was fired and he became Rhodes's coadjutor and closest friend. Rhodes and Jameson were men after the heart of the arch-imperialist, Joseph Chamberlain, Colonial Secretary in Salisbury's 1895 administration. Jameson must also have struck a sympathetic chord in Carson, for he was an imperialist too, and a disciple of Chamberlain. He, like Jameson, but fifteen years later, was ready to flout the law for the greater good of Empire. They were to become close confederates during the Ulster crisis.

By the 1890s only the independent Boer republic in the Transvaal stood in the way of northward expansion. But within the republic there was an influential minority of 'Uitlanders' (foreigners), mainly British, who were there to exploit the gold on the Rand. They had many grievances against the government of President Kruger, but he stubbornly refused to contemplate any reform. Rhodes, by then the Prime Minister of Cape Colony, actively fostered the Uitlanders' grievances with his purse and his influence. By the autumn of 1895, the Uitlanders had decided on an armed rising to overthrow Kruger. With Rhodes's approval, Jameson mustered a force of some five hundred mounted police on the border of the Transvaal under the command of Sir John Willoughby, a major in the Royal Horse Guards. The force was to be used to help the Uitlanders, but only if necessary. Jameson, however, convinced himself that the rising could not succeed unless he made a pre-emptive strike and invaded the Transvaal. On 29 December, in spite of warning messages from the Uitlanders and from Rhodes to hold off, he embarked on the adventure. It was a fiasco. The small force was quickly surrounded by Boer commandos and compelled to surrender. Jameson and Willoughby might have been tried by Kruger, but he handed them over, with others involved in the adventure, to the mercy of the British authorities.

They were charged in England under the Foreign Enlistment Act, a statute which made it a criminal offence to fit out a military expedition against a friendly state. The British public would not have agreed that the republic of the truculent Boers was a friendly state, but in law it was. The trial came on in July 1896 before three judges and a jury. Both law officers, the Attorney-General and the Solicitor-General, prosecuted for the Crown. This unusually heavyweight team demonstrated the importance of the case, and great public excitement was aroused. Jingoism was at its height and Britain was spoiling for a fight with the Afrikaaners. There was much sympathy for the defendants. The country had been humiliated by the abject failure of the

Raid, and the pain was made the more acute by the Kaiser sending Kruger a congratulatory telegram.

For the defence, Carson was led by Sir Edward Clarke, who had been his opponent in the Oscar Wilde libel case in the previous year. Clarke was a silver-tongued orator, but he was not a good court tactician. There were apparently serious differences between the two over the conduct of the case, but Carson had to defer to the seniority of his leader.[2] Clarke insisted on taking technical points, which Carson thought ill-advised, and which were summarily dismissed by a strong court led by Lord Russell, the Chief Justice. Carson was for attacking the prosecution frontally, and arguing that the raid was justified to protect British citizens within the Transvaal. But his advice was not taken, and the evidence for the prosecution was scarcely challenged. These differences of view cannot be gathered from the law reports,[3] and are probably derived from Carson's own recollection, passed on to Marjoribanks. But whether or not there were differences between the two counsel, it is unlikely that any different tactics would have resulted in an acquittal. The reports make clear how straightforward Russell thought the case was.

The jury convicted both defendants, but only after pressure from Lord Russell. They answered all the questions in his summing up in a sense which was consistent only with a guilty verdict. But when asked to say whether they found the defendants guilty, the foreman said that the jury wished to append a rider that the state of affairs in Johannesburg presented a great provocation. It became difficult to maintain order in court. Over Clarke's objection, the Lord Chief Justice directed the jury to bring in a verdict of guilty without more ado. Jameson and Willoughby were each sentenced to fifteen months' imprisonment without hard labour. Jameson fell dangerously ill in Holloway Prison and was released in less than six months. He recovered and his reputation was completely rehabilitated. In 1904 he became Prime Minister of Cape Colony, and in 1911 he was knighted.

Three years before the Jameson trial, at the time of the debates on the second Home Rule Bill in 1893, Carson had met Sir William Harcourt, the Liberal Chancellor of the Exchequer, at a reception. Harcourt prophesied that Carson was in for a painful disillusionment: the Tories would let him down. The Conservative Party, said Harcourt, never yet had taken up a cause without betraying it in the end.[4] Harcourt's gloomy prophecy was soon to be realised – at least as Carson saw it.

The issue, as so often, was Irish land. While the Liberals were still in power, Carson had been the leading Unionist spokesman on Morley's cross-party committee to decide how further to reform Irish land law – which meant improving the lot of the tenant farmers. Carson's own view was that the process was going too far. He saw the landlords as a beleaguered company, faithful to the Union, who little by little were being deprived of their rights in an over-anxious search for peace. When he found that all his proposals were being rejected by the Liberal-dominated committee, he withdrew the whole Conservative representation on his leader's advice, leaving the Liberals to themselves to draw up a report. The Conservatives then returned to power and, pursuing their new policy of beneficent reform, stole the Liberals' clothes. The Morley Report became the basis for Gerald Balfour's Irish Land Bill of 1896. The Bill made it easier for the tenants to buy the land they were working. It enabled them to have the benefit of any improvements they had made to the land themselves and so would reduce the price they had to pay.

This was a step too far for Carson. What was unforgivable was that it marked an about-turn since the Conservatives were in opposition. He resolved to attack the Bill from the back benches. He moved amendment after amendment in committee. He filibustered and made long speeches in the weary days of argument. He irritated the Balfour brothers. On the other hand, his tactics were much appreciated by Colonel Saunderson, whose mainstay he became. The Colonel considered that his 'keen intellect and trained habits of examination were invaluable in minute criticism'.[5] *Punch* was watching it all and saw 'fragments of Carson darken the sky'.[6]

Finally, Carson's attacks reached their climax. He observed that it was extraordinary how 'his friends' seemed to have changed their views in one short year because they had removed from one side of the House to the other – from opposition to government.[7] The implication was clear and Arthur Balfour was stung. He said he could not allow such observations coming from an old friend and colleague to pass without remark. The accusation was that the government had changed its opinions in the last year, 'as he would generously imply, for the sweets of office'.[8] Carson did not reply, as he had obviously been invited to do. He sat immobile with his hat over his eyes. When he was called to move the next amendment standing in his name, he replied that he had no intention of moving that or any other amendment. 'It is quite apparent that no amendments of any importance will be accepted, and that, if they are accepted, the government will go back on them.' Then he stalked out of the Chamber.

He wrote to Balfour the next morning, protesting that he did not intend to infer that Balfour's opinions could be affected by the 'sweets of office'. 'So mean a thought never crossed my mind.' It was unconvincing. He reminded his leader that he had given a pledge to his constituents in his election address that he would resist to the best of his abilities any further interference with landlords' property in Ireland. 'If I have gone too far in carrying out this pledge it will no doubt justify a change in your opinion of my

1. Sir Edward Carson. (*Getty Images*)

2. Edward Carson Senior. (*Carson Family*)

3. Isabella Carson (née Lambert), Carson's mother. (*Carson Family*)

4. Annette Carson, Carson's first wife. (*Carson Family*)

5. Theresa, Lady Londonderry, Carson's patroness.

6. Gladys Carson, Bella Robinson (Carson's sister) and Aileen Carson. (*Carson Family*)

7. Aileen, Walter (behind) and Harry Carson. (*Carson Family*)

8. Arthur Balfour in the early 1890s. (*National Portrait Gallery*)

9. Herbert Asquith. (*National Portrait Gallery*)

10. Ulster's Appeal. A postcard circulated at a Unionist rally. (*Tessa Hawkes*)

11. Donegall Place, Belfast, under Home Rule. A postcard from the time of the Home Rule crisis. (*Linen Hall Library, Belfast*)

12. A study in hats. Walter Long, Lord Londonderry, Andrew Bonar Law and Edward Carson watch a march past. (*House of Lords Record Office*)

13. Carson about to speak at the Blenheim Palace rally. (*House of Lords Record Office*)

14. Ruby Carson, Carson's second wife. (*Carson Family*)

judgment and wisdom but I hope it will not lead you to think I am the less grateful or devoted to the Leader to whom I owe so much.'[9] Balfour replied at once, saying gracefully that he had watched Carson's brilliant career at the Bar with satisfaction, 'but in my eyes it has been somewhat dearly purchased at the cost of the severance of our old official relations ... I do not get accustomed to seeing you off the front bench. I am delighted at the success to which that absence is due.'[10]

Balfour's soft words, however, were not what he thought. In his letter to the Queen the same day, he reported 'one episode of rather sharp controversy between Mr Carson and Mr Balfour. Mr Carson has always taken a very exaggerated view of the possible injuries to Irish landlords which the Irish Bill may possibly produce; he is a man of great ability, and has a somewhat bitter tongue.'[11] And in plainer language he told Sir Joseph Ridgeway, his old Dublin colleague, that 'there never was a more remarkable instance of the power which one able man has of doing infinite mischief. I really believe that if Carson had not put his finger in the pie, we should not have had the slightest difficulty with the measure ...'[12]

The depth of the rift was soon beyond doubt. Carson went to the Conservative Chief Whip and told him that he no longer wished to receive the whip or daily notice to attend. The whole episode was highly significant. Carson had given notice that the regular compromises, shadings off and changes of direction of party political life were not for him. Although his difference with Balfour was patched up soon enough, he would show again and again that inflexibility which drove him to independent action.

Carson never understood or, if he did understand, never accepted the implications of the two-party system. The party out of power has always to demonstrate its fitness for office, the one in power its credibility as a government. For this, party unity was indispensable and a split an unthinkable disaster. Carson's public life was not based on this premise. It was founded instead on the sanctity of the Union of Britain and Ireland. On this, any compromise, whether or not an exercise in the art of the possible, was weakness. This overriding principle had been dominant in Carson's make-up for as long as he had been in politics, and he made it quite explicit more than once in private correspondence with Lady Londonderry.

On Irish landlords and tenants, even his admirers considered that in 1896 Carson was wrong for the right reasons.[13] But to Arthur and Gerald Balfour the reasons were wrong too. They saw the removal of the still running sore of agrarian discontent as the best chance of peace in Ireland. If that meant a change or even a reversal of policy, so be it. The landlords would have to accept the price. But the landlords were not willing, and no more was Edward Carson.

His views were moulded by his Anglo-Irish origins on his mother's side, and the Galway society which he knew from his youth. The Ascendancy continued to command local society in spite of the class hatred engendered by the Land League, and in spite too of the land reforms which were intended to pacify the country by cutting into their landed interest. The atmosphere in the country was paternalistic. The stories of the early twentieth century in the Irish RM series by Somerville and Ross show how durable it was. In 'The Finger of Mrs Knox', Stephen Casey, a tenant in course of buying his land, is in debt for £15 to one Goggin, a notoriously sharp local tradesman. Goggin has put in the sheriff to satisfy Casey's debt by seizing his livestock. Casey seeks the protection of his landlord, the redoubtable Mrs Knox. 'I have no tenants,' Mrs Knox tells him tartly; 'the Government is your landlord now, and I wish you joy of each other!' 'Then I wish to God it was yourself we had in it again', laments Casey, 'it was better for us when the gentry was managing their own business. They'd *give* patience and they'd *have* patience.' 'Well, that will do now', says Mrs Knox, 'go round to the servants' hall and have your tea. I'll see what I can do.' Carson thought of people like Mrs Knox as a garrison in need of reinforcement. They were the one class in Ireland competent to govern. Parnell and his gang, the very ones he had encountered time and again in court on the wrong side of the law in the years of coercion, had shown themselves profoundly unfit to rule.

Such a view carried the implication that the Anglo-Irish could sail on forever as a governing class within the Union. Unfortunately for them, they could not. The Ascendancy would have no chance of survival unless it could change, and in some way contribute its knowledge, prestige and experience to a new kind of political structure. Few of them realised that their class was doomed if they clung to the old ways and the old life. That life was English or, at least, depended for its existence on the Union with England. Therefore everything which threatened the Union must be resisted by all possible means. Carson's standpoint was exactly that. He shared the view of the large majority of the Protestant gentry who did not see that change must come.

Having thrown over the Tory whip, Carson made full use of his freedom. In 1897 he added his voice to those, mainly the Nationalists, who complained that Ireland was being treated unfairly by the Imperial Exchequer. He complained of the inadequacy of the provision being made by the Chancellor for Irish teachers. For this he received the unusual compliment of Nationalist cheers in the House.[14] Not for the last time he was a back-bench thorn in the side of the government.

In February 1898, John Dillon, an influential Nationalist politician who in 1900 was to form a highly effective team with John Redmond, moved a resolution for a separate Catholic university in Ireland. Carson made a significant departure by supporting Dillon's motion.[15] Trinity College, Dublin, had long been open to Catholics, but it was a strongly Protestant institution and few Catholics applied to it. Carson told the House that Irish Catholics were a people passionately devoted to their own religion, who would not accept any institution for the education of their children which was in conflict with their views. He thought that the English had never understood this. They continued to aim at a mixed denominational university education. But this was idealised theory, and it was necessary to deal in facts. A mixed system had been tried (at Trinity) and it had failed. He asked whether Catholics would be worse off with further enlightenment; and whether they would make any further progress if they were deprived of the chance. It was a strong speech but it failed in its object. Dillon's motion was withdrawn.

At last, in 1908, the Liberal government announced that it would bring forward legislation under which a Roman Catholic university could be established. Carson welcomed it, saying, as he had ten years earlier, that he had no fear of his Catholic fellow-countrymen, but he preferred them educated and highly educated to uneducated.[16] In the substantive debate on the Bill, he begged the House to come to the reform of Irish universities in a spirit of generosity and frankness. He acknowledged that he would not think of sending his own son to a university which did not have a Protestant atmosphere: could not Catholics be forgiven for feeling the same about their own religion?[17]

The struggle for a Roman Catholic university in Ireland was a long one, ending successfully only in 1909. Carson had long wanted it. But the proposal awoke vehement anti-Catholic prejudice among Protestant Unionists, who feared that it would extend the already pervasive influence of the Pope. Colonel Saunderson was typical of Orange opinion when he said that it would be 'an infatuated blunder' to allow Catholics their own university. He thought nothing of the assurance that the governing body would have a majority of Catholic laymen, for what layman would dare risk the condemnation of the hierarchy?

Carson was concerned about Catholic education. Ireland dominated his public life, but his vision was not a sectarian one. Ireland had a majority of Catholics. He could not see why they should be discriminated against in higher education – or in any other way. As a Southern Irishman, he felt an instinctive sympathy for his Catholic fellow-countrymen, and he responded emotionally to the romance of their faith and their rural lives. In 1900 he wrote an introduction to a book of stories, 'The Heart of the Peasant', by Georgina O'Brien, the daughter of the Attorney-General, Peter O'Brien, under whom he had served in the time of coercion. The O'Briens were a

Catholic family and the stories were of the credulous beliefs and unspoiled morality of young Catholic girls. The tone was thickly sentimental and the content undistinguished. But Carson's introduction is revealing. Under a quotation from Horace extolling the virtues of country life, he wrote:

> There is nothing we are more proud of than the simplicity of life, the deep-rooted affection, the passionate religious feeling, the romantic sentiment and the sensitive pride in untarnished morality of our own people in Ireland. Do you then expect me, as a politician and a law maker and expounder, to become enthusiastic over the benefits which, under the name of 'progress', we are supposed to be conferring from day to day on such natures as these? ... With all my heart I wish you at the hands of the public a true appreciation of 'The Heart of the Peasant'.[18]

How surprised would those who later saw him as the personification of Ulster obduracy have been by these sentiments; and how far were those sentiments from the cast of mind of the northern Presbyterians who were to become his followers.

The coolness between Carson and Arthur Balfour did not last – at least in what Balfour had called 'our official relations'. Privately, however, Balfour told his sister-in-law in April 1900 that Carson had behaved badly over the Irish Land Act in 1896, both to his brother Gerald and himself, 'to myself chiefly on account of a bad liver and irritable nerves: to Gerald largely through a misconception that ought never to have been entertained'.[19]

None of this prevented Balfour from persuading his uncle, Lord Salisbury, that Carson should be appointed Solicitor-General when a vacancy occurred in the spring of 1900. He was too valuable for his knowledge of Ireland, as well as his growing authority in the House, for his personal foibles to interfere with his advancement. Carson received the rare courtesy of a handwritten note from Hatfield House: 'Arthur Balfour will have communicated to you our hope that you will be willing to accept the offer of the Solicitor-Generalship which is likely to be immediately vacant. Your acceptance would strengthen the Administration. I trust you will see your way to do so.'[20]

Carson accepted, and with it the customary knighthood. Acceptance involved a drop in income. His earnings from the Bar in the previous year, 1899, had reached the extraordinary amount of £20,000.[21] This was the equivalent of about one and a quarter million in today's money, and worth a great deal more in real terms, with income tax at eight pence in the pound and living very cheap. The Solicitor-General's salary was £6000 (about £375,000 today), and he could expect at least the same amount from other advisory or court work from the Crown, including much dreary tax work.

The importance of the appointment, however, had nothing to do with money. Carson wrote back to Salisbury, saying how sincerely appreciative he was of all that Balfour's generous friendship had done for him. Indeed, his continuing debt to Balfour can hardly be exaggerated. Balfour was steady in his recognition of Carson's worth to the party, and in his willingness to ignore his caprices for the greater good. He was a good friend. The promotion of the wayward Carson in preference to the loyal and safer Charles Cripps (later Lord Parmoor) did not go unnoticed by *Punch*. Observing that in politics it was no good being docile, *Punch* commented: 'As for Carson, he, with a finely confused metaphor, would let you know that though he does not spurn the fatted calf, he is not to be muzzled. It is a new kind of situation – a Solicitor-General retaining the privilege of criticising the Ministerial action from the Treasury Bench.' [22]

It was true, as Balfour had told his sister-in-law, that Carson's poor health persisted, as did his intense preoccupation with it, and that this may have given an acerbic edge to his behaviour. At the beginning of 1901, Carson told Balfour that he had been advised by his doctor 'to lie up for a few weeks and do absolutely nothing'. If it should prove inconvenient, 'you will, of course, consider that you have in your hand my resignation'. Balfour replied kindly, and, knowing his man, ignored the offer of resignation. In the summer of that year, with the strain of his double life in the Commons and the courts telling on him, Carson went for the first time to Homburg, a watering spot in the Rhineland. Edward VII, as Prince of Wales, had made the place popular with English visitors who wished to combine that rather self-regarding solicitude for their health which 'taking the waters' implied, and the pleasures of the casino and the tennis club. It was to become an annual event for Carson.

In November 1900, George Wyndham became Irish Chief Secretary in place of Gerald Balfour. Wyndham had been Arthur Balfour's disciple and private secretary. He had toured Ireland with him and seen for himself the appalling conditions of life in the west. He was a man of attractive character: a poet and visionary with a strong sense of honour. His administration in Ireland was the high water mark of the Unionist policy of benign rule. Although the Crimes Act was still on the statute book, Wyndham's heart was not in coercion. His aim was finally to solve the perennial land problem, and so bring to an end for ever the long cycle of violence, boycott, and cattle driving and maiming. He hoped as well to achieve a solution to the whole question of Ireland which had dogged political life for so long. Wyndham's Act, as it became known, was passed in 1903. Landlords were encouraged, but not compelled, to sell their estates whole, and would receive enhanced prices funded by the Imperial Treasury. By this Act and its predecessors, most of Ireland's agricultural land was transferred to those who worked it. The Act succeeded in its aim of ending the Land War. For a time there seemed to be solid ground for optimism.

Carson's attitude to the Act was, for once, equivocal. On one side, he acknowledged the generous provision being made for landlords persuaded to sell. But he did not believe the claim that this was the last Irish Land Act, or that it would bring an end to the Irish question. He had to explain to Balfour why he had said that he would give the Bill only 'the minimum support which my official position required' – praise so faint as to be inaudible. His excuse was that his constituency, Dublin University, did not like land purchase at all, a view in which, he said, he concurred. He hoped Balfour would understand, and protested that he never could intentionally commit a disloyal act.[23] It was surely too much to hope that his chief would understand such sentiments from a front bench colleague.

If Wyndham's heart was not in coercion, Carson's certainly was. And, as he had confessed to Balfour, he did not like land purchase, which would eventually destroy the landed interest of the Anglo-Irish. He was therefore at odds with the policy of the government of which he was a member. Always preferring the smack of firm government, the fear of chaos if the Irish were left to govern themselves overshadowed everything else in his mind. He was, however, right to be sceptical about killing Home Rule by kindness. It would not die so easily. John Dillon and other leading Nationalists did not respond with enthusiasm to the Unionists' benign embrace. They knew that the object of conciliation was to maintain the British connection, and were fearful that betterment would blunt the edge of demand for an Irish Parliament. The prize the Irish more and more sought was not so much the alleviation of grievances as a separate nationality. Carson saw this more clearly than most. 'They call this the last Irish Land Bill', he said of Wyndham's Bill, 'I have been hearing of a last Irish Land Bill, and of a permanent solution, all my life, and I have no doubt I shall hear of them again.'[24]

In 1904, a group of reform-minded Irish landlords, led by the notably eccentric Lord Dunraven, conceived the idea that it might be possible to reach a compromise solution to the Irish political problem. This they called 'devolution' – possibly the first use of that now modish word. While maintaining the Union, the idea was to give increased power to local government. Wyndham was sympathetic. They enlisted the help of the Under-Secretary at Dublin Castle, Sir Antony MacDonnell, an Irish Catholic with strong Liberal sympathies. Writing on Castle notepaper, MacDonnell helped Dunraven to produce a document which looked forward to the creation of various 'devolved' institutions including financial and legislative councils.

Was not this Home Rule by another name? A storm broke. Carson was the fiercest critic. At Manchester in February 1905, he described devolution as 'a fatuous, ridiculous, unworkable, impracticable scheme, lately set going in Ireland by certain gentlemen whose names had been attached to it'.[25] A group of Ulster Unionist MPs told the Whips that they no longer had confidence in the government. Carson, although a member of the government, took their part, saying that their grievance was that the scheme originated with a permanent official retained under a Unionist government in Dublin Castle.[26] The complaint was unanswerable, but the string of adjectives Carson had used at Manchester was meant to serve as a warning that creeping Home Rule would not be tolerated. He told Balfour, who had by then succeeded Salisbury as Prime Minister, that he could no longer remain a member of an administration whose Chief Secretary was in any way committed to a scheme of this sort.

The episode ended in an odd way. Wyndham, whose health was broken, had to resign. Rather than accept Carson's resignation, Balfour offered him the position of Chief Secretary. It seems that he accepted, but held the office only for a single day. Then, discovering that the Irish Attorney-General was senior to him and accordingly first entitled to preferment, Carson withdrew rather than embarrass his former colleague at the Irish Bar.[27] Walter Long, a future leader of the Irish Unionist Party, became Chief Secretary in his place. Carson remained Solicitor-General. Unfortunately, we can only speculate how Balfour came to offer the Chief Secretaryship to someone who, as he knew, was opposed to the conciliatory policy of his government. Perhaps the Prime Minister simply thought Carson the best informed and most experienced man for the job. What sort of an Irish proconsul Carson might have made, if he had had the chance, is an intriguing question. But in any case, the Unionist government had less than a year to run.

Arthur Balfour inherited an already weakened administration in 1902. Joseph Chamberlain, who had already split the Liberal Party over Home Rule, now threatened to split the Unionists as well. He proposed a system of 'Imperial Preference' or 'Tariff Reform' for imports. It was with a sense of shock that his listeners understood that free trade, the rock on which England's Victorian prosperity had been built, was to be abandoned. Only goods from the Empire would be permitted to enter without customs duties. The Unionist Party was divided. Balfour attempted to ride out the difficulty by delphic utterances which did not say, one way or the other, whether he was in favour of this tariff reform. But he did not like tariffs. 'Personally, I am not a protectionist', he told Sir Joseph Lawrence, a Conservative MP and tariff reformer, 'and it would be neither right, nor fair, to pretend that I was.'[28]

Chamberlain's scheme was the economic aspect of imperialism. It naturally appealed to Edward Carson. It would be good for an Ireland within the Union. In any case, he was magnetised by Chamberlain. He might now have to choose between him and Balfour. 'I loved and revered Arthur Balfour,' he said, 'and owed him so much; but Joe was different; he had qualities which Arthur Balfour lacked. He was a great man.'[29] Joe was indeed different. In Winston Churchill's incomparable phrase, he was the one who made the weather. In the character of this electric figure grand design and brash showmanship mingled. As for Carson, the Union took precedence over Liberalism in Chamberlain's make-up. He had crossed the floor of the House for it. He had earned the implacable hatred of the Irish Party for it and endured their taunts of 'Judas!' He was the prophet of Empire. Carson spoke out for tariff reform, describing it as a 'glorious edifice of a worldwide united economic Empire', and the press began to place him in Chamberlain's camp. But he did not desert Balfour.

The Unionist administration, divided as it was, weakened steadily during 1905. At the beginning of the year Halsbury, the Lord Chancellor, offered Carson a senior position in the judiciary, President of the Probate Divorce and Admiralty Division of the High Court. He consulted Balfour, who gave him a free hand. But Carson had probably already decided to refuse. The chief reason, he wrote to Halsbury, was 'because I am devoted to politics especially under the leadership of the PM and I feel a great distaste to retiring when the ship is in troubled waters'.[30]

As the year ended, Balfour knew that defeat at the polls was inevitable. He resigned on 4 December and Sir Henry Campbell-Bannerman became the new Liberal Prime Minister. Campbell-Bannerman dissolved at once and in January 1906 won an earthquake of a victory. In his safest of safe seats, Carson was returned again for Dublin University. But when the polls were declared the Liberals were found to have won 400 seats, the Conservatives and Liberal Unionists only 157. Hardly less significant were the successes of the new Labour Party, which increased its tally from two to forty seats, and the Irish Nationalists eighty. The people had given their votes for social revolution.

Had they also voted for Irish independence? It was less clear. Campbell-Bannerman was a Home Ruler, but the issue had wrecked a Liberal government twice. He was cautious. Above all, he did not need the Irish votes. Carson tried to smoke him out in a letter to *The Times*: 'Will the Prime Minister or any of his colleagues answer this single question? Have they abandoned the policy of setting up a separate Parliament in Ireland, with a separate Executive accountable to such Parliament?'[31] Of course there was no answer. But Carson went on warning of the danger.

The country and its government were more interested in other things – the taxation of the rich, the beginnings of a welfare state, and the legal position of the trade unions. The unions were first on the agenda. A decision of the House of Lords (the highest court in the land) led by Lord Halsbury, decided in 1901 that a trade union was responsible for all acts done on its authority.[32] In practice this rendered strikes impossible. For at common law strikes were conspiracies to injure employers. They could therefore be stopped by injunction, and union funds were not immune from damages awarded against the union. This was wholly unforeseen and struck at the heart of trade union action. If the decision stood, workmen dare not strike for higher wages or to prevent their wages being lowered – then not merely a hypothetical possibility. Trade Unions, which had won their very right to exist by a long and painful campaign through the nineteenth century, would be rendered nugatory.

The Liberal government had to repair the damage. It first put forward a compromise Bill under which trade unions could be sued if illegal acts were done under express orders from the union, but not otherwise. At once the Labour Party, and many Liberals, were up in arms. The trade unions must have complete immunity. Nothing could safely be left to the hostile ingenuity of the judges. The government gave way and accepted the demand for complete immunity. Carson led the attack on the hapless Attorney-General, who had the disagreeable duty of explaining the *volte-face*. He accused the Attorney of allowing himself to be used as a catspaw, and so degrading his profession. The Attorney might have said that the King can do no wrong: neither can a trade union. 'I want nothing more to condemn this proposal than the words of the Attorney himself, and which he has now ignominiously eaten.'[33]

Carson's invective was of a bitterness seldom heard in the House of Commons. It was correspondingly effective. After the decimation of the Unionist ranks in the 1906 election, he had become one of the few on that side who could command the House. But the question raised by the Taff Vale case deserved better than Lord Halsbury's perfunctory judgment, running only to two short paragraphs, and, perhaps also, Edward Carson's flailing attack. Whether and how far trade unions can and should be 'above the law' is a question which would return to haunt future governments. The issue was both more difficult and more delicate than either Halsbury or Carson allowed.

The old Queen and Lord Salisbury had left the scene within a year of each other at the beginning of the new century. They both had been there for ever, it seemed. With their departure the era of peace and aristocratic rule ended. There would be no more Unionist governments and only one more

Liberal administration. The extensions of the franchise in 1867 and 1884 had worked their way into the body politic, and the new force of democracy was beginning to make itself felt. Political parties would have to take the working man into account.

Empire was to be another casualty of the new century. Salisbury had said that the first Home Rule Bill had woken the slumbering genius of imperialism. The rejection of that Bill in 1886 and the consequent triumph of the Union had given a new impetus to imperialism. The Empire and the Union with Ireland were not merely linked. The latter was the most vital part of the former. But Empire was in gradual terminal decline – although few saw it. What then would be the fate of the Union? The Irish question had been quiescent during the years of Unionist government, but it was about to rise again to distort and shake English political life.

6

The Naval Cadet

On 18 October 1908 the Bank of England's agent in the West Country, Martin Archer-Shee, received a surprising and most unwelcome letter from the Secretary to the Board of Admiralty. It informed him curtly that a postal order had been stolen at the Royal Naval College, Osborne, in the Isle of Wight, and afterwards cashed at the post office. Investigation of the circumstances had left no other conclusion possible than that his son, Cadet George Archer-Shee, had taken it. The Admiralty therefore requested Mr Archer-Shee to withdraw his son from the college.

George was a boy of thirteen in his first year at Osborne. His achievements in the classroom were modest, but he was of excellent character. Martin Archer-Shee replied immediately that nothing would make him believe his son to be guilty of the charge, which, he said, 'shall be sifted by independent experts'.

On 7 October a cadet named Terence Back, who had the next bed to George in their dormitory, received from home a postal order for 5s. and put it in his locker. During the afternoon he found the postal order missing. Two cadets had been given leave to go to the Post Office that day. One was George Archer-Shee. He had drawn some cash in order to get a postal order to pay for a model steam engine which he had long coveted, made by the celebrated model makers Bassett-Lowe. The other cadet was called Arbuthnot. Back reported the loss to the Chief Petty Officer, who went down to the Post Office at once to see the postmistress, a Miss Tucker. She told him that one cadet had come in to buy a postal order and then about an hour later another cadet had asked her for an order for 15s. 6d. The same second cadet had also asked her to cash an order for 5s. There was then an identification parade. Several cadets including Archer-Shee and Arbuthnot were lined up, but Miss Tucker could not identify either of the cadets who had been to the post office. The Commander of the College then sent for George and asked him to write down Back's name on a piece of paper. George wrote 'Terence H. Back' which was Back's usual signature. This paper and the postal order on which Back's name had been written in the space provided for encashment were sent to a handwriting expert. The expert's opinion was that the two signatures were in the same hand. On this evidence the Admiralty wrote their letter to Martin Archer-Shee. 'All I can say', George repeated again and again, 'is that I never did it.'

George had a half-brother, Martin, by his father's first marriage, with whom he was on close terms. The younger Martin Archer-Shee had served in the Boer War as a major and was now a Unionist MP. He told his father that Edward Carson was the only man who could help. So Major Martin, George and their father went to Carson's chambers in Dr Johnson's Building in the Temple. If the London November afternoon was bleak, so were Carson's chambers. There Carson saw the boy alone and subjected him to a three-hour examination on all the circumstances. At the end of the ordeal Carson declared that he was convinced of the boy's innocence.*

Throughout the long case Carson did not waver in his admiration for the boy's fortitude. He considered that the facts of the case were in his favour. Apart from his irreproachable character, there were other circumstances pointing to George being innocent. He had asked another boy to go with him to the post office. It is hardly likely that he would have wanted to be accompanied if his errand was to cash a stolen postal order. His own locker had been broken into. The postmistress had paid out two half crowns when the stolen postal order was cashed. George had not used half crowns to pay for the 15s. 6d. order he himself bought, and there was no suggestion that he had used half crowns at any time afterwards.

There were, however, two difficulties. The opinion of the handwriting expert was against George, but Carson was inclined to dismiss the value of this type of expert evidence. The second was more substantial. Miss Tucker had said that the same boy who had bought the postal order for 15s. 6d. had cashed one for 5s. Although she had failed to identify George at the identification parade, she was almost certainly honest. She might be mistaken. She might be obstinate.

On studying the case as a whole, Carson felt that the officers at Osborne had persuaded themselves of George's guilt without any proper basis. It seemed that they had reconstructed events with a bias in their minds. Overall there was a good chance of persuading a court that the circumstances pointed to an acquittal. But there were formidable legal difficulties. The passage to a successful result was obstructed by the half-submerged wreckage of the royal mystique. An action against the Admiralty was an action against the Crown. The courts were the king's courts; and he could not be brought before them because, according to law, the king could do no wrong. In order to get round these obstacles and ensure that justice was somehow done, the

---

* The dramatic possibilities of this extraordinary and unequal encounter were so striking that Terence Rattigan adapted the story for his play *The Winslow Boy*.

medieval kings admitted what became known as Petitions of Right. These were petitions by a subject which the Crown voluntarily submitted to a decision by the courts. The king's consent was given by his endorsing the petition with the words 'Let Justice be Done' (*fiat justitia*). However, the remedy was not available in all cases. There was no logic about it.[1] Moreover, if George had completed his course at Osborne and become a midshipman, he would have been entitled to trial by court martial; but the position of a cadet was uncertain.

Fortified by a detailed opinion written by Carson, the family demanded an enquiry by the Admiralty. Two leading Counsel, George Elliott KC and R. D. Acland KC, the Judge Advocate of the Fleet, went down to Osborne separately to conduct enquiries. No legal representation was permitted in either enquiry, and so the assertions of witnesses could not be tested by cross-examination. These inadequate attempts to look into the case were later and not unfairly characterised by Carson as 'hole-in-the-corner' enquiries. Predictably, the Admiralty refused to alter its decision.

It was obvious that the naval authorities would use every means to obstruct and delay, so Carson decided to proceed by Petition of Right.[2] The petition was endorsed with the time-honoured words 'Let Justice be Done' and the case came on for trial on 12 July 1910, nearly two years after George had been expelled from Osborne. The Admiralty was represented by Sir Rufus Isaacs, Carson's old adversary in many cases, and now Solicitor-General in the Liberal Government. He immediately took the legal point that a Petition of Right did not lie (that is, it was not appropriate for this case), arguing that the Crown was immune, having an unqualified right to dismiss anyone in its service.

A characteristic row flared up. Carson protested that the Crown was shirking the issue of fact. Not to allow the real circumstances to emerge and to hide behind a legal technicality was, he said, a scandal and the grossest oppression without remedy that he had known since he had been at the Bar. But the judge was against him and gave judgment for the Admiralty. Carson at once appealed. It was heard in less than a week by three judges in the Court of Appeal. Carson opened the appeal by saying that the charge of theft against the boy was devoid of any foundation. It had been trumped up and raised serious questions of fact which ought to be tried. 'Yes, yes', said Lord Justice Vaughan-Williams, the presiding judge, 'Where are the facts? We want to see the facts.' The Court of Appeal sent the case back for trial by a judge and jury. Carson went immediately to the Lord Chief Justice for a speedy trial and the second hearing started nine days later.

Taking the facts first, with the opportunity to cross-examine witnesses, before legal argument, was crucial in the Archer-Shee case, as Carson knew.

It would have saved time and trouble to hear legal argument first if Sir Rufus Isaacs had had a complete answer in law to the claim. But if that were done, it would never be known whether this boy was innocent of theft. The Court of Appeal was persuaded by Carson's argument that justice to the cadet was more important than establishing a point of law.

The outcome of the case now depended on Carson's cross-examination of the Admiralty witnesses, particularly Miss Tucker, the postmistress. She told Horace Avory, junior counsel for the Crown, that she was 'perfectly sure' that it was the same cadet who cashed the 5s. postal order as bought the one for 15s. 6d. Carson faced a delicate task. It would be dangerous and wrong to attempt to impugn Miss Tucker's honesty. She was transparently honest. He had to get her to concede that she could not be certain and might have made an honest mistake,.

He elicited from her that it was the Chief Petty Officer who had first suggested to her that it was a cadet who cashed the 5s. order. 'Did he say that such people were not wanted in the Navy?' 'Yes.' 'Was he in a very excited condition?' 'I thought so. I have said he was almost raving.' 'Did you say a word to anyone that evening about it being the same boy who bought the 15s. 6d. order who had cashed the 5s. order?' 'I did not say it to the petty officer.' 'Did you even say it was a cadet who cashed the order, before you saw Commander Cotton [the Commander of the Naval College] the next day?' 'If I said I did not to Mr Elliott KC, it must be correct.' 'Can you remember anyone else at all having a transaction or conversation with you at all that day?' 'No.' 'Do you remember the appearance of anyone at all who called that day?' 'No.' 'Do you remember if any of the cadets' servants called?' 'No.' 'So you paid no attention to anybody else that day?' 'No.' 'And no one has ever attempted to test your memory on that point until now?' 'No.'

When Carson sat down, he had virtually demolished the primary evidence of the postmistress – and without any bullying or casting any shadow across her character. He had broken the back of the Admiralty's case. Other witnesses followed, cadets and officers and staff of the college. But it was the postmistress's evidence which was decisive.

That evening, Isaacs and Avory went to see Sir Charles Inigo Thomas, the Secretary to the Admiralty Board. They told him, as he later reported to the First Lord, Reginald McKenna, that acquittal was almost certain, and that the moment had come when they should try to settle the case. They proposed that the Admiralty should concede that the cadet was innocent, on terms that Carson would agree on his side that the Admiralty had acted in good faith and had reasonable ground for its belief. The naval witnesses were so weak, they said, that they risked a finding that the Navy had no reasonable basis for expelling Cadet Archer-Shee. That would be sure to lead to very embarrassing publicity.[3]

The next morning the case was settled on that basis amid scenes of joy and relief in the Archer-Shee family. Unaccountably, Carson did not deal with the questions of compensation and costs. These outstanding issues dragged on for months more and were eventually raised in the House of Commons. Finally, it was agreed that the Archer-Shees should be compensated with a payment of some £7000. But even after the trial was over, the Admiralty showed no generosity or remorse for the injustice it had caused. McKenna in particular was a dog in the manger. In the House, his manner was smug and he offered no apology. Balfour's secretary, J. S. Sandars, wrote to Carson about McKenna's part in the affair. 'How he came to be drawn into the blunder over the earlier stage of the Osborne case, and having blundered to throw up the sponge before the final round is perfectly amazing. The result is that he gains no credit for magnanimity in his treatment of the plaintiff, while he is charged with abandoning his officers at the last moment.'[4]

Carson had a special interest in the case because his own son, Walter, had been through Osborne. He was also strangely impressed by the boy himself. George had endured nearly two days of cross-examination by Sir Rufus Isaacs with complete self-possession. But he was not in court when the case finished. When he saw him afterwards Carson asked him why. 'Well, sir, I was taken to the theatre last night, and I overslept.' 'What a strange boy you are. Didn't you feel too nervous to go out to the theatre?' 'I didn't. When I got into a court of law I knew I would be all right. Why, I never did the thing.'[5] The boy could not be reinstated at Osborne. He completed his education at Stonyhurst and then joined the army. He was killed at Ypres in the first year of the First World War.

Carson put a great deal of his emotional self into the case. It exhausted him. His brother Walter Carson saw him at his home in Eaton Place immediately after the hearing was over. He found him sweating and anxious. He had had to put political duty on one side while the case was on.[6] He carried the burden of the case, with all its crises and anxieties, struggling against the resources of the Admiralty and its unfeeling policy of bureaucratic obstruction, with the utmost professionalism. Replying to a telegram of congratulation from Lady Londonderry, he wrote, 'You know how I appreciate it. It has been a great victory and I feel quite tearful over it. I was always convinced of the boy's innocence, and I know it all arose from the blundering suggestion of the officers-in-charge. You should have seen the boy when he came to thank me. He was so frank and honest. My regret is that the Navy will have lost so promising a boy.'[7]

He was under great strain while the case was on. His wife Annette was becoming seriously ill. His eldest boy, Harry, had returned from the Boer War with a new wife but sadly unreformed. He continued to plague his father with his debts and gambling losses. His daughter Gladys, attractive and intelligent, was found to have tuberculosis. And in February 1910 Carson had become the leader of the Irish Unionist Party at a time when the Irish Nationalists held a controlling vote in the House of Commons. It must have been a hard thing at just this time to concentrate on the long drawn out case and carry it through to a triumphant end. J. L. Garvin, the editor of the *Observer*, paid him a singular tribute in an editorial in the issue for 31 July 1910.

> There is not a parent in the land who has not been amazed by the crudity of the procedure adopted in this business at Osborne ... But the acquittal of the cadet [has] not been so much the triumph of law as the triumph of a great lawyer, and Sir Edward Carson's whole conduct of the case has been one of the finest things in the annals of the English Bar. Even law may be dead and impotent without personality. A good cause has been lost again and again by weak handling. The abstract justice of a cause is not necessarily any one's security ... If his health had been always as robust as his mind and character, Sir Edward Carson, as every Unionist knows, might have held a far greater position in political life than he has ever cared to assert. But he has won this time something above party distinction. His splendid courage and will have ensured his permanent place in public regard, and make him a national figure.

There is no doubt that the acquittal of the naval cadet owed everything to Carson's fighting qualities as an advocate. He has been compared with his contemporary and frequent opponent, Rufus Isaacs. They were very different lawyers. Isaacs liked to settle cases and knew the exact moment to do so. Carson preferred to fight. He had great flair and confidence. His cross-examination was often brief, always to the point. He knew how dangerous was the superfluous question. He could dominate a witness, not by bullying but with an impression of power. No judge made him flinch or deflect from his course. If the case was one of life and death, or on which a reputation or a career might depend, as with George Archer-Shee, then as his half-brother Martin said, there was only one man to choose.

7

The House of Lords

At the end of 1909 Carson took Annette to Madeira. He was exhausted by court work and by the demands of the House. F. E. Smith, the young blade who was making a name for himself in the Unionist ranks, told Lady Londonderry: 'Your Solicitor is very sorry for himself; he has stuck to it splendidly, but I think he should have allowed himself a month's holiday.'[1] He was taking holidays now whenever he could, obsessed by his health and his encroaching age. A visit to Homburg in the summer season featured regularly in his diary, where he was sometimes accompanied by his daughter, Gladys. And, as was becoming conventional, he went to Monte Carlo as well. But when he was away, he complained of being out of it. 'I am wondering what is going on in England and how the campaign is going on', he wrote to Lady Londonderry from Madeira. 'I am sorry I came away as it is difficult to realise the loneliness of isolation ... there is nothing to do. I play roulette all the afternoon to pass the time – not very intellectual! Is it?'[2] He was becoming something of a malcontent and Annette could not help. Reading the letters to Lady Londonderry, it is impossible to resist the sense that he let himself gratify his feelings.

The correspondence with Lady Londonderry at this period exposes Carson to a cruel light. We read only one side, as no letters from her survive. He wrote formally 'My Dear Lady Londonderry', and in his rare references to Annette, she is 'Lady C'. He visited the Londonderrys frequently at Wynyard Park on the Tees, and, especially during the period of the Ulster Crisis in 1912–14, at Mount Stewart, often at his own suggestion and always alone. He was made welcome, and he enjoyed the life in these houses among the grand personages he met there. Life at home was humdrum by comparison. The letters are not good letters, and he almost always apologises for them. The theme running through them is complaint. There is no honour left in politics. On the whole the Bar is more rewarding but even that is not immune. 'I plod along at the Law Courts and am deadly sick of feeling nervous and anxious over other people's affairs ...'[3] Rottingdean bores him. Sometimes he lashes out at his family. 'My family came up and I am settled down here – and "the usual routine" is the murder of individuality and so I perish – Rot!'[4] His hypochondria intensified and he describes himself as a dyspeptic pessimist. He could make himself sound like a small boy who kicks at the nearest object.

Perhaps it is too easy to be censorious about the letters of this period, but they show a side of him that cannot be denied. They describe the course of the most important personal relationship in his life, at least until he met his second wife, Ruby. Unless Theresa Londonderry thought he was worth supporting, she would not have given the time. In any case, she enjoyed his company. She sometimes disagreed with him, as when he wrote that he thought the Bar was better than office, 'but you don't agree',[5] but she bore all his complaints, believing that this neurasthenic who was her protégé was the strong man the country needed.

When 'FE' told Lady Londonderry that Carson was 'sticking to it splendidly', he meant the struggle over the Budget that was the brainchild of David Lloyd George, the Chancellor of the Exchequer. The Liberal programme was laying a foundation for the beginnings of a welfare state. The 'People's Budget' of 1909 was the chosen battlefield between the two Houses. Money was needed for the Navy (to keep ahead of Germany), for old age pensions, and for roads for the new motor car. Lloyd George relished the task of raising it. He increased death duties and income tax, and he introduced a supertax. Most provocatively, he proposed a new tax of 20 per cent on the increment in the value of land whenever it changed hands. He declared war on the rich and on the landowners, with the peers at their head. It would be an understatement to say that he trailed his coat in front of the House of Lords. He informed a packed and rapturous meeting in Limehouse that ownership of land was not merely an enjoyment but a stewardship. No country, however rich, could afford to have quartered upon its revenue a class which declined to do its duty. 'Finally, I say to you, without you we can do nothing, with your help we can brush the Lords like chaff before us.'[6]

He wanted to enrage and exasperate his opponents. They duly obliged. In November the Lords threw out the Budget. Since the seventeenth century they had accepted that they had no power to amend a Money Bill. And since 1860, when the practice was adopted of dealing annually in a single Finance Bill with the funding of the whole of the government programme, the Lords had never thought to reject a Budget *in toto*. Was the People's Budget a Money Bill? It was arguable that the attack on land values made it something different. But whether that was right or wrong was hardly the point. By rejecting the Liberals' Finance Bill, the Lords had asserted a right to make the business of government impossible. Could they, whenever they chose, insist on an election to ascertain the views of the people? The Commons replied to the Lords' contumely by a declaration on 2 December, passed by a large majority, that the action of the Upper House amounted to a breach of the constitution and a usurpation of the rights of the Commons. Herbert Asquith, who had replaced Sir Henry Campbell-Bannerman as Liberal Prime Minister in 1908, asked Edward VII to dissolve.

The results of the election in January 1910 were deeply disappointing to Carson. Gone was the overwhelming Liberal majority which Campbell-Bannerman had won in 1906. The numbers of Liberal and Conservative seats were found to be almost exactly equal, with forty Labour and eighty-four Irish Nationalists. The Irish were therefore now in a position – as they had not been before the election – to hold the government to ransom. It did not take much percipience to see that the price of cooperation would be Home Rule. As Carson wrote to Lady Londonderry, so long as Asquith did not waver on this, the Irish would simply do as they were told and would act solidly with the government,[7]

One result of the election was that Walter Long, who until then had been the Chairman of the Irish Unionist Party and who had sat for South Dublin, was returned for a London seat. A replacement had to be found because by convention the chairman held an Irish seat. Carson was invited to fill the vacancy. He was then fifty-seven. He had attained an unqualified and lucrative supremacy at the London Bar, and, if he wished it, he also had the most promising political prospects. All this would have to be foregone if he became leader of the Irish Unionists. Moreover, he knew that the leadership of the Irish Unionist Party must mean, in effect, leadership of the Ulster Unionists, for it was in Ulster that the real Irish opposition to Home Rule was concentrated. He must have wondered whether he, neither an Ulsterman nor a Presbyterian, nor a fire-eating leader, nor even a politician from choice, was cut out for the job. Nonetheless, he accepted.

He met the Irish Unionist members on 21 February 1910, the day Parliament gathered to hear the King's Speech, saying simply, 'I dedicate myself to your service, whatever may happen'. Three days later, he wrote to Lady Londonderry to tell her that he liked being Chairman of the Irish Unionists and that they were a very good lot. This was a casual way to record a change which, as he knew, would fix the future course of his life. Ireland and the Union were now formally what they had been in fact since he entered public life: his lodestar.

There was not much in the King's Speech. The government promised to define the relations between the two Houses of Parliament so as to secure the 'undivided authority' of the Commons over finance, and 'its predominance' over all else. John Redmond, the Irish Nationalist leader, at once declared that his objective was to remove the last obstacle to Home Rule: the Lords.

In the same week as Carson became Chairman of the Irish Unionists, Redmond presented his ultimatum to the government Chief Whip, the Master of Elibank. The government must proceed immediately with resolutions in both Houses to clip the powers of the House of Lords. If the resolutions were rejected or 'hung up', the King must be asked for 'guarantees' (a euphemism for a promise to create enough new peers to secure a reduction in the Lords' powers). These steps must precede the introduction of the Budget. If the government did not promise all this, the Nationalists could not support the Liberals in a forthcoming by-election and would be free to give any advice they liked to Irish voters. In case that was not clear enough, he added: 'Further, we would feel bound to vote against the government and oppose them consistently in the House of Commons.'

On 20 March at Liverpool Redmond was explicit on the relationship between the powers of the House of Lords (which he referred to as 'the veto') and Home Rule. 'With us this question of the veto is the supreme issue. With us it means Home Rule for Ireland.'[8] That was the bargain which ever after would be characterised by Unionists as corrupt. Carson and Redmond faced each other in a dispute that was now in the open.

The problem of the House of Lords could be tackled in one of two ways. The Lords' powers could be restricted by legislation, which would preferably be carried through by agreement between the two Houses; or the composition of the Upper House could be changed by the creation of enough peers to swamp the Conservative majority. Asquith preferred the former – if only because the latter would need the active concurrence of the King. So on 19 March he put three resolutions before the Commons. The first proposed to disable the Lords from rejecting or amending a Money Bill; the second provided that any other Bill which had passed the Commons in three successive sessions, and each time had been rejected by the Lords, would automatically become law, if no more than two years had elapsed from the date when the Bill had first been introduced; and the third shortened the life of Parliament from seven to five years. It is worth noting that neither the idea of reducing the Lords' veto power to one of delay, nor the creation of new peers to carry radical legislation was at all new, let alone revolutionary. In 1835 a young Radical member, Arthur Roebuck, had prophesied that in consequence of the Great Reform Act of 1832 the two Houses were bound to conflict. He proposed that the House of Lords should have only a power to delay rather than an absolute veto. Fifty years later John Bright put forward the same idea. Similarly, the threat of creating more peers was made during the struggles over the Reform Bill of 1831.[9]

In April, Carson's Irish Unionists tested the temperature of the water.

James Chambers, the Unionist member for Belfast South, moved an amendment to the second resolution, that restricting the Lords' powers over non-Money Bills, to a delaying power only.[10] The amendment was framed to ensure that the Lords would continue to have unrestricted power to block Home Rule. Winston Churchill, lately appointed Home Secretary, was put up by the government to deal with the amendment. He said that Home Rule would accord with the will of the electorate, which had been so recently ascertained by the election. In any case, great changes had passed over English opinion on Ireland. The new generation was 'not going to be frightened out of its wits by the nightmares and bugbears of a vanished past'. In the opinion of the government, Home Rule would add benefits to the strength, unity and prosperity of the Empire. Carson had not intended to speak, but Churchill provoked him to get to his feet. His impromptu intervention was mordant. 'You have had it twice rejected, and now, by your bargaining with the Irish Nationalists for the sake of your Budget, for the sake of remaining in office, you want to sneak this Bill through, breaking up the United Kingdom, without the people having an opportunity of expressing an opinion upon it ...'[11] He told Lady Londonderry that before Churchill spoke he had no idea that he was leading up to a row. 'I feel boiling with rage and I hope there will be violence ...'[12]

Winston Churchill made him particularly angry. He had not been forgiven by Unionists for crossing the floor and joining the Liberals in 1904, and when he was defeated in a by-election in 1908 on his appointment to a Cabinet post, Carson exulted. 'I felt almost a savage satisfaction', he told Lady Londonderry, whose views about Churchill agreed with his own. 'I think W. Churchill really degrades public life more than anyone of any position in politics and I doubt if he will ever mature into the kind of serious and reliable politician the majority of people have confidence in ...'[13] Churchill crossed back to the Conservative Party in 1924, but his reputation for opportunism and untrustworthiness lived on in the minds of mainstream Conservatives until 1940 and after. But the personal relationship between Carson and Churchill was to undergo a surprising change in the remaining decade of Carson's career.

Chambers's amendment was defeated. Amid scenes of uproar in the House and shouts from the Conservative benches of 'Redmond' and 'Dollar Dictator' (a reference to the American funding of the Irish Nationalist Party), the Prime Minister had difficulty getting a hearing. When at last he made himself heard, he said that if his government was not in a position to give effect to its policy on the Lords, they would either resign or recommend a dissolution; but, he added, he would not ask for a dissolution 'except under such conditions as will secure in the new Parliament that the judgement of the people as expressed in the election will be carried into law'.[14] It was a good example of his habit of expressing himself with apparent firmness, but in fact with delphic equivocation. The statement was read as meaning that he would make sure of his policy by asking the King to create enough new peers to carry it – or leave the Opposition to form a government if they could. Balfour denounced this anticipation of what advice Mr Asquith would give the King as destructive of the constitution. The price the Prime Minister had paid for the Irish vote, he said, was 'the dignity of his office, and of all the great traditions which he, of all men, ought to uphold'.[15] Carson naturally agreed. It was a public outrage, he told Lady Londonderry, to disclose advice given to His Majesty on a hypothesis.[16] But the Irish Nationalists were satisfied and the budget passed. Parliament then rose for the Spring recess.

At this point, when the battle on the future of the House of Lords was about to be joined, Edward VII died unexpectedly. Carson returned from a break in Paris in time for the funeral. He chose to mark the occasion quietly in the little parish church at Rottingdean rather than attend the solemn obsequies in London and Windsor. 'I do not care about great shows – they afflict me unnecessarily and in an inordinate degree', he said characteristically. 'But I quite admit ... that people ought not to shirk, and if I had been of the least importance I would have remained in town.'[17] Although he could madden his sponsors and friends by his lack of ambition, he was at bottom a modest man.

The new King, George V, had been brought up to be a sailor and was in striking contrast to his predecessor. A man of respectable, narrow, almost middle-class attitudes, patriotic and conservative, he could nonetheless show unexpected decision. He was to be sorely tested by the crisis that was already impending when he came to the throne.

Neither side wanted another election. When Asquith proposed a conference between delegates from both parties, Balfour readily agreed. The King was relieved. The delegates were Asquith, Lloyd George, Lord Crewe and Augustine Birrell on the government side, and Balfour, Lord Lansdowne, Austen Chamberlain and Lord Cawdor for the Unionists. The deliberations were confidential and were wide-ranging in the search for an agreed solution. One possibility canvassed was a coalition of both main parties; but there was insufficient common ground, particularly over Home Rule, and the talks ended in failure in November.

While the conference was on, the air was thick with rumours. Carson was alarmed about what might be being agreed behind closed doors. In August he complained that it was impossible to fight whilst the generals are in friendly conference.[18] And in October he wrote that he was 'sick to death of this Home Rule tragedy [that Unionists were tending to soften on Home Rule] – it is weakening the position every day and from what I can gather there is truth in it. But what I hate most is the number of our people who are apparently quite ready to fall in with the idea'.[19] His worst fear was of politicians who blew with the wind.

In the same letter he told Lady Londonderry that he had written to Balfour to say that he was being pressed by the Irish Unionists to deny rumours that the leadership was weakening on Home Rule. He had had no reply, but he would, he said, wait a few more days and then take his own course. He added: 'It will split the party to pieces and should it turn out to be true I earnestly hope the Conservatives will never again be in office during my life. How can anyone suppose that those of us who have fought all our lives to prevent a separate Parliament and executive in Ireland now turn round and allow so base a surrender?' He hated being in the dark with nothing for company but his fears of treachery. And he would not scruple to split the party if treachery there was.

His fears were allayed at the beginning of November. A meeting of senior Unionists, including Carson, was called by Balfour to decide whether or not to continue the negotiations. It was agreed that they should be broken off. At the Conservative Constituency Associations' meeting in Nottingham Carson was able to say: 'Let us make an end of all this nonsense about any section of the Unionist Party flirting and coquetting with Home Rule. For my own part I would rather, for the rest of my life, stay in the honest Division Lobby of the Opposition than surrender one particle of my principles to obtain the highest office in the land.'[20] The trouble was that so few believed that, when the time came, he would be as good as his word.

The attempt to arrive at an agreed solution having failed, the Liberal Cabinet decided on an immediate dissolution. This would establish whether there was an electoral mandate in favour of reducing the Lords's powers, and on Home Rule. Asquith obtained a promise from the King that, if the Liberals won the election, and if it should prove necessary, he would sanction the creation of a sufficient number of peers to carry the forthcoming Parliament Bill in the Upper House. In this way, Asquith proposed to ensure that the Lords could not frustrate the will of the people. To protect the Crown, the King's promise was to remain secret until the actual occasion arose.

The election took place on 28 November 1910. Interest was low. People had had enough of elections. Politicians might describe the constitutional issue as a crisis or a revolution, but the electorate was unimpressed. The public considered that the issue was already decided. The House of Lords would be emasculated one way or another. Their verdict at the polls gave the clearest possible indication of indifference. The House of Commons which was returned was almost identical in composition to the one which had been returned in the January election. The Liberals, combined with the Irish Nationalists and Labour, increased their majority over the Unionists from 124 to 126. The Parliament Bill began its stormy journey. It was not through the Commons until May. In June the Lords mutilated it in committee. It looked as if the King's promise to create more peers would have to be redeemed.

Asquith informed Balfour and Lansdowne, the Unionist leader in the Lords, that, having first invited the Commons to reject the Lords' amendments, he would advise the King to exercise his prerogative to secure the passing of the Bill in the form in which it left the Commons. He then went down to the House on 24 July to try to make a statement to that effect. He stood at the despatch box unable to make himself heard. Balfour sat impassive while his followers disgraced themselves. The Speaker had to suspend the sitting. The worst offender was Lord Hugh Cecil, known in his circle as 'Linky'. In her diary for 28 July, Violet Asquith, who was in the gallery to witness the scene, wrote 'Linky sat there snow white and gibbering execrations – like a baboon, epileptic and suffragette rolled in to one. He has the excuse of insanity – not so FE who is a mere political adventurer . . .'[21]

The public was now witnessing a curious phenomenon. While the Liberals looked on as spectators, the Unionists were tearing themselves apart. They divided into two factions: 'Hedgers', who were for a tactical retreat which would prevent the creation of new peers; and 'Ditchers', who were for resisting into the last ditch. The two factions began to fight in public and through the correspondence columns of *The Times*. In June, before the Bill had been savaged in the Lords, Carson, an arch-Ditcher, wrote from a sanatorium in Baden-Baden, where he had been ordered by his doctor for a month: 'I hope the Lords will stand firm and let the Radicals make their filthy Peers and then become ridiculous.'[22] Balfour, Lansdowne, Bonar Law, Walter Long, Curzon and, perhaps surprisingly, Lord Londonderry were Hedgers; Carson, F. E. Smith, the brothers Robert and Hugh Cecil, their brother-in-law Lord Selborne, George Wyndham and Austen Chamberlain were Ditchers or 'Diehards' under the leadership of the crusty octogenarian Lord Halsbury.

The battle between the factions intensified during the stifling summer of 1911. Arthur Balfour was distressed by the public display of division in the party. He began even to doubt the sanity of the Diehards, particularly his kinsmen, Robert and Hugh Cecil. His view of the policy of 'fighting to the last' was that it was unrealistic and essentially theatrical. But he admitted in a memorandum he had prepared for the shadow cabinet, but did not send, that 'the Music Hall attitude of mind is too widespread to be negligible'.[23] His waning confidence in his colleagues and general weariness of the hot air he heard and felt around him hastened his decision to retire from the fray.

Carson was all for fighting on. But unless he and his fellow Diehards thought that Asquith was bluffing in his threat to create peers – and he had no reason to believe that he was – it was a futile quest. To have the Lords swamped with new Liberal peers would only discredit the Upper House. And from the point of view of Ireland there was much more to be gained from making use of the delaying power which the Lords were in any event to retain.

On 24 July there was a grand dinner in honour of Lord Halsbury at the aptly named Cecil Hotel. Carson was one of the organisers, and afterwards he wrote to Lady Halsbury to say that he hoped her 'splendid Earl' was none the worse for the banquet, and that he found her husband's arguments 'unanswerable'.*

The final act came on 10 August when, in a temperature of 100 degrees, thirty-seven Conservative peers and thirteen bishops secured a government majority of seventeen in the crucial vote which sealed the fate of the Lords.[24] Lansdowne and the remaining Hedgers had abstained.

Carson was bitter about the peers who had voted with the government. 'It will do a deep and lasting injury to the party', he wrote to Lady Londonderry. 'I think the King has gone too far in trying to save himself at our expense ... I have no feelings whatever towards Lansdowne's adherents, they were just as much entitled as I was to their opinions and no more. But as for the Judas Peers I hope they will be posted in every Unionist Club in the country until their names are a byword ... and so ends the House of Lords!'

As the crisis over the House of Lords moved to its inevitable conclusion, Edward Carson's letters to Theresa Londonderry took on a more resolute

---

* Lady Halsbury was even more Diehard than her husband, if that were possible. Lord Halsbury described his wife's reaction to the final demise of the Lords in a letter to his daughter of 24 August: 'We only arrived last night about 9 o'clock and of course your mother was almost worn out with fatigue and excitement. If she could only catch a recreant Unionist peer or better still a bishop to slaughter, I believe she would get strong again directly.' Quoted in Robert Heuston, *Lives of the Lord Chancellors, 1885–1940* (Oxford, 1964), p. 71. Carson was one of the founders of the Halsbury Club later in the year, but the club petered out within weeks of its inauguration.

tone. Although he remained a die-hard to the end, he recognised that the last constitutional bulwark against Home Rule was bound to go. On 30 July 1911, before the final vote in the Lords on the Parliament Bill, he wrote to say that, after going to Scotland to see his daughter Gladys, who was being treated for tuberculosis there, and to have a few days fishing, he would go to Belfast where the people were very anxious that they should have some serious consultations with him about the course to be taken in resisting Home Rule. 'We cannot I think depend even on "The Lords" throwing out a Bill and if anything is to be done the Ulstermen must do it for them-selves.'[25] The Ulstermen had earlier reached the same conclusion, that whatever was to be done must be done by themselves – at latest in Decem-ber 1904 when the Ulster Unionist Council had been formed. What was new was that Edward Carson had decided to be at their head.

The day before he wrote to Lady Londonderry he had written a letter to James Craig in Belfast. Craig was the Unionist Member for East Down, whom Carson already knew and who was to become his right arm. The letter makes it very clear what was then in Carson's mind.

> I am engaged for a visit to Scotland on 13 September or thereabouts. I should stay there a week or ten days and therefore any day after the 23rd would suit me. I will have no difficulty in staying a few days in Ireland if that is necessary. What I am very anxious about is to satisfy myself that the people over there really mean to resist. I am not for a game of bluff and unless men are prepared to make great sacrifices which they clearly understand the talk of resistance is no use. We will you will find be confronted by many weaklings in our own camp who talk very loud and mean nothing and will be the first to criticise us when the moment of action comes. For this we must be prepared and as far as possible we ought also to be sure of our Press – which unfortunately is not unimportant. Personally I would be prepared to make any sacrifice – my time, business, money or even my liberty if I felt assured we would not in the end be abandoned – I am glad to have so good and true a friend as you are to work with and if we get sufficient help we ought to be able to call a halt. I think the action of the Leaders in the present cri-sis is lamentable – it will damp all enthusiasm for a long time – and the open way in which the official party is joining hands with the government is a positive calamity.[26]

Craig was Carson's partner in Belfast, and ultimately his successor and the first Prime Minister of Northern Ireland. His character and experience were vital for the success of the campaign to block Home Rule, or at least to pre-vent its applying to Ulster. Neither Carson's prestige as one of the leading advocates of the day at the Bar and a member of the inner circles of the Unionist Party, nor his charisma as a political orator, was enough in itself.

Craig supplied what was needed besides. He interpreted the hopes and fears and prejudices of the Ulster Protestants for Carson. A four-square, dependable, unflappable man, he looked like a Blimp and seemed to embody in himself the character of the Presbyterian of the North. He had served with distinction in the Boer War. The son of a millionaire whiskey distiller, he was a stockbroker before he took to politics and was returned to Parliament in 1906. He typified the business and professional class in Belfast who were to provide much of the drive and all the money for the Ulster campaign. Craig had something of a genius for organisation and stage management. He was entitled to more credit than any other person for the fact that, when the crisis came, resistance to Home Rule in Ulster was credible, and something which no one in Westminster could treat lightly.

Carson was fortunate to have a man of this character beside him. They fought the crisis together and saw eye to eye with an extraordinary consistency. In attributes they were opposites. Craig had no charisma and little imagination. But he needed no reassurance that what he was doing was right. His was a stubborn courage, and he was all of a piece. By contrast, Carson's character was shot through with inconsistencies. He had the histrionic gifts of the jury advocate. His rhetoric could rise to rare heights. But his confident public self hid an unceasing desire for reassurance. As his letters to Lady Londonderry show, his self-pity could seem impossible to assuage. He had no talent for administration. The personalities of the two men fused together into a formidable leadership.

Until the Unionist Party split over the House of Lords, Carson had been able to work hand in hand with its leadership, but it was now clear that he could not rely on them. On 28 August he told Lady Londonderry that he so much wanted to have a good chat with her. He was very doubtful about the way the leaders intended to fight Home Rule, 'but in any event I will lead for myself this time ... The whole country is in a shocking state, everyone is demoralised and weak and still the country is calling out for a strong man. Will it be at Belfast?' [27]

If it was to be at Belfast, it would be him. And if the fight was to be won, it would have to be carried on outside as well as inside Parliament. Although he was the leader of the Unionist MPs for the whole of Ireland, the heart of the resistance must necessarily be in the North, where the Protestant Unionists were massed. Belfast, the principal city of Ulster, was to be the command centre, the place with which Carson became inseparably identified.

Carson had been to Belfast to hold a public meeting in 1910 and had presided over the Ulster Unionist Council in January 1911. By the rules of the Council, he was its Vice-President through his chairmanship of the Irish Unionist Party. But he did not know Belfast well until September 1911.

He found the Unionists were well prepared. They had been making their dispositions over a period of more than two decades.

In 1886 Lord Randolph Churchill had advised the Protestants of Ulster to watch and wait, organise and prepare, so that the catastrophe of Home Rule might not come upon them as a thief in the night. They had taken the advice. They took the first steps to defend themselves against 'Rome Rule' in that year. After the second Home Rule crisis in 1893 Unionist clubs sprang up across Ulster. But then the danger seemed to recede with the Conservative victory of 1895 and the ten years of Unionist government which followed.

In December 1904, when danger loomed again, the Ulster Unionist Council was formed to unite in one body all the disparate elements of Unionism in the province. Its original membership of two hundred was divided between a hundred members representing the local associations, fifty the Ulster MPs and fifty representing the Orange lodges. The Orange Order was not the main or sole element in Ulster Unionism, but it was an important resource, and it had always been formally represented on the Ulster Unionist Council. Founded in 1795, it had a membership approaching a hundred thousand within three years. Its purpose was to perpetuate the name of William III of Orange, and its published aim was to preserve the triple foundation of the Protestant establishment in Ireland: Church, Crown and Constitution. It became associated with Protestant sectarianism, and at first had an unsavoury reputation for violence. As a secret society it drew on the rituals of the Freemasons. It was suppressed and then dissolved during the early nineteenth century, but later it revived and attracted members from all classes of the Protestant community. Orangeism was given a massive boost by the Home Rule crisis of 1886. By the beginning of the twentieth century, two thirds of the adult male Protestant population were members. The Order gave both colour and cohesion to Loyalism through its lurid pageantry and its social pervasiveness.

By 1911 the membership of the Ulster Unionist Council had risen to 370. Although it was concerned only with Ulster, it became the engine which drove the entire Unionist movement and was its most intransigent voice. It numbered able people among its membership, but in the autumn of 1911 it lacked a strong leader. Edward Carson and the Ulster Unionist Council might have been made for each other.

As he had promised, Carson went to Belfast for talks with James Craig and others. Annette went with him and they stayed with the Craigs. It was her only visit to Ulster. The result of the talks was the first great gathering of the faithful on Saturday 23 September. Carson wrote to Lady Londonderry beforehand. He told her that he was nervous about how it would come off. He was upset by the condition of his daughter, Gladys, whom he had just visited in Scotland. Her lung was healed but she was in a neurotic state. He was also jarred by Lady Londonderry's warning that his policy and attitude might foment unrest in Belfast and split the party. But he was unrepentant. 'I do not know why you ask me whether I want another split', he wrote, 'If you mean do I want the party to be more active and show more life and fight I certainly do ... I would rather be out of it altogether if we are to dribble along in the old lines ...'[28] But he agreed with her about the danger of rioting, and he assured her that everything would be organised and orderly. It always was, so long as Carson and Craig were in charge. Both knew that a community that was disciplined was much harder to coerce than an unruly mob.

The gathering took place at Craigavon, Craig's home on the southern shore of Belfast Lough. Craig had organised everything meticulously. No policemen were present and none were needed. These Unionists saw themselves as the upholders of law and order. The lawns and fields of the grounds of Craigavon sloped down in a valley towards the shore. The speakers stood on the terrace above the slope, with the Union Jack floating above them. The enthusiastic and committed *Belfast News-Letter* estimated that at least a hundred thousand were there, representing the Unionist clubs and the Orange lodges. They had marched with clockwork precision in column of fours from the marshalling centre at City Hall in the middle of the city. The scene was brightened by regalia, flags and bannerettes. It had been decided that the Orangemen should dispense with their side drum parties for the day, but 'the shrill notes of fife and the inspiriting sound of the kettledrums were to be heard, while the skirl of the bagpipes rose now and again ...'

During the morning it was Belfast grey and wet, but providentially the sun came out in time for the ceremonies. A resolution was proposed welcoming Carson as their leader and a number of formal addresses were presented to him. Carson rose to speak. His soft brogue contrasted with the harsh accent of the North. Many who were gathered there could not hear what he said. There were no loudspeakers. But they could see the tall gaunt figure standing above them, whose gestures and granite presence were to become so familiar.

He told them that he knew full well what the resolution and the addresses meant, and what responsibility was being put on him. He cheerfully accepted it, grave as it was:

> I now enter into a compact with you, and every one of you, and with the help of God, you and I joined together – I giving you the best I can, and you giving me all your strength behind me – we will yet defeat the most nefarious conspiracy

that has ever been hatched against a free people ... Mr Asquith, the Prime Minister, says that we are not to be allowed to put our case before the British
electorate. Very well ... We must be prepared, the morning Home Rule passes,
ourselves to become responsible for the government of the Protestant Province
of Ulster.

He asked their leave at the meeting of the Ulster Unionist Council the
next Monday to set to work on a constitution for that eventuality. On the
Monday, a conference of over four hundred delegates passed a resolution 'to
take immediate steps, in consultation with Sir Edward Carson, to frame and
submit a Constitution for a Provisional Government for Ulster, having due
regard to the interests of the Loyalists in other parts of Ireland'. The powers and duration of the Provisional Government were to come into
operation on the day of the passage of any Home Rule Bill, and to remain
in force 'until Ulster shall again resume unimpaired her citizenship in the
United Kingdom and her high position in the great British Empire'.[29]
Carson had lost no time in setting the political agenda. If the government
forced through Home Rule, Ulster would declare unilateral independence.
But it was rebellion with a difference. As soon as right thinking prevailed
again, the province would be readmitted to the United Kingdom, restored
to its position in the Empire, and its independence would fall away.

The Craigavon rally set the tone for the forthcoming crisis. The Ulster
Protestants were to be organised and ready. It was not going to be a matter
of words only. Carson had told Craig that he was not for a game of bluff.
Nor were his new followers, whatever Asquith and his Liberal colleagues
might think. The phrase 'Protestant Province of Ulster' which Carson had
used at Craigavon was significant. The faithful gathered at Craigavon were
Protestant to a man. What was to be the fate of the Catholics, who in the
eastern counties of Ulster formed a minority within a minority, and for
whose university education Carson had been so solicitous and so forceful?

The gathering also set the theatrical tone for the series of rallies which
were to come. Carson had hit precisely the chord which resonated in the
minds of his hearers. He had shown at the first opportunity that he had the
true gift of popular oratory. He was no Ulsterman and no Presbyterian, but
he knew as if by instinct how to play on the emotions of that audience. And
how formidable were those emotions – a mix of grim resolution and the
involuntary elation felt by a people under siege – the strange duality of
Calvinism on the march.

Carson wrote to Lady Londonderry from Craigavon the day after the
gathering, telling her that 'it was all magnificent and Craig managed everything splendidly'. She could not be there to see his triumph, but her

husband presided at a lunch on the Monday after the Craigavon gathering. Carson said that he was so glad to see him – 'it is too absurd to think there is even a scintilla of feeling about the Lords veto business'. This referred to Lord Londonderry's having been a 'Hedger' – as Lady Londonderry had also been.[30]

Carson stayed in Ulster to make more speeches. At Portrush he asked: 'Are we going to fight the army and the navy?' A voice in the crowd called out: 'They are on our side.' 'No,' he replied, 'it is not that we mean to fight them. But, believe you me, any government will ponder long before it dares to shoot a loyal Ulster Protestant, devoted to his country and loyal to his King.'[31] It was an awkward question and one which would be asked again.

In this fateful visit he had made himself plain. Protestant Ulster would stop at nothing to remain British and hold off the nightmare of going under Catholic Dublin; and he would lead them. What was the strategy underlying this? Was he already contemplating that it might be necessary to split off Ulster, or was it a wrecking tactic to block Home Rule, because Ireland could not be independently viable without Belfast? On the face of it, it seems more likely that as a Southerner devoted to the Union of the whole of Ireland with Great Britain, Carson would at this early stage of the crisis be using Ulster as a tactical 'Orange Card'. But there is one piece of strong evidence that Carson was thinking about partition as early as the autumn of 1911.

Among the Bonar Law papers is an undated memorandum in Carson's hand. He wrote:

> The question is a very difficult one and also one of delicacy. Ulster Unionists have always declared they would not desert those in south and west. Unionists are prone to be very jealous and suspicious that they will be deserted and that the whole opposition to Home Rule will be run from Ulster. Even after the Craigavon demonstration I found a great deal of dissatisfaction in Dublin at the line I took in Belfast as many thought it meant separate treatment for Ulster. I am sure that north-east Ulster is the key to the situation and that the government dare not propose separate treatment and that Redmond could not accept it, and it may be necessary at some stage to raise this question by an amendment but I feel certain to agitate it now would be to alienate support in Ireland outside Ulster.

He added that the question of separate treatment for Ulster had been discussed in the Home Rule crisis of 1893, but the Irish Unionist members would not agree to it.[32]

This is the sort of note that a new leader like Andrew Bonar Law (appointed on 13 November 1911) would want to have as early as possible. It seems therefore that as early as November 1911, and possibly even earlier, Carson was thinking of 'separate treatment', or some form of partition, as a desirable outcome, although tactically a difficult initiative to take. If Ireland were to be split, the line might be drawn to exclude north-east Ulster from Home Rule. But nothing more was to be heard of this from the Unionist side for another year or more.

8

The Conservative Leadership

Carson's complaint about the leadership of the Conservative Party had been grumbling for a long time. In the summer of 1911 there had been weakness over the Parliament Bill, and his disaffection increased into the autumn. When he returned from Belfast he met a number of his Diehard colleagues. He told Lady Londonderry that they were resolved to keep their forces together and to gain others 'with a view to active work and pressing forward in better fighting spirit and to cooperate in supporting each other in the House, on the platform and in the press ... We are of course working within the party and there is no idea whatever of any hostile attitude ...' For the first time in the correspondence he criticised Balfour by name. 'I feel quite nervous as to what AJB will say – milk and water won't satisfy the thirst of the party.'[1]

It would not have been politic for Carson to be too open in his criticisms of his leader in his letters to Lady Londonderry. Her husband had been Balfour's fag at Eton – a notable and sometimes enduring relationship – and was his friend. Londonderry had been President of the Board of Education and Lord President in Balfour's administration. Balfour disliked the Ulster Protestants and their moral earnestness, but this did not interfere with the friendship, even though both Londonderrys were much involved in the Ulster movement from the beginning.

It was predictable that Carson and his colleagues in the Halsbury Club would be attacked for intriguing against Arthur Balfour. It seems that Carson was among the most vocal in calling for a new leader.[2] Lady Londonderry warned him that he was courting a split. He characteristically dismissed the allegation of intrigue. 'All this criticism', he wrote, 'comes to this that everything should be let run on in the old miserable non-fighting groove. The "do nothing" attitude but be gentlemen is what many of our followers would like ...'[3] Carson never forgot the debt he owed to Balfour, but the trouble was precisely the 'be gentlemen' attitude. The time for that was past.

In fact, by July Balfour had decided to go. He was fatigued by the foolishness or mischief-making of many of his colleagues. He had done everything he could to prevent the ultimate disaster of a split in the party, but Austen Chamberlain and Halsbury's Diehards seemed almost perverse. He did not wait for the final vote in the Lords on the Parliament Bill, but left for Bad Gastein the day before, where he tried to forget politics amid the cataracts and pines of the Austrian mountains. He was writing an article on philosophy.[4] His was a liberal outlook, and those who were to replace him spoke for much of the frustration and bitterness in the party – and a certain crudeness that was new.

On 7 November Balfour informed the King that he intended to resign as leader of the Unionist Party. The choice of his successor seemed to lie between Joseph Chamberlain's elder son, Austen, and Walter Long, the one representing the Birmingham brand of commercial imperialism and the other the older traditions of Conservatism. They ran close and there was no love lost between them. There was therefore a clear opportunity for a third candidate. It appeared to Lady Londonderry that that third might be Edward Carson.

According to her own account,[5] she had a letter from Jack Sandars, Balfour's private secretary, in the middle of October saying that he thought 'the Chief will be like Ajax – killed by his friends'. She took this, correctly, to mean that Balfour had decided to give up the leadership, but she hardly thought that he would choose to go when a Home Rule Bill was imminent. She thought she would sound Carson out. He had demonstrated his powers of leadership at Craigavon. And in a letter to her of 23 October he said he thought that next year he must give up the courts if he was to work properly in politics.[6] That was a good sign. There could be no doubt that he would take the extreme threat of Home Rule as seriously as anyone in politics.

When she was in London on 26 October she dined with him and told him that Balfour might be going. 'I must own (as before I have done)', she wrote, 'that I did not expect he would do it very quickly. I then discussed with Sir Edward the question of Leadership, telling him I thought [Walter Long] wanted it and would probably get it; but that [Austen Chamberlain] and his friends would do all they could to prevent it. I suggested to him that in the event of the fight being too violent and the possibility of the Party's being split, that he (Sir Edward), in view of Home Rule, would be a very suitable Leader. He did not appear to dislike the prospect, but talked much about his health and the Ulster Party.'

In the same memorandum Lady Londonderry recorded that on 31 October Balfour came to Wynyard, her house on Teesside. He looked pale and tired but was in good spirits. Neither she nor her husband wanted to talk politics unless he wished to do so. But on the last evening, he came to talk to her for a moment. 'In my sitting room, he put his hands on my shoulders and said, "My dear, you know I am going!" ... Although I was not intellectually surprised, I must own that in an emotional sense I was. I asked him if he would reconsider it, and he said "No, I cannot". On no account would he indicate, by word or sign, who he thought should succeed him.'

On 10 November she was in London again. There she heard, 'to my utter astonishment and greatest regret, that Mr Long and [Austen Chamberlain] had agreed to stand down in favour of Mr Bonar Law'. She thought the whole thing had been mishandled. Her estimate was that Walter Long would have had a large majority if there had been a vote, and that everyone 'seems now to forget that the Tory Party existed long before we paid the Liberal Unionists so very handsomely for sticking to their principles'. Her dislike of the Chamberlain clan, whom she described variously as 'Birmingham' or 'importations', was fearful to contemplate. The antipathy was warmly returned by Austen Chamberlain. He once said that he could tell the state of his political fortunes by the number of fingers, from two to all ten, she extended in greeting.[7] And she did not know Bonar Law at all.

As to Carson's candidacy, her opinion was that:

> had Sir Edward Carson been properly approached at the beginning of the crisis, he undoubtedly would have led the Party; but as far as I can make out Mr Campbell [J. H. Campbell, later Lord Glenavy, a Trinity, Dublin, friend of Carson's] went to see him on the Thursday [9 November] morning, and told him Bonar Law would not stand if he [Carson] wanted to. He was ill in bed; and we know people of emotional temperament and feeling change their minds; but the idea being new, he sent a message back to say he would not stand. He did not feel at that moment that he wished to be Leader, and I must say has said so consistently since.

Lady Londonderry's judgment of the leadership stakes was clouded by her conviction that the party should be led by 'a gentleman of the WL [Walter Long] type'. Her own feeling was that Long or Carson should have succeeded, which would have been 'a tremendous thing for me'. They were both members of her salon. She was probably wrong about Long's chances. The issue between him and Austen Chamberlain was far from clear cut. Chamberlain was Balfour's choice – although he was at pains to conceal his preference.[8] The late runner, Andrew Bonar Law, whose success derived from the deadlock between Long and Chamberlain, took her completely by surprise. W. M. Short, another of Balfour's secretaries, wrote to Balfour's sister, Alice, that Bonar Law's methods were open to much criticism. 'In this struggle he has been run by Max Aitken, the little Canadian adventurer who sits for Ashton-under-Lyne.'[9] There was some truth in this, but Aitken's machinations were unknown to Londonderry House.

She was also wrong about Carson. In the same memorandum, and after the crisis had been resolved, she recorded that Carson thought Bonar Law would be a great success, and seemed 'quite pleased at having the Home Rule question to fight for, without the leadership'. That exactly reflected Carson's state of mind. He would not have been persuadable. Bonar Law had sent a message to him during the contest saying that he, Law, would not stand if Carson wished to do so. But Carson would not. He was ill in bed once more. On 15 November, he wrote to Lady Londonderry, 'Here I am stuck in bed feeble and miserable and if you saw me you would thank heaven I was not the Leader!'[10] In any case, and although his position was already solid among the Irish Unionists, it must be very doubtful whether Carson had any real chance of securing general support in the party.

In the event, Long and Chamberlain both withdrew in favour of Bonar Law. On 13 November 1911 a meeting of Unionist MPs took place at the Carlton Club to choose the new leader. Bonar Law was the only candidate. Carson led him into the meeting to prolonged applause. Aitken, who had accompanied Bonar Law to the Carlton Club, urged him to behave like the great man he now was. 'If I am a great man,' said Bonar Law, 'then a good many great men must have been frauds.'

It was a bizarre choice. A Presbyterian of Canadian origin, who had spent most of his life in the iron trade in Glasgow, had become the leader of the party of the Anglican Church, the country squire, broad acres and hereditary titles. There had been nothing like it since Disraeli became leader.[11] When Bonar Law began to concern himself with the Home Rule crisis, further ironies would emerge.

Lady Londonderry lost no time, through Carson, in inviting the new leader to dinner. He reported that Bonar Law would accept her invitation, 'but not with pleasure'.[12] He did not like to dine out and found social grandeur disagreeable. Since the death of his wife in 1909 he had shown a complete indifference to the society and charm of women. But Theresa Londonderry was merciless and bombarded him with invitations. Austen Chamberlain reported to his sister, May, that she had pursued Bonar Law even to his room in the House, where he was conferring with Chamberlain, to ask him to dine. After she had withdrawn crestfallen when he declined, Bonar Law observed, 'She's very kind but she's an awful nuisance'.* Londonderry House

---

* Chamberlain went on to describe a row he had had with Lady Londonderry: 'She has always been mischievous, and now with her arts and graces applied to Bonar Law when Londonderry & Long have broken in her hands, she is not only ridiculous but ... Bah! I begin to get angry again when I think of it!' Chamberlain Papers, AC4/1/248, 16 March 1913.

was the social centre of the Tory Party and its mistress was the greatest Tory hostess. No member of the Conservative hierarchy could afford to ignore her or decline her invitations. Bonar Law would gladly have avoided the grand dinners and glittering receptions, but he could not.* Much political business was done on these occasions. Lady Londonderry's personal political influence, however, was perhaps not as great as some, including herself, imagined.

The differences in taste between Carson and the new leader about social life were, however, of no account. Bonar Law soon proved to be a man after Carson's heart. He was a fighter. Although cautious in triumph, he was resolute in time of difficulty. He was a Presbyterian, too, and the son of a Presbyterian minister. His father was born and had died in Ulster. Bonar Law got to know Ulster when he visited his father there almost every weekend during the last five years of his life until he died in 1882.[13]

Bonar Law's views about the Ulster question were commendably simple. The population there was determined to be treated in exactly the same way as any other citizens of the United Kingdom. In his opinion, they had every right to that attitude. They were Protestants, but to Bonar Law, that, although important, was secondary. He was no more a bigot than Carson. Their attitude to their Protestant faith was not rabid or theatrical, as it was in the case of many of their Ulster followers. Like Carson, he preferred the peculiar situation of Ulster to be used as a tactic to block Home Rule entirely. But he was ready, if necessary, for a solution in which Ulster would be separated from the rest of Ireland. It was natural that they would work easily together.

Bonar Law's style was also agreeable to Carson. It was blunt and sometimes crude. He had no personal magnetism. His manner on the platform was modest, even self-deprecatory. But he could hit hard. Carson's sombre presence and ability to bring a mass audience to an almost religious fervour would complement his leader's plain speaking. After Balfour's elegant adversarial style, all this came as a shock to the cultured Asquith. At a speech

---

* Robert Blake draws a vivid picture of Bonar Law's preference for the simple. 'Formal luncheons and dinners bored him profoundly. In those days a dinner party seldom had less than five or six courses with appropriate wines, followed by dessert and port. But what Bonar Law liked was a quick meal, preferably soup and chicken followed by milk pudding, washed down with ginger ale. Having consumed this barbarous repast he was impatient to leave the table and smoke a large cigar. To someone of these strange tastes the ordinary routine of hospitality was a painful and tedious infliction.' Blake, *The Unknown Prime Minister*, p. 88.

in Belfast on 9 April 1912, Bonar Law accused the government of turning the House of Commons into an exchange where everything could be bought and sold. The commodities included Ulster, the constitution and even themselves. A few days later in the House, Asquith asked him if he was prepared to repeat it there. 'Yes.' 'Let us see exactly what it is: it is that I and my colleagues are selling our convictions.' 'You have not got any.' 'We are getting on with the new style!'[14] The 'new style' was well adapted to the impending Home Rule Bill, where battle was going to be joined with some violence outside as well as inside Parliament.

On 18 December Carson told Lady Londonderry that 'Bonar Law has so far given great satisfaction both on the platform and in the House of Commons'.[15] On the same day he wrote to invite Bonar Law to come to Belfast on the Tuesday in Easter week for the greatest demonstration yet held against Home Rule – 'we will then be in the thick of the fight'.[16] It was Carson's intention to use that occasion to bind the entire Unionist Party into an absolute commitment, without any ifs or buts, to attack Home Rule by every possible means. Bonar Law's response exceeded his most optimistic expectations.

Just over a week after the Craigavon demonstration, on 3 October 1911, Winston Churchill, then not quite thirty-seven, First Lord of the Admiralty, and by far the most energetic member of Asquith's administration, spoke at Dundee. He told his audience that the government intended to bring forward a Home Rule Bill in the next session and to press it with all its strength. We must not attach too much importance, he said, to 'all these frothings of Sir Edward Carson'; and he ventured the opinion that, when the worst came to the worst, threats of civil war would evaporate into uncivil words.[17] He may have believed that Carson and his Ulster Unionists were bluffing; but, if so, he was wrong. For in January 1912 Colonel R. H. Wallace, the Grand Master of the Belfast Orange Lodge and a member of the commission appointed to draft a provisional constitution for Ulster, obtained from the Belfast magistrates leave to drill and practise 'military exercises, movements and evolutions'. Wallace was a serious soldier. He had commanded a battalion of the Royal Irish Rifles in the Boer War and he had taken the precaution of consulting Carson and his colleague, James Campbell, before applying to the magistrates. This was the origin of the Ulster Volunteer Force which was to play a pivotal role in the developing crisis.

Churchill took the – for him characteristic – view that the war should be carried into the enemy heartland. He therefore accepted with some enthusiasm the invitation of the Ulster Liberals to speak for Home Rule in the Ulster Hall in Belfast on 8 February 1912. It was the very spot at which in

1886 his father, Lord Randolph, had warned his Loyalist audience that the catastrophe of Home Rule might come upon them like a thief in the night. The Unionists were outraged. The standing committee of the Ulster Unionist Council met on 16 January under the chairmanship of Lord Londonderry. Wallace informed the committee that, if it did not prevent Churchill's meeting taking place in the Ulster Hall, the people would take matters into their own hands and the result would be disorder and bloodshed. The committee passed a resolution expressing astonishment at the challenge thrown down by Churchill, and resolving to take steps to prevent his meeting being held. Carson was anxious. Writing from the Carlton Club, he told Lady Londonderry, 'Everyone here is very much exercised about the Council's action ...' F. E. Smith and he were prepared to hold a meeting in the Ulster Hall the night before Churchill's (7 February), and then another the next day in west Belfast. 'Certainly if the thing goes on I will go over as I could not have it said I stayed comfortably in London.'[18]

Although the situation was dangerous, he thought the Council had overreacted. On 25 January he wrote to Bonar Law from Mount Stewart:

> Everything here in Belfast is in a very serious condition and it is difficult to see a way out ... I fear each day makes it more difficult for the leaders to control the situation, and from what I now know I feel certain the action of the Ulster Council was forced upon them, although the wording of the resolution might have been different ... I will stay here at all events for a few days to see if I can be of any use.[19]

That was an understatement. His presence in Belfast was essential to ensure that order was maintained. Nothing could be worse for the cause of Unionism than a riot. The case against Home Rule depended heavily on the Loyalists representing the forces of order and good citizenship. There had been riots in Belfast in 1886 and the threat of sectarian violence always lay just below the surface.

Dublin Castle too was alarmed by the risk of rioting. Five battalions of infantry and a detachment of cavalry were sent into Belfast. On the same day that Carson wrote his letter to Bonar Law, however, Churchill made a tactical withdrawal. He wrote to Lord Londonderry to say that he would be willing to speak anywhere in Belfast. It need not be at the Ulster Hall. He added with some gall that he desired to choose whatever hall or place was least likely to cause ill-feeling to the Orange Party. For whatever reason, it now proved mysteriously difficult to find any suitable place where Churchill could hold his meeting.[20] It was eventually decided that he should speak at the Celtic Park football ground in the Nationalist quarter of the city.

Carson continued to try to lower the temperature. On 28 January, again from Mount Stewart, he told Bonar Law that he would try to get a resolution passed deprecating any interference with Churchill's meeting, 'but I must say there is a very difficult feeling here to control . . . I have had a very difficult and anxious time'.[21] He got his resolution passed. But it was a narrow line that he had to tread. On one hand, he alone could inspire his followers and bring out the determination that was in their character. On the other, the excitement which his oratory and the unfolding crisis had provoked must be kept under control.

Winston Churchill, accompanied by his wife, came ashore at Larne in the morning of 8 February. Crowds had been gathering early in the centre of Belfast, singing and waving Union Jacks. They intended to give him a hot reception that he would not forget. The couple had to run the gauntlet of the demonstration from the railway station to the city centre in order to reach their hotel. After lunch, a crowd of shipyard workers advanced menacingly on the Churchills' car in Royal Avenue with the apparent intention of turning it over. But when they saw Mrs Churchill sitting beside her husband, they fell back with shouts of 'mind the wumman'.[22] The Churchills behaved with exemplary coolness. They moved on and crossed the sectarian line. Effigies of Churchill and Redmond were replaced by grotesques of Carson and Londonderry. The growling and catcalls gave way to cheering. Perhaps fortunately, the day was wet and windy. In any case, the police decided that discretion was the better part of valour. After the speeches at the football ground, they took the Churchills to the station by a different route through back streets in Nationalist territory, while the Protestant crowd waited in vain in the wet.

Carson had been in London in the days immediately before Churchill's visit, but he decided to join Craig and Londonderry in Belfast and be on hand on the 8th in case of trouble. In the event it was not necessary, but the incident in Royal Avenue showed how near violence came. Churchill's attempt to show that the Ulster Unionist movement was hollow had failed thoroughly. He and his wife had had an unhappy – and dangerous – day in Belfast. Although the experience did not deflate his pugnacity, it must have strengthened the feeling, which he and Lloyd George shared, that the best course would be to treat Ulster differently from the rest of Ireland.

Parliament met on 14 February. Serious labour troubles preoccupied the government. The King's Speech stated that a Home Rule Bill would be introduced during the session but it gave no further details. It was widely expected that the Bill would see the light of day before Easter; and upon that assumption the Unionists planned their big demonstration during the recess, on the Tuesday of Easter week. Bonar Law was to come over and speak.

Carson now fell ill again and had to retire to Dr Dengler's Sanatorium in Baden-Baden. These melancholy surroundings induced a speculative mood, reflected in his letters to Lady Londonderry.

> I do not remember any time when politics were so interesting and it is a ray of consolation that (I think) English Common Sense is again asserting itself ... I should not wonder if there is a great reaction even amongst the poorer people and that they would realise that a body politic is or ought and must be a harmonious whole or it will cease to exist. How I long to see Home Rule defeated – it is I think a passion with me ...'

Then he added, less harmoniously, 'I cannot bear the hypocrisy of so called political toleration – I would make it as hot as h— on any occasion – socially or politically for the demagogues'.[23]

On March 12, he told his correspondent that every day he felt greater contempt for Asquith. He had so many chances of showing himself great but would not do so – 'and what a backing he would have from all reasonable men. I imagine he suffers from indolence and also from the consequences of his lack of means should he have to retire'.[24] In the same letter he told Lady Londonderry that he was feeling better, but that it was lonely in Baden. Then in a memorable shaft of self-recognition – 'Still I think my energy is less than it was and if Home Rule was killed I would be glad to take it easy. I have always worked up the hill with the collar hurting me. How I wish I had done more! That you will understand.'[25]

By the end of March he was back in London. Although he was better, he continued to complain about his 'trials'. These included Annette's health. 'My wife suddenly asked me ... "How is Lady L?" and I said you were in Ireland and she said "You ought to go there for a change". I thought her better but in the evening she lapsed away and has since not been so well and indeed sometimes [is] almost comatose.'[26] From this time until her death in April 1913 she was seriously ill, with only momentary rallies. She had become addicted to betting on horses and was careless about money. It was pitiful. She became very heavy and sustained a stroke. She lay in bed for weeks 'unable to raise her hand to brush a fly away.'[27]

In spite of these anxieties, Carson's political resolution was hardening all the time. On 27 March, he told Lady Londonderry that he was to dine that night with Craig to meet Earl Roberts. 'This is very private. I have made up my mind to recommend very drastic action in Ulster during this year and also in the House when the Home Rule Bill is on. There is a growing feeling we do not mean business and I certainly think this is the crucial year and am prepared for any risks.' He ended with a side-swipe at George V – which perhaps showed that he was restored to health. 'I am told he is saturated with the idea of "constitutionalism" which he translates into doing everything his Prime Minister tells him – what a good King!'[28] Events would show that this was a good deal less than fair to the King.

Bonar Law arrived at Larne as planned on Easter Monday. His progress to Mount Stewart, where he was to stay with the Londonderrys, was triumphal every mile of the way. Carson was staying at Mount Stewart as well, apparently recovered from illness. Their hostess had also been quite unwell, but she was fit enough to attend the demonstration the next day. It took place at the agricultural show ground at Balmoral, a suburb of Belfast. As usual with the Ulster Protestants, it was organised superbly. Rudyard Kipling had written a poem for the occasion, 'Ulster 1912', whose last stanza was quoted by Carson in his speech. It was not among Kipling's best verse, but it stirred its readers by its angry response to betrayal.

> What answer from the North?
> One law, one land, one throne.
> If England drives us forth
> We shall not fall alone.

In sheer size, Balmoral put Craigavon in the shade. The excited *Belfast News-Letter* reported that 'Two hundred thousand adult male representatives of about the toughest race on earth passed before the Unionist leaders in a procession for which it would be hard to find a parallel'. There was an intense religious feeling about the gathering. The *Belfast Telegraph* caught the mood of theatrical piety: 'at the highest point on the platform was the conspicuous and manly form of the Primate'. He began the proceedings by leading a prayer for deliverance from 'these great and imminent dangers by which we are now encompassed ... and continue to protect Thy true religion against those who seek to overthrow it'. The whole two hundred thousand breathed a deep Amen. The throng then sang 'O God Our Help in Ages Past', the battle hymn of the Ulster Unionist movement. As if to underline the message of a people facing bondage, postcards were circulated with a picture of the biblical Ruth, sick for home amid the alien corn, entitled 'The Whole Story on a Postcard: Ulster's Appeal'. The biblical text was printed on the face: 'Intreat me not to leave thee; or to return from following after thee: for where thou goest I will go; and where thou lodgest I will lodge: thy people shall be my people, and thy God, my God'.

Carson spoke. According to the *Belfast Telegraph*, itself carried away by the Old Testament atmosphere of the occasion, 'he mounted into the sight of the people'. He waved a Union Jack on a blackthorn stick. 'Raise your hands. Repeat after me: "Never under any circumstances will we have Home Rule." ' There was a thunderous response. He was followed by Bonar Law, whose speech was eagerly awaited. He rose to heights of eloquence which were above and beyond his usual utterance. His theme was the threat of canker in the body of Empire, and Ulster's role in the struggle to repel it. To set up a separate Parliament at the heart of the Empire, he said, would be to destroy the nation's unity of purpose. If that were allowed to happen, then, as always, England's difficulty would be Ireland's opportunity. These were the arguments of the younger Pitt in his original advocacy of the Union in 1800, and Bonar Law adapted Pitt's words in his often-quoted peroration:

> Once again you hold the pass for the Empire. You are a besieged city. Does not the past, the glorious past, with which you are so familiar, rise again before your eyes? The timid have left you. Your Lundys have betrayed you,* but you have closed your gates. The Government have erected, by their Parliament Act, a boom to shut you off from the help of the British people. You will burst that boom. That help will come, and when the crisis is over, men will say to you, in words not unlike those once used by Pitt – 'You have saved yourselves by your exertions, and you will save the Empire by your example'.

It is not hard to call up in the imagination the fervour and excitement of the occasion. Symbolism, both religious and secular, was everywhere, brought about by the disciplined choreography of the occasion. None was more potent than the handshake in the sight of the multitude between Edward Carson and Andrew Bonar Law, representing the mystical union of Conservatism and Unionism, of London and Belfast. Carson himself was moved. 'The whole proceedings at Balmoral seem like a dream', he wrote to Lady Londonderry, 'it was the most thrilling experience I ever had or will have ...'[29]

---

* In Protestant mythology, Governor Lundy was the traitor who left Londonderry to its fate when it was besieged by the forces of James II in 1689. The gates of the city were then shut. A boom was placed across the River Foyle to prevent help from coming to the besieged garrison by sea.

9

Asquith's Home Rule Bill

Whether by accident or design, Asquith did not introduce his Home Rule Bill until after the Balmoral demonstration. But he allowed only two days to elapse afterwards before doing so. The Bill's introduction marked the formal opening of hostilities between Home Rulers and Unionists. It was the beginning of the crucial phase of Edward Carson's life, in which it would at last be decided whether the Union could survive.

The man who forced Asquith's hand to bring forward new proposals for Home Rule was John Redmond, leader of the Irish Nationalist Party since 1900. Redmond was a man who inspired trust and was a dignified orator with a strong sense of constitutional propriety. With John Dillon as his second-in-command, he was able to enforce discipline on the party, which had been riven by the fall of Parnell. Because of his authority over his parliamentary colleagues and his success in raising funds in the United States, he earned the nickname of 'Dollar Dictator'. He was to play a strong and consistent hand through the crisis precipitated by Asquith's Bill.

Like its predecessors, the Bill was a modest measure. The new Dublin Parliament was to have power to legislate for the internal government of Ireland, but with only a little exaggeration this amounted to hardly more than the powers of a county council. The Imperial Parliament was to remain supreme, and would retain power over all the major areas of policy: defence, peace and war, relations with the Crown, and the vital question of finance, including Customs and Excise. As if to symbolise the subordination of Dublin, Irish Members were to continue to sit at Westminster. There was no thought of Ireland leaving the Empire.

Such a Bill did not seem to call for heroics or cries of pain. But both Irish Nationalists and Unionists treated it as provisional only. It was a thin edge of the wedge. Carson put the point when, on the first day of the debate, he quoted Lord Derby: 'I hold, and have held all along, that there is no middle course possible. If Ireland and England are not to be one, Ireland must be treated like Canada or Australia. All between is delusion and fraud.'[1] He and Redmond agreed that there could be no legislative autonomy without financial independence. For the one that would be a disaster, for the other an essential prize.

Asquith's Bill was the third attempt by the Liberal Party to satisfy Irish national aspirations. In one sense the passage of time had moved Asquith into a more favourable position than his predecessors had enjoyed. Gladstone's first attempt in 1886 had failed at the first hurdle when he was defeated in the House of Commons. His second Bill in 1893 passed the Commons but failed in the Lords. Now the Lords could do no more than delay. And although the first two Bills had been followed by an adverse verdict at the polls, the more widely enfranchised public was showing signs of being bored by Ireland, and treating Home Rule as a foregone conclusion, leaving only the question of when.

There were other things weighing on people's minds. Captain Robert Falcon Scott had reached the South Pole on 16 January 1912, only to make the heart-breaking discovery that Amundsen had got there first and the Norwegian flag was already flying there. Scott made the last entry in his diary on 29 March and not one of his polar party returned. The public knew early in March 1912 that Scott had failed in his attempt to be first to the Pole, but the tragic circumstances of his death with all his colleagues in the polar party were not known until February 1913, when the rest of the party finally returned to New Zealand. On 4 April, the *Titanic*, built at Belfast and regarded as 'absolutely unsinkable', hit an iceberg in the North Atlantic and sank with the loss of 1600 lives.[2] These two tragedies deeply affected Britain and damaged its international prestige.

In spite of his favourable position in Parliament on Home Rule, the Prime Minister faced opponents who were more intransigent even than Lord Salisbury, Lord Randolph Churchill and Joseph Chamberlain. Carson and Bonar Law had already made plain their intention to fight Home Rule without regard to the law of the constitution. They were to go further and show that nothing would stop them. They had powerful and vocal allies, Milner the proconsul and Kipling the poet among them. Sentiment among the officer class in the Army was also sympathetic to the Unionist cause. So was a timid King, conscious of his position as Commander-in-Chief and worried by the nagging voice of duty.

Ireland had been in the foreground of English politics for more than a century. It had been like a fever racking the body politic. There were spasms and crises. At other times, when the Unionists were practising benevolent rule, or the Liberals could temporarily afford to ignore it, the malaise was quiescent. It now erupted again. The Lords could prevent Asquith's Bill from passing into law until 1914, but not beyond. Like every Prime Minister since, Asquith had no intention of honouring the rash promise in the preamble to the Parliament Act that wholesale reform of the Upper House 'brooked no delay'. So the parliamentary struggle could not be short and sharp. It would be prolonged guerrilla warfare. As it intensified with the approach of the endgame in 1914, Carson and his ally, Bonar Law, saw to it that tension was wound up like a coiled spring in Belfast as well as in Westminster.

Asquith was not well endowed by nature to deal with hostilities of this character. By education and experience he was a parliamentarian and a constitutionalist. He could be relied on to play by the rules. Now that the bulwark of the House of Lords was dismantled, Carson and Bonar Law would use any weapon to hand. Asquith's disposition was not to try to seize the initiative, but to wait for a favourable conjunction of circumstances. With Ireland that conjunction never came. Having opponents who aimed to hold the initiative, Asquith was mostly on the back foot. His famous 'wait and see' policy made him a poor leader in time of crisis or war.

It is a curious feature of the long struggle for Home Rule that no Liberal statesman ever took the Protestants of Ulster seriously. For Ireland posed two questions, not one. And, although it was always vehemently denied by the proponents of Home Rule, there were two nations living in one island. Provision would somehow have to be made for both. In introducing his Bill, Asquith warned against refusing to recognise the constitutional demands of 'the vast majority of the nation'. What nation, he was asked. 'What nation? The Irish nation'.[3] He did allow that opinion was genuinely divided in Ulster. Taking the province as a whole, he said, Ulster is represented in Parliament by seventeen Unionists and sixteen Home Rulers. 'These figures in themselves are quite sufficient to show the misleading character of the pretence that Ulster would die rather than accept Home Rule.'[4] That was correct but it missed the point. It was *north-east* Ulster, where the Protestant Unionists were in a majority, and not the province as a whole, which was the key to the situation. Carson had said as much in his note to Bonar Law of 18 November 1911, and added that the Liberal government dared not propose separate treatment for this part of Ireland. It would have been impossible for Asquith to maintain his alliance with the Irish Nationalists if he did.

Separate treatment for the north east was nevertheless discussed openly in Parliament, for the first time in the entire history of the Home Rule movement, on 11 June 1912, when T. G. Agar-Robartes, a Liberal back bencher, moved an amendment to exclude the four counties of Antrim, Armagh, Down and Londonderry from Home Rule.[5] He intended the amendment to be a genuine attempt at a solution, but neither side was willing to treat it in that way.

For the Unionists, as Carson had predicted, it posed a difficult and delicate question. Bonar Law called a meeting at Londonderry House for

10 June to discuss it. The debate was awkward. The southern Unionists were sensitive about being abandoned by the north. Walter Long, who was a landowner with many friends in Munster and Leinster, wrote to Bonar Law ahead of the meeting and described the Agar-Robartes amendment as a 'very open trap'. He told Bonar Law that if the Ulstermen fell into the trap it would mean that 'for the first time in the history of the HR question our Party will be divided. As an Englishman, I cannot assent to HR in any form ...'[6] This would be the most persistent difficulty in the way of partition.

On the other hand, if northern Unionists opposed the amendment, they could hardly fight later for what they had been offered in peace. It was decided to vote for the amendment, but to use the opportunity to attack the whole basis of Home Rule; in other words, to treat it as a wrecking move. After three days' debate, the amendment was defeated. Carson repeated what he had said earlier in Dublin. 'If Ulster succeeds Home Rule is dead.'[7] He was not yet ready to fall back on the north east and, at any rate in public, was still using Ulster as a blocking tactic.

For Asquith, the amendment presented an opportunity to smoke out the Unionists, and to find out whether there might be the basis for agreement by treating north-east Ulster separately. But he declined to take it. The government preferred to taunt the Ulster Unionists with saving their own skins and leaving the scattered Protestant minority elsewhere in Ireland to their fate. On 14 June, at the Albert Hall, Carson described this as a declaration of war – which he and his supporters were happy to accept. At a dinner at the Criterion restaurant ten days later, he observed, amid laughter, that it had been said that he ought to be sent to gaol. But after what had been said in the House from the government side about Ulster, he intended, when he went over there, to break every law that was possible. Let the government take its own course.[8]

In the following month, the Unionists organised a great demonstration at Blenheim Palace. Bonar Law said that the people of Ulster feared that under a Dublin government neither their civil nor their religious liberty would be safe. 'They say it and they believe it.' If the unthinkable happened, and the government used troops to shoot down men who demanded no privilege other than was enjoyed by citizens of Britain, they would succeed only in lighting fires of civil war. 'I can imagine no length of resistance to which Ulster will go in which I shall not be ready to support them and in which they will not be supported by the overwhelming majority of the British people.' Carson was no less belligerent. Speaking after Bonar Law, he said 'we will shortly challenge the Government to interfere with us if they dare, and we will with equanimity await the result ... They may tell us if they like that

that is treason; it is not for men who have such stakes as we have at issue to trouble about the cost. We are prepared to take the consequences.'[9]

The language chosen by Carson and Bonar Law at Blenheim was incitement to sedition. It could not be read any other way. Nothing like it had been heard in England from a political leader since the republicans of the seventeenth century had turned the world upside down; and Carson was aptly described as the Cromwell of the new movement.[10]

Did they themselves think that they were preaching sedition? Bonar Law believed that any means were justified to deprive the unholy alliance of Liberals and Irish Nationalists of the power which they had usurped. They had made a corrupt bargain to unman the House of Lords, and concealed from the electorate that the real purpose was to break up the Union and sell out Ulster. They were, he said at Blenheim, 'a revolutionary committee which has seized upon despotic power by fraud'. A view so extravagant will not bear examination. The alliance was no more corrupt, and involved no more expediency, than any other coalition. The electorate knew perfectly well that Home Rule was in the Liberal programme. Carson, on the other hand, did not bother to argue the constitutional basis for his course. His adversaries were fond of pointing out that, while preaching lawless rebellion, he owed his career to the law. But he was not deflected. The preservation of the Union justified the means, whatever they might be.

A. V. Dicey was the theorist of Unionism. He was a highly respected constitutional lawyer and the author of *An Introduction to the Study of the Law of the Constitution*, one of the greatest textbooks on the subject. He was an apostle of the rule of law, and he had formulated the fundamental of parliamentary sovereignty. Parliament (meaning Crown, Lords and Commons), he pronounced, had under the English constitution the right to make or unmake any law whatever; and no person or body is recognised by the law of England as having a right to override or set aside the legislation of Parliament. How was this resonating, *ex cathedra*, and wholly unqualified statement to be reconciled with Bonar Law and Carson's assertion that a Home Rule Act passed by Parliament and having the royal assent would not be valid and could be resisted by all and any means?

Dicey, who was a passionate Liberal Unionist, wrote a book to refute each Home Rule Bill as it was introduced: *The Case Against Home Rule* (1886); *A Leap in the Dark* (1893); and *A Fool's Paradise* (1913). In the last one, *A Fool's Paradise*, he argued that Asquith's Bill would violate the principle, which he described with little conviction as "tacitly and practically" recognised, that no Bill which changes the foundations of the constitution should pass into law until it has obtained the assent of the electors. Much complaint was made by Unionists that the electorate had not had a clear and proper chance to vote on Home Rule. But it was dubious theory, to say the least, that that would vitiate the Bill. And what if the electors sanctioned Home Rule? Dicey was as uncomfortable with the question as were the Unionist leaders. He wrote: 'I will not give, because I have not formed, any certain opinion about how to react to that monstrous iniquity.'[11]

In truth, Dicey was troubled by the practical application of his theories. He wrote endlessly to the Unionist leaders and sympathetic editors during the crisis, putting hypothetical cases, and not helping at all. In July 1912, he posed the question to J. St L. Strachey, the editor and proprietor of the *Spectator*: how would Ulster carry out its resistance? 'A very sagacious and very cool-headed Englishman', he thought, might perhaps manage a successful campaign of passive resistance. But Carson was not the sort of man to conduct such a difficult operation. 'When I met him', said Dicey, 'I liked him but it is impossible to trust his judgment and his temper.'[12] While Dicey havered and worried, Carson had the responsibility to decide and to act. The theory could look after itself. 'I am daily dubbed a rebel and a traitor', Carson said in Belfast to his followers, 'but at all events I shall never be a rebel or a traitor to you. Names cannot alter realities. What is right is right, and no Act of Parliament can make it wrong.'[13]

Asquith described the speeches at Blenheim as a 'reckless rhodomontade'. He was well justified, but his intellectual disdain was unfortunate, for it made him unable to realise that what had been said by Carson and Bonar Law was seriously intended. But other Liberals were uneasy about the storm blowing up in Ulster. Churchill, who had early taken the view that some settlement ought to be possible, wrote to Redmond on 31 August: 'The opposition of three or four Ulster counties is the only obstacle which now stands in the way of Home Rule. You and your friends ought to be thinking of some way round this. No doubt you are, with your usual political foresight.'[14] In the same letter Churchill proposed the option of a moratorium for several years for the Protestant counties before acceding to the Irish Parliament. He admitted that he was apprehensive about the 'combination of the rancour of a party in the ascendant and the fanaticism of these stubborn and determined Orangemen'. Unfortunately, Redmond was not thinking of a way round the 'opposition of three or four Ulster counties'.

Carson went off to Bad Homburg in August as usual, telling Lady Londonderry before leaving that he hated going, but he supposed 'we cannot always stick at home'. The place was becoming more German and less English every year. It was a strange contrast, he said, to have returned from Belfast to 'the air of apathy and unreality in England ... But the next few months will bring us all into the open ... I hope we will have the biggest row there ever has been and be done with it one way or the other ... I will write to you from Homburg – if there is anything or anybody of interest which I hardly expect.'[15] That expectation proved false. While he was sitting watching tennis, a young woman came and occupied the empty chair beside him. She was not shy. They began to talk and he was charmed. She was Ruby Frewen, thirty years younger than he, the daughter of an army officer from Somerset, and staying in Homburg for 'the Season' at the house of her friend, Mrs Hall-Walker.

Carson returned home at the end of August from Homburg. Annette's long slow decline was relentless. 'All here is depressing', he wrote from Rottingdean, 'tho' my wife progresses slowly I think but I find it hard to realise and get accustomed to her being an invalid.' He had stayed the night with Bonar Law on his way home. 'He is full of fight and pluck – I think he is the most modest man I have ever met.'[16] Bonar Law also admired Carson and there was no thought of rivalry. Each recognised in the other someone absolutely straight and not 'on the make'. The purpose of the meeting was for Carson to tell his leader all he knew 'as to the arrangements in Ireland'. Bonar Law was worried about the state of Ulster, but Carson told him that he did not think there was any ground for fearing there might be 'any premature unwisdom in the North'.[17]

There was reason for Bonar Law's apprehension. Fear was abroad again in the North, and the vicious cycle of sectarian outrage had begun once more. At about this time Violet Asquith's friend, Hugh Godley, wrote to her from County Cavan.

> All the people I have talked to of whatever station, from the Archbishop of Armagh to the boy who weeds the garden, are passionately anti-Home Rule. They really think that if it passes there will be a serious rising in Ulster and that all the Protestants in a little outpost like this will be set upon and murdered ... It is very difficult till one gets among them to realize that all these deep feelings are not merely invented by politicians for party purposes.[18]

Trouble started at the end of June when children on a Sunday School outing in County Londonderry, carrying Union Jacks and banners bearing biblical texts and accompanied by a band, were set upon by members of the Ancient Order of Hibernians, a Catholic association revived to counter the Orange Order. On the following day, a Sunday, the minister who had accompanied the children told his congregation not to talk about the incident and stoke up feeling against their Catholic neighbours. Nonetheless reprisals took place within days in the always volatile shipyards. Catholic workmen were told to get their coats and go home. They were pelted with 'Belfast confetti', the metal discs punched out by riveters. Ill-feeling and sporadic violence then rumbled through the summer until it blew up in

September at a match between Catholic and Protestant teams at the Celtic football ground, where Churchill had spoken in February. There was a pitched battle and sixty casualties had to be treated in hospital.[19]

Carson was profoundly concerned about it. The movement that he led was always in danger of spilling over into uncontrolled disorder. If there were to be any 'premature unwisdom', it would come from the urban working class on both sides of the religious divide, who lived and worked dangerously close to each other. It was vital that Carson should prevent it if he could, lest it destroy all he was striving for; but although not sectarian, his own words were inflammatory. Some safety-valve was needed. The means which were chosen were well suited to the Ulster Protestant community. They combined solemnity, religiosity and military discipline.

From the Spring of 1912 Carson had been discussing with James Craig and others the idea of the whole body of Ulster Protestants swearing a solemn oath to resist Home Rule.[20] The idea that the document should be called a Covenant came from a suggestion made to Craig by the Secretary of the Ulster Club in Belfast, B. W. D. Montgomery. He proposed that its wording should be modelled on the old Scottish Solemn League and Covenant.[21] The word 'Covenant' was well chosen. The Covenant of the Old Testament was made with God, and the Promised Land, to which the Israelites would be led from Egypt, was the Land of the Covenant. Calvinist teaching had always laid emphasis on the Old Testament. Now, in the struggle against Home Rule, the conception of God as a strong refuge against the threat of exile seemed precisely in point.

The word was lodged in Presbyterian historical memory. The Scottish Presbyterians, to whose Covenant Montgomery had referred Craig, were in the forefront of the seventeenth-century struggle against domination by the Stuart Kings and the taint of popery. They had repelled the attempt to Anglicanise the Scottish Church with ritual and vestments, and had signed a National Covenant which bound them to maintain the purity of Holy Writ. When civil war came, the parliamentary forces needed the Scots to help them to defeat Charles I. The Scots were willing to do so, but only if their English allies would introduce Presbyterianism south of the Tweed. The Solemn League and Covenant of 1643 was a formal agreement to reform religion in the kingdoms of England and Ireland, and to 'endeavour the extirpation of popery, prelacy ... superstition, heresy, schism, profaneness, and whatsoever shall be found to be contrary to sound doctrine and the power of godliness'. The ornate language meant simply the establishment of Calvinist government.

Sir Walter Scott thought that these people committed the sin of arrogance. In *Old Mortality* he wrote of the envoy of the Covenanters, that 'to judge by his mien and manners, seemed fully imbued with that spiritual pride which distinguished his sect'. There were contemporaries of Carson, like Arthur Balfour, who disliked the northern Presbyterians for the same reason, and for their moral earnestness. Others thought the Ulster Covenant portentous. But Carson had no qualm about the plan to sign a solemn Covenant. The Ulster document, however, did not pretend to be made with God. It appealed to temporal rather than divine majesty and its final invocation was 'God Save the King'.

The text ran:

Ulster's Solemn League and Covenant

Being convinced in our consciences that Home Rule would be disastrous to the material well-being of Ulster as of the whole of Ireland, subversive of our civil and religious freedom, destructive of our citizenship, and perilous to the unity of the Empire, we whose names are underwritten, men of Ulster, loyal subjects of His Gracious Majesty King George V, humbly relying on the God whom our fathers in days of stress and trial confidently trusted, do hereby pledge ourselves in solemn Covenant throughout this our time of threatened calamity to stand by one another in defending for ourselves and our children our cherished position of equal citizenship in the United Kingdom, and in using all means which may be found necessary to defeat the present conspiracy to set up a Home Rule Parliament in Ireland. And in the event of such a Parliament being forced upon us we further solemnly and mutually pledge ourselves to refuse to recognise its authority. In sure confidence that God will defend the right we hereto subscribe our names. And further, we individually declare that we have not already signed this Covenant. God Save the King.

Carson entered into the preparations for the ceremonial signing with enthusiasm. During August it was announced that Saturday 28 September had been fixed as the day for the ceremony, and would henceforth be known as 'Ulster Day'. As usual, Carson, who had neither the talent nor the inclination for administration, left all detail to Craig, who was assisted by the Secretary of the Ulster Unionist Council, Richard Dawson Bates. Bates was an unassuming man, but he held all the threads of the organisation of Unionism in his hand. He had a gift for detail. Everything was meticulously organised. There were to be ten days of meetings throughout the province culminating in the mass act of self-dedication in Belfast. Carson would speak at all the principal towns, and would be accompanied as fellow speakers by F. E. Smith and Lord Londonderry. The mounting excitement can be sensed from the despatches of the journalists of Unionist persuasion as the bandwagon moved on. Their prose heightened as the day of signing approached.

The progress began on 18 September with a gathering in Enniskillen, the frontier town of the province which Carson described as 'one of the outposts, nearer to the zone of danger, and amongst our enemies'. A troop of mounted yeomanry met him at the railway station carrying lances and banners, and wearing rosettes. *The Times* correspondent was there to see 'these young Fermanagh men, bronzed, self-confident, with a look of colonials, riding the horses of their farms and wearing slouch hats and gaiters'.[22] They escorted Carson to Portora Hill, where forty thousand members of the Unionist clubs marched past in military order. The event did not escape the attention of pickpockets. Two Birmingham men were found loitering at the railway station and brought before a magistrate. Their inventive solicitor suggested that they were English Liberals studying the Irish question and visiting Enniskillen to see the demonstration. It was in vain. They were sentenced to two months with hard labour.[23]

The next day at Craigavon Carson, 'standing bare-headed and smoking a cigarette', read out the text of the Covenant to assembled journalists.[24] Meetings followed at Lisburn, Londonderry, Coleraine and other towns. Lisburn was gay with bunting. Union Jacks and other loyal emblems were displayed from almost every house. Swinging arches hung across the streets. The platform in the Grain Market in Lisburn, where the rally was to take place, was draped in blue and crimson, with gold fringes. Streamers hung on Venetian masts in the enclosure, and the entrance gates were ornamented with trophies which 'flaunted gaily in the evening breeze when the distinguished speakers arrived on the scene'. The Lisburn Temperance Silver Band and the Conservative Flute Band headed the procession and played 'Boyne Water' and 'Protestant Boys'. The Volunteers carried dummy rifles and lighted torches. Carson read out the text of the Covenant and told his audience that they would be asked to sign 'with religious deliberation', and that this would be 'the most solemn step that a God-fearing and a law-abiding people have ever been asked to take in defence of their civil and religious liberties'.[25] *The Times* correspondent was moved to purple prose by the sight of the working men here. 'They seemed to be animated by a more desperate resolve,' he wrote, 'and as they carried the resolution with a roar of cheers, the multitude looked as dark and forbidding as the sea with a storm brooding over it.'[26]

On the eve of signing, the Ulster Unionist Council formally ratified the Covenant in the Old Town Hall in Belfast. It had already been approved by the leaders of the Protestant churches. Then in the evening there was a rally in the Ulster Hall. F. E. Smith was one of the speakers. His 'caustic satire' drew salvoes of cheers. As the crowning act of symbolism, Colonel Wallace, the Grand Master of the Belfast Orange Lodge, handed Carson a faded yellow banner, said to have been carried before William III at the Boyne. 'If that flag ever saw the Battle of the Boyne,' remarked the *Irish News* sourly, 'all we can say is the man who manufactured it deserves undying fame for the strength and durability of the material.' *The Times* correspondent thought the comment unseemly.[27]

No one could fail to appreciate the seriousness of what was happening in Ulster, not the scoffing Radical press nor the Liberal front bench. The dangerous head of steam that had been building between Ulster Catholic and Protestant was – for a time at least – damped down. But the character of the monster rally on the eve of Ulster Day was more than anything else religious. It was well described at first hand by Ronald McNeill, a leading Ulster Unionist MP and a member of the Ulster Unionist Council.

> The mental atmosphere, he wrote, was not that of a political meeting but of a religious service – and in fact the proceedings had been opened by prayer, as had become the inevitable custom on such occasions in Ulster. It was felt to be a time of individual preparation for the *sacramentum* of the following day, which Protestant Ulster had set apart as a day of self-dedication to a cause for which they were willing to make any sacrifice.[28]

On the following morning, Ulster Day, 'O God, Our Help in Ages Past' was sung in Protestant church services across the province as ministers and their congregations identified themselves with the Unionist cause and the solemn act of dedication to be performed that day. In Belfast, factories, shipyards and workplaces lay idle. Boxes of copies of the Covenant for signature had been distributed throughout Ulster and beyond. Each box contained a large-scale copy of the text printed in Old English typeface with the Red Hand of Ulster at the head. In heraldry, the badge of Ulster is a sinister hand, erect, open and couped at the wrist, gules. The hereditary title of baronet was instituted by James I in 1611, the sale of which was to provide funds for the defence of the Ulster plantation. The Red Hand became the badge of the baronetcy, and so of Ulster.

Carson was the first to sign. The image of that moment is burned in public memory. He looks up as he prepares to sign. On his right hand is the lugubrious figure of Lord Londonderry, on his left a younger, defiant Craig, the organiser of victory, both looking straight ahead; behind, a wall of grimly determined faces. All are men; only Carson, the southerner, has a clean-shaven upper lip.

After the temporal and spiritual leaders had signed, the doors were opened to admit the public in batches of some five hundred who formed orderly queues inside the City Hall to come up to the tables to sign. As at the earlier rallies, there were no policemen on hand and none were needed.

Ronald McNeill was one of the signatories. He described the scene inside the City Hall. All was quiet within the sunlit hall; while 'through the open door could be seen a vast forest of human heads, endless as far as the eye could reach ... whose blended voices ... were carried to the ears of those in the hall like the inarticulate noise of moving waters'.[29]

All over Ulster it was the same. In every town and village there were signing ceremonies. Everyone was out in his Sunday best. Outside Ulster, more than two thousand men signed in Dublin, and signatures were collected in London, Liverpool, Glasgow and other cities on the mainland. In Ulster almost a quarter of a million men signed the Covenant, and a similar number of women signed a corresponding form of declaration.

After it was all over Carson dined with the Lord Mayor of Belfast at the Ulster Club. The steamship *Patriotic* was to leave at 9.15 to take him to Liverpool. He was carried in a wagonette from the club to the quay. As he and the other leaders arrived at the dockside a great shout went up. The crowd was so densely packed that he could not go on board. 'Don't leave us. You mustn't leave us', they shouted. Someone called out that he had work to do in England as well, and the press of people gave way at last. As he leaned over the rail on the upper deck they sang the National Anthem and 'Come Back to Erin'. Some hundred thousand had seen him off.[30]

Afterwards Carson told Lady Londonderry, who was unable to be in Belfast for the ceremonies with her husband, that everything had gone without a hitch, and that he was especially pleased at the great good order of the people: 'they are the finest I have ever seen'. He had never imagined, he said, that the Covenant would be such a success both in Ireland and Great Britain.[31] From Liverpool, where the boat from Belfast docked, Carson went on to Glasgow, where he addressed a crowd of over six thousand at an indoor meeting. Many of the audience were of Ulster origins, and he was continually interrupted by cheering and the waving of the Union Jack. When he had finished, the entire assembly rose to its feet and cheered him to the echo for five minutes.[32] He told Lady Londonderry that the Glasgow demonstration had been the most magnificent and enthusiastic he had ever seen.

He was entitled to feel that the Covenant rallies had been just as much a political success as a triumph for good order. J. L. Garvin, the editor of the *Observer*, was so excited by Carson's plans that he went to Belfast to see the event for himself. He loved Carson as he had loved Parnell for the big men they both were, and in the *Observer* for 29 September he summed up magisterially: 'The spirit of Ulster has been made plain in the past week. Home Rule is dead, killed by the resistance of Sir Edward Carson and his followers.'[33] The conclusion was wildly off the mark.

By the ceremony of the Covenant Carson attained an extraordinary ascendancy over the Protestants of Ulster. He was an outsider, but it made no difference. It may even have been an advantage for the leader to appear as a messiah from far off. In any case the leader and his followers trusted each other and had plenty in common. These people were clear, austere, hard working, the ones to be with in a tight corner. So was he. He was not for a game of bluff, as he had told Craig at the outset. Nor were they. For, with those qualities, they were 'determined never to amalgamate with the race of babblers and merry Andrews', as the French historian, Halévy remarked mischievously, 'whose follies and vices the new school of Irish literature delighted, it would seem, to depict as though in defiance, a spectacle for the respectable Protestants of the north.'[34] Their belief in the Union and its untold benefits was no greater than his. They knew what he had sacrificed for it, and they were prepared to do the same.

A year later Bonar Law explained to an audience in Newcastle that the Ulster movement was greater than its leader.

Now Sir Edward Carson and I are friends, he said, in his presence I shall say no word in his praise. His influence is greatly, in my opinion absurdly, exaggerated by our opponents. They think, or pretend to think, this movement in Ulster, to which they have given his name, is due to him, and without him would disappear. There never was a greater delusion. That movement rests on forces far deeper and stronger than the personality of any man.[35]

For all that, Carson's ascendancy over his followers was a personal one, and his oratory held them. His style of speaking was very plain. Although he used a bitter sarcasm, he avoided ornament, artifice and imagery. His sentences were short and straightforward. His meaning was never in doubt, whoever formed his audience. Written down, his speeches can appear commonplace, but to someone who was there, and heard and saw him, his sombre presence and hatchet face were not to be forgotten. 'His mobile expression – so variable that his enemies saw in it a suggestion of Mephistopholes, and his friends a resemblance to Dante – his measured diction, and his skilful use of a deep-toned voice, gave a remarkable impressiveness to all he said'.[36] Carson was no mob orator. He enunciated a simple Old Testament morality and an old-fashioned view of manly virtue which were entirely agreeable to the Calvinists who made him their leader. He gave them a sense of fellowship which they felt as hymn singers. But more than that, he gripped them with his power. They went home filled with a hot resolve never to give way.

When the editor of the *Irish Times*, a steadily Unionist paper, came to write Carson's obituary notice more than twenty years later in 1935, he made

an extraordinary remark. The career of Edward Carson, the obituarist considered, had been one of the tragedies of Irish history. 'If he had been forty
years younger, Lord Carson of Duncairn might have been a British Hitler,
or even a Mussolini ...'[37] At that time the British public, and the Irish people – more so – did not begin to comprehend the nature of Fascism and its
leaders. But the observation, which was made without a trace of irony, is still
shocking. There was nothing Fascist about the Ulster Unionist movement.
But some of its methods and tactics bore some resemblance to those which
became familiar in the Germany of the 1930s, among them the cult of the
charismatic leader and the techniques of propaganda. The line between an
inspirational leader and one who can loose dangerous charges of emotion
in his followers is a thin one.

10

Ulster

As soon as Parliament reassembled in October 1912, Asquith moved a resolution to allot specified periods for the remaining stages of the Home Rule Bill. He was wearied by the interminable debates and yet somehow he had to maintain momentum in order to keep faith with his Irish allies. Redmond himself was uncomfortable. He was being pressed by a faction of his Irish Nationalists on the weaknesses in the Bill, particularly the financial clauses. Some Liberals, led by Churchill and Lloyd George, were pulling in the other direction. They were looking for some way of treating Ulster separately, and the weight and determination shown by the Unionists in the episode of the Covenant added strength to their argument. But the guillotine resolution did not improve tempers. In November they frayed and snapped.

On 11 November the government was taken by surprise and defeated on a financial amendment.[1] On the 13th, Asquith moved a resolution to rescind the amendment, saying that it did not represent the considered judgment of the House. In that atmosphere, it was not an observation likely to endear him to Members. A shambles ensued and, amid cries of 'civil war', the Speaker adjourned, saying that a state of grave disorder had arisen.[2] After the Speaker withdrew, and before the House was emptied of Members, there were further ructions. Churchill taunted the opposition, waving a handkerchief at the benches opposite. Ronald McNeill aimed a book at him and scored a direct hit. Churchill advanced towards his assailant across the floor, but was persuaded to leave the Chamber. The next day apologies were tendered and accepted.

As Carson was aware, the combined effect of the Parliament Act and the guillotine meant that the report stage of the Bill might be the last opportunity in the Commons for a full debate on Ulster's special position. The remainder of the committee work would be guillotined. And when their turn came to consider the Bill, the Lords could do no more than hold up progress. With guillotine and Parliament Act, Asquith had a complete armoury, since, as Lord Londonderry succinctly said, 'while the House of Commons can vote but not speak, your Lordships can speak but cannot vote effectively'.[3] The two further passages of the Bill required by the Parliament

Act would be a formality. With all this in mind, how could Carson and Bonar Law maintain effective resistance to the Bill?

Carson decided that it was time to float openly the idea of splitting off Ulster. It had been in his mind for at least a year. In December he went over to Belfast to discuss the idea with the Ulster Unionist Council. His proposal was that he should move an amendment during the report stage of the Bill to exclude the whole province, leaving Ulster as part of the United Kingdom. As he would have expected, it was not warmly welcomed, for it cut across the so far undeviating policy of 'No Home Rule'. And it left the Unionists of the south and west to the mercies of a Popish Dublin Parliament. There was a long discussion, but Carson's proposal was in the end accepted unanimously. It was a mark of his authority. The resolution of the standing committee included its 'firm belief' that, by the exclusion of Ulster, 'the interests of Unionists in the three other provinces of Ireland will be best conserved'.[4] It was perhaps more a hope than an expectation that those other Unionists would agree.

What was in Carson's mind was a two-pronged attack on the Bill. While intensifying and making more credible the threat of resistance in Ulster, he would for the first time make a formal move to separate the province from the rest of the island. He proposed his amendment on 1 January 1913. In a speech which Asquith described as very powerful and moving, Carson explained his reasons. He told the House that he was convinced that without the use of force the Ulster Protestants could not be compelled to submit to Home Rule. The events surrounding the signing of the Covenant showed that these men were grimly in earnest. 'Can any man measure beforehand – if you once try to drive people out of a Constitution they are satisfied with into another – where the forces of disorder if once let loose will find their objective, or what will be the end of it? ... there is time yet left in this case to avert disaster.'[5]

The speech was meant as a sober warning. But Asquith was not temperamentally inclined to treat it at face value. As Carson must have known, it was certain that he would dismiss it as a mere tactic. 'What is this amendment?' Asquith asked. 'The Right Hon. Gentleman knows perfectly well what it means. It means the wrecking of the whole Bill.'[6] The amendment was lost. The Bill pursued its way, passed its third reading on 16 January, and was then duly rejected by the House of Lords by a huge majority at the end of that month.

The credibility of splitting Ireland along the line of the provincial border of Ulster was damaged by the by-election in Derry City on 30 January, which was won by a Home Ruler. This put the Unionists into a minority of the MPs returned for the province. If there was to be a split, it was likely that it would have to be drawn along a narrower front.

Before the vote on Carson's amendment was taken, Bonar Law said, incautiously, that he believed that the people of the north east would prefer to accept the government of a foreign country, rather than submit to the Irish Nationalists.[7] Churchill pounced, derisively calling Bonar Law's remark 'the latest step in Imperial statecraft'. 'This then is the latest Tory threat. Ulster will secede to Germany' (Hon. Members: 'Why Germany?' and 'Who said Germany?')[8] There was a reason. In January 1911, James Craig had referred to a feeling in Ulster that Germany and the Kaiser might be preferred to 'the rule of John Redmond, Patrick Ford and the Molly Maguires'.[9] Patrick Ford was a veteran of the Fenian movement; 'Molly Maguires' was the name popularly given to the Ancient Order of Hibernians. Against the rising tide of German militarism, what Bonar Law and Craig had said was scandalous.

Carson missed the vote on third reading. He had cancelled all his engagements and was down at Rottingdean where Annette lay helpless and dying. On 18 January he wrote to Lady Londonderry that she had lost much ground since the previous week, and he did not think he could leave her. 'Oh how I suffer with it all. But you are the kindest of friends and understand so well.'[10] His daughter Aileen was staying with him. She was a stalwart, and he wrote truly when he said that, but for her, he could not go on.[11] Annette died on 6 April 1913 after thirty-four years of marriage, and was buried in Rottingdean churchyard. He allowed a week to pass before writing again, from Eaton Place, where Aileen had gone with him: 'My dear and good friend ... I felt it so horrible to see my wife die in a few minutes even tho' I had really gone thro' it nearly every night for some months. I was so glad I was at home as a few hours before she died the last thing she said was "I want to see my old man" and altho' she did not speak she put her face up to be kissed and put her arm round my neck.' Then, with the remorse which was inevitable, 'she was with me all my career and I did the best I could for her and her happiness'.[12]

Since January 1912, magistrates in Ulster had authorised drilling and military exercises. As an advocate, Carson knew that the way to a good settlement was to show strength. He encouraged the drilling and militarism in every way he could. He inspected and presented colours to Orangemen and volunteers from the Unionist clubs. By the beginning of 1913 there were tens of thousands of men who were undergoing military training. Drilling was going on in public places, in Orange halls, and in the farms and parks of sympathetic landowners, many of whom took part themselves. For the most part, the volunteers used wooden dummy rifles. This caused hilarity in some parts of the Nationalist press. But the men who trained the volunteers were serious enough and had gained experience in the South African war. And not all the rifles were dummies. The magistrates licensed not only drilling, but also training in small arms, and a small quantity of rifles was being imported – which was at this stage perfectly legal.

In January 1913 the Ulster Unionist Council decided that these local groups of volunteers should be organised into one body to be known as the Ulster Volunteer Force. Numbers were to be limited to a hundred thousand and every volunteer must have signed the Covenant. The structure of the new army was based on the model of the British Army, in its division by county and by district, into regiments, battalions and companies. The Orange Lodges and Unionist clubs were invited to undertake local recruitment and organisation. The response was highly enthusiastic and recruitment went on apace.

The organisation of the volunteers was in place very quickly, as is well vouched by the papers of Captain Roger Hall, in charge of dispositions at Newry. On 20 January 1913, he had a letter from one of his subordinates, Joseph Orr.[13] 'I got your letter before the LOL [Loyal Orange Lodge]' Orr wrote, 'and they appointed the WM [Worshipful Master] of each Lodge as a committee to confer with your humble. We had a meeting and divided each district into six localities ... I appointed leaders ... I attended Altnaveigh on last Friday night for the first meeting and got twenty-five volunteers ... I could get in each locality about 150 in all and when they are drilled, if there were too many, I could pick whatever number was required'. Rifles were in short supply, and a Belfast merchant offered dummy ones in all wood, 'shaped as nearly as possible like a service weapon' in pitch pine at 1s. 8d. or spruce at 1s. 6d. each.[14] In October another correspondent told Hall that the BSAs, rifles manufactured by the Birmingham Small Arms company, were in great demand and that he needed more. Only four men could be instructed at one time and it was very slow work.[15] Pressure for real weapons was growing.

The new army now needed a Commander-in-Chief. Colonel Hickman, an English Unionist MP, who was taking a special interest in Ulster, agreed to get advice from Earl Roberts, the most distinguished and decorated soldier in the United Kingdom, who was known to be sympathetic to the Unionist cause. Roberts, universally and affectionately known as 'Bobs', had been born in India but both his parents were southern Irish Protestants. He wrote to Hickman on 3 June to say that he had been a long time finding a suitable senior officer, but he thought he had one now. His name was Lieutenant-General Sir George Richardson. He was not an Irishman, said Roberts, but had settled in Ireland, and was ready to meet at any time.[16] Richardson had retired the service in 1907. He turned out to be a very sound choice.[17]

Richardson found that his staff were already in post. They were local gentry, accustomed to command and determined to preserve their way of life. They were also men with considerable military experience, gained in India or South Africa. General Sir William Adair, who commanded the Antrim division, was a good example. A tall, chilly, retired Royal Marine, he was later to command the landward side of the illegal gun-running, but would not have spent a moment to reflect on the ethical or political consequences. The Chief of Staff was Colonel George Hacket Pain, like Richardson an Indian Army officer. Others, like Colonel T. V. P. McCammon, a member of the Orange Order, were closely involved in the political organisation of the Ulster movement.

When the new Commander-in-Chief went to the north in July to see his troops for the first time, there were more than fifty thousand of them. After a number of parades at which Carson accompanied the General, there was a grand review in Belfast on 27 September. Richardson took the salute, Carson, Craig and Lord Londonderry were on the platform with him and, while an entire division marched past in review order, the bands played the 'British Grenadiers'.[18] F. E. Smith, mounted and in a bowler hat, acted as the general's 'galloper'.

There was much here to be taken seriously by the Liberal front bench. The temper of the officer class in the regular army (what other ranks may have thought never seems to have been taken into account) and the potential of the Volunteer Force were matters worth study; and the more so since the threat was being assessed as a grave one by men on the spot. The monthly report for July 1913 from the Commissioner of the Royal Irish Constabulary in Belfast to the Chief Secretary's office noted that religious and political feeling had intensified over the past twelve months, and that between the Orange body and the Unionist clubs some 20,000 men had been drilled in Belfast.

> To sum up the situation you have in Belfast some 300,000 Protestants and 100,000 Catholics – the latter mainly dependent on the former for a livelihood – of the Protestant population all are bitterly opposed to Home Rule ... I am convinced that there will be serious loss of life and wholesale destruction of property in Belfast on the passing of the Home Rule Bill.

The County Inspector for Antrim agreed. He reported that Carson had been inspecting the UVF around the county, and he did not think that the businessmen of Ulster would decline to take an active part for fear of injuring their business. 'There is no doubt that the cry of "bluff" must be laid aside.'[19] But Asquith continued to doubt the reality of the threat.

There were other belligerent developments. The commission which had been appointed to draft a constitution for the provisional government of Ulster completed its work. The draft was approved by the Ulster Unionist Council in September 1913; but the text of the constitution was not published, and then only in part, until July 1914. If the Home Rule Bill passed into law, the constitution would come into operation immediately. On that happening, the Council would become a 'Central Authority', with Carson as chairman. Departmental affairs would be delegated to a number of committees and boards. Carson was the first named in each. There was provision for an independent judiciary and a military council.

The whole scheme was drawn up as an ordinance in the form of a parliamentary Bill, whose opening words were 'It is hereby Enacted by the Central Authority in the name of the King's Most Excellent Majesty ...' The hapless George V cannot have enjoyed discovering what had been done in his name. The constitution went on to state that the government in Ulster would be held 'in trust for the Constitution of the United Kingdom', and that 'upon the restoration of direct Imperial Government, the Provisional Government shall cease to exist'.[20] By these legal gymnastics the Unionists strove to preserve their Loyalist allegiance. Asquith's acute sense of irony must have been strained by the shameless appropriation of the clothing of lawful authority.

As the RIC Inspector for Antrim had forecast, the Belfast business community were prepared to back these arrangements. An indemnity fund was established to compensate members of the UVF in case they should suffer any loss or disability. Contributions were invited, and by the end of the first week £387,000 had been subscribed. By the beginning of 1914 the figure stood at over £1,000,000.

Meanwhile, on 27 March 1913 a letter signed by a hundred Unionist peers and 120 commoners had appeared in the London press.[21] It announced the formation of a British League for the support of Ulster and the Union. This was the first step in a movement of great significance. It would grow rapidly and demonstrate that, if Ulster were to be forced, it would not fight alone. It would have friends not only in Britain but also throughout the Empire, the integrity of which was one of the most important and emotive elements of Unionism. The members of the League intended to be an active force in politics. They also helped the UVF in its military preparations. Colonel Hickman, who had helped to find a Commander-in-Chief, was also a member of the commission that drafted the constitution for the rebel province. Hickman went further into territory of dubious legality, and involved himself in gun-running and in recruiting English officers for the Volunteers.[22] The story of the growth of the League, its adoption of a British Covenant mirroring the Ulster Covenant, and the adherence of many public figures in

Britain belongs to 1914. But there was enough earlier evidence of tangible support in Britain for Carson and his Ulster Protestants to give Asquith pause. If the talk of civil war was not just alarmist, it might spread from the north of Ireland to the mainland.

Carson's tactic was to demonstrate that he was in earnest. During 1913 he had established the framework for a separate 'provisional' government for Ulster, if Home Rule passed. The mechanism was in place and it was fully staffed. A military arm with 100,000 troops was in an advanced state of readiness. As yet it had no real weaponry; but, even without, it presented an obstacle to any attempt to force Home Rule on the province. That itself was increasingly implausible. Sending regular soldiers to put down the rebellious Ulstermen was widely regarded as unthinkable. In any case, the reliability of the army in these circumstances was doubtful. And any doubts were reinforced by the presence of men in public life, led by the Leader of the Opposition, willing to back Carson by any and all means.

It was a strong hand. But even so, it was a risky course. The rising excitement in Ulster had to be contained, lest it spill out into sectarian violence. Carson was careful always to avoid polarising the dispute so that it became religious, telling his followers that they had no quarrel with individual Irishmen, whatever their creed. It is much to his credit that, so far, serious trouble had been avoided. As Bonar Law was to say, it was due to him alone, and to the confidence the people of Ulster placed in him, that they had been restrained.[23] To date the northern Catholics had been little more than interested spectators. But they might not remain so. That threat would come closer if Redmond's precarious hold on his Nationalist followers were to be prised loose by men less scrupulous. The lessons being taught in Ulster of the leverage to be gained by a show of force would not be lost on men growing impatient of waiting for Irish independence by constitutional means. It remained to be seen whether Carson's tactics would yield a settlement by agreement.

Bonar Law and Order in Belfast.

11

Marconi

In March 1912 the Postmaster-General, Herbert Samuel, announced that, subject to the approval of Parliament, the government had accepted a tender from the Marconi Company to build a chain of wireless stations throughout the Empire. Wireless telegraphy was a new and reliable means of communication, of great interest to the government both in its civil and military applications. The announcement gave a sudden boost to Marconi shares, to which the *Titanic* disaster in April gave further impetus. That tragic event showed in the most dramatic way possible the need for wireless telegraphy on shipboard.

The Managing Director of Marconi was Godfrey Isaacs, the brother of the Attorney-General, Sir Rufus Isaacs. The English Marconi Company had a number of associated companies operating in various countries, including the United States. In view of the frequent assertions that the American company was completely independent of the English company, their relationship is of some importance. It is not easy to say precisely what it was, but this much can certainly be said. The English company had a controlling interest in the American company, amounting to 57.9 per cent of its shares; and Godfrey Isaacs was a director of both companies.

Marconi decided to expand the activities of its American company, and to fund the expansion by introducing shares in the American company on the London market. The new issue would increase the share capital by more than six times, and Godfrey Isaacs and Guglielmo Marconi were to underwrite the whole issue. This was to be done on 19 April 1912 at a price of £3 5s. per share.

But before this, on 9 April, Godfrey Isaacs met his two brothers, Rufus and Harry. He told them of certain contracts which the American company had entered into, and that he had 100,000 shares of the new issue to dispose of. He said that the shares were certain to go to a premium. They could have as many as they liked. Rufus declined to take any shares but Harry agreed to take 50,000 at £1 1s. 3d. Meanwhile the price of the shares in the English company was rising, which in turn affected the demand for shares in its American subsidiary company. Harry urged Rufus to take some American shares, and eventually persuaded him to take 10,000 of his own 50,000 at £2.

On 17 April, Rufus offered to Lloyd George, his colleague in the Liberal government, and the Liberal Chief Whip, Alexander Murray (the Master of Elibank), 2000 of the shares he had agreed to buy from Harry, giving them the same information about the American company he had had from his brother Godfrey. They agreed to take them. When the American company's shares were introduced to the market on the 19th they jumped immediately to nearly £4. All three ministers promptly sold. They subsequently bought again, the Chief Whip buying for the Liberal Party Fund, and eventually made losses.

Insider trading, which these dealings clearly were, was not then a criminal offence, as it is now. Nonetheless it was improper for Ministers to engage in such transactions. It was also imprudent to a point almost beyond belief. It was especially so because rumours that the contract between the government and the English Marconi Company was corrupt, and that ministers were gambling in the shares, were circulating freely in the City and beyond. The gossip involved two prominent Jewish members of the government, Rufus Isaacs and Herbert Samuel, and was made more ugly by an undertow of anti-Semitism. It was not long before these suspicions found their way into print in a scurrilous journal called *Eye Witness*, edited by Hilaire Belloc and Cecil Chesterton, G. K. Chesterton's brother. In face of these rumours and suspicions, the Prime Minister promised, during the summer, to appoint a select committee to investigate the circumstances surrounding the Marconi contract. On 11 October Herbert Samuel moved the appointment of the committee.[1] The committee met for the first time on 25 October.

Rufus Isaacs made a personal statement in the debate, in the course of which he said: 'Never from the beginning, when the shares were 14s. or £9, have I had one single transaction with the shares of that company.'[2] In that passage Isaacs referred to the English company, and was so understood. But he said nothing about his dealings in the American company's shares. He also made it clear that he was speaking not only for himself, but also for Herbert Samuel and Lloyd George. The latter did not make a speech.

On 12 February 1913 Leo Maxse, the editor of the *National Review*, gave evidence to the select committee. Maxse was a Diehard Tory whose sister had married a Cecil and whose widow was eventually to marry Lord Milner. He appeared to know about the dealings in the American company, but he was careful in what he told the committee. He pointed out that, since the rumours began, Ministers had done nothing to dispel the mist of suspicion overhanging the affair. One might have conceived, he said, that those under suspicion would have appeared before the committee at its first sitting, clamouring to state in the most categorical and emphatic way that they had

had no transactions in any shares in *any* Marconi company throughout the negotiations with the government.[3]

Two days later the French newspaper *Le Matin* published an account by its London correspondent of Maxse's evidence. It was a travesty of what he had said.[4] The account was defamatory of Herbert Samuel, who was in any case blameless, and of Rufus Isaacs. Samuel and Isaacs decided to sue. Carson and F. E. Smith accepted briefs to appear for them.[5] The case came on for hearing in a court besieged by a curious public on 19 March 1913. There was no defence to the action and *Le Matin* was fortunate to escape with an apology and costs, but no damages.

It was, however, at the hearing that the public learned for the first time of the dealings in the American company's shares. Carson volunteered the information, although it was not germane to the libel action. He did so on the explicit instructions of Rufus Isaacs, as the House learned later.[6] Isaacs said that he 'insisted' on its being disclosed then, although that only added point to the question why it had not been made clear to the House when the matter was debated in October 1912, nine months earlier. Carson made much of the fact that the Ministers had made a loss on the investment. He said that the American company was independent and had no interest in the profits of the English company, 'although the English company has shares in it'.[7] This was a poor way to make a clean breast of things. The fact that the result of the purchase of the American company's shares turned out to be a loss was irrelevant to the propriety of the transaction. And the description of the American subsidiary was a half truth. The close connection between the two companies had been demonstrated by the way the American company's share price had been affected by movements in the price of those of the English company.

The belated disclosure of the share dealings had political consequences. The select committee summoned Rufus Isaacs to appear within a week of the revelation in court. In his evidence he stubbornly maintained the independence of the American company from its English parent. Lloyd George did not dissent from this view. The Chief Whip, however, did not give evidence, since he had gone away to the implausible destination of Bogota. By this means, he seems to have escaped all censure.

The committee divided on party lines and the majority exonerated the Ministers. That, however, was not the end of the matter. In June, George Cave, a Conservative back bencher and a future Lord Chancellor, moved a resolution in studiedly moderate terms, regretting the conduct of the Ministers not only for their share dealings, but also for their want of candour before the committee.[8] Isaacs gave the House details of the transactions in the American company's shares, saying that, at the time of the share dealings, he had thought them unobjectionable, but that if he had known then what he now knew, he would not have entered into them.[9] Eventually, the Ministers were acquitted of bad faith and their expressions of regret were accepted.

Bonar Law had been handicapped in the debate by the absence of Carson and F. E. Smith. Carson wrote to him to excuse himself. 'I want to explain that I consulted Lord Halsbury about voting and he advised me not to do so as it would be open to hostile criticism and so I thought it best to go the straight line.'[10] His leader replied: 'I quite understood when you did not take part in the division that you felt you could not honourably do so, and I was sure that your decision in any case would be the right one.'[11]

It was not quite what Bonar Law thought. There was much disquiet, and some anger, in the party about Carson's and Smith's position, which Bonar Law privately shared.[12] Many did not think that Carson had 'gone the straight line'. James Campbell, Carson's old friend, had asked Bonar Law beforehand whether or not he should take a brief, which he had been offered, for *Le Matin*. Carson and Smith had not asked. They took the view that legal etiquette precluded them from refusing. Carson published a statement:[13]

> I believe in what I did I acted in accordance with my duty as a barrister, and I think I also did so according to the highest traditions of the Bar. We are given a monopoly of advocacy not for this person or that person, or this side or that side, and I think myself (I may be wrong) that it will not be a good day for the administration of justice when the judge or jury or counsel may be looked upon as taking political sides.

But Sir George Younger, the Unionist Scottish Whip, spoke for many Tories when he wrote to Bonar Law in May: 'Legal etiquette may be what it pleases, but it could never be held right to utilize it in order to close the mouths of prominent politicians whose duty to their constituents is paramount, and who have no business thus to handicap themselves ... This feeling is very strong amongst our men.'[14]

The argument about what Carson and Smith should or should not have done was carried on in the press. *The Times* devoted an editorial to it, and gave its opinion that the advocates had taken the independence and brotherhood of the Bar too far, and that it was confusing to the ordinary man. FE replied in a long pompous letter, saying 'You speak of the "ordinary man". I do not in this connexion recognize such a tribunal ... *The Times* would be better employed in informing his mind than appealing to his judgment'.[15]

There is no doubt that a debate on the conduct of Ministers who had dealt in Marconi shares presented a great opportunity for the opposition. It was even possible that a concerted attack in the House might have brought the government down – the very object which the Ulster leaders most wanted. Yet here were the two greatest lawyers and masters of invective on the Conservative side, absent from the House and defending the miscreants, giving the impression, as the public might think, that there was nothing in the Marconi scandal after all. What might not Carson have done, when Cave's motion was debated, with the statements made by Isaacs to the House of Commons and the select committee, when compared with his transactions in the American Marconi shares? Lady Londonderry joined Carson's critics. We do not know what she wrote, but its tenor can be gathered from his exasperated reply. 'It is no use my explaining again the position I am in as a barrister. You would not listen! However, as I *know* I was right in my action, I am unrepentant.'[16]

Understandably, Isaacs was very grateful to Carson. 'My Dear Ned', he wrote, 'You behaved to me with all that nobility which is characteristic of you – there I must leave it – it almost overwhelms me.'[17] One must hope that Carson did not warm to this oleaginous tribute. By then Isaacs had become Lord Chief Justice, by favour of his Prime Minister. He was the leading one of three Ministers who had placed themselves in a position in which their public duty was at odds with their pecuniary ambitions; and they had done so by accepting favours from a company which was contracting with the government of which they were members. Isaacs knew the law as well as anyone, but he did not apply its principles to himself. Rudyard Kipling thought the whole thing 'stank pretty much', and that the 'tomfool' Unionists had been stupid and incompetent.[18] He saluted Isaacs's appointment as Lord Chief Justice and his elevation to the peerage as Lord Reading with one of the bitterest poems in the language, *Gehazi*, the untrustworthy servant of Elisha.

'Whence comest thou, Gehazi,
So reverend to behold,
In scarlet and in ermines,
And chain of England's gold?'
'From following after Naaman
To tell him all is well,
Whereby my zeal hath made me
A Judge in Israel.'

In August 1913 Carson was at Homburg as usual when a curious incident occurred. He sat next to the Kaiser at a lunch party. Carson found that he took 'an extraordinary interest' in everything and 'loves a joke'. He was much fascinated by the Emperor's personality, he told Lady Londonderry.[19] The Kaiser remarked that he would have liked to go to Ireland, but that his grandmother, Queen Victoria, would not let him. 'Perhaps she thought I wanted to take the little place.' Carson replied: 'I think, Sir, you are well out of it.'[20] He seemed to forget that the German Emperor was by then the single greatest threat to European stability.

By the beginning of September 1913 there had been no worthwhile attempt to resolve the Ulster crisis by agreement. The Home Rule Bill had been grinding noisily through Parliament, and preparations for war were going on apace in Ulster. But, with the doubtful exception of Carson's own amendment to exclude the whole of Ulster from the Bill, no one had made a move for peace.

At that point, however, Lord Loreburn, a former Liberal Lord Chancellor and, until then at least, a committed Home Ruler, dropped a sizeable stone into the pond. On 9 September Loreburn wrote to *The Times* to suggest that there should be a conference between the leaders on both sides behind closed doors. The editor gave it the heading, 'Lord Loreburn's Appeal to the Nation'. The letter was a long one but the gist was simple. If the government went on with its Bill there would be unprecedented disturbance and violence in the North of Ireland. Is there, then, Loreburn asked, really nothing that can be done except to watch the play of irreconcilable forces in a spirit of indolent resignation? Surely it would be better to talk.

The letter took everyone by surprise. Asquith told his daughter Violet that Loreburn had not consulted him beforehand. 'Would the conference be any good?', she asked. His answer was characteristic: 'Not at this stage – there is nothing to confer about – no common ground to meet on. It's no good all meeting round a tea-table.'[21] Asquith was privately irritated by 'this typical elder statesman's show of non-partisan wisdom'.[22] If the Prime Minister was annoyed, Redmond was appalled. It showed how successful Carson's tactics had been, he thought, and had greatly stiffened the Ulster resistance. It showed too the consequences of the Liberals' want of resolution.[23]

Carson was impressed by the Loreburn letter. He told Ruby Frewen, with whom he had been in touch since their encounter in Homburg, that of course the letter was important. He thought (wrongly) that it must have been inspired by the government to secure peace, but that it was difficult to see whether it could lead to anything.[24] He became more optimistic as the autumn wore on about the prospects of peace, although cautiously so. In the middle of October he told Lady Londonderry that he doubted if, after Loreburn's intervention and Churchill's hints of a settlement, the Cabinet could really intend to go on to the bitter end.[25] But a good deal had happened before he wrote that last letter.

The King was much troubled by the way events were being allowed to drift. He had been embroiled in one turbulent episode over the House of

Lords, and now another was looming up. Bonar Law was not averse to prolonging the royal discomfort if by so doing he could further the Unionist cause. Speaking at Edinburgh in January, he asked his audience to suppose that the Bill had passed all its stages and was waiting for the King to decide whether or not it should become law. What would then be the position of the sovereign of this country, he asked. Whatever he did, half of his people would think he had failed in his duty.[26] George V took this to heart. In a memorandum for the Prime Minister of 11 August, he said: 'Whatever I do I shall offend half the population ... I cannot help feeling that the Government is drifting and taking me with it.'[27]

The King had an opportunity to make his views known when Churchill was at Balmoral in the middle of September, and when Bonar Law was there too. Asquith had asked Churchill to sound out the Unionist leader. He wrote a word of friendly advice to his young colleague. 'You will find the royal mind obsessed, and the royal tongue exceptionally fluid and voluble.' Asquith did not have a high opinion of the King's grasp of affairs, and had just sent him a memorandum on 'what are, and *what are not* the functions of a Constitutional Sovereign in regard to legislation' – doubtless to counteract any heresies that Bonar Law might insert into the royal mind. Asquith told Churchill that the important thing was 'to emphasise the dangers of rejection, when the ship is just reaching port. An ungovernable Ireland is a much more serious prospect than rioting in four counties – serious (and if possible, to be avoided) as the latter is.'[28] Nothing could show more clearly how blinded by optimism the Prime Minister was.

Churchill duly had his talk with Bonar Law, which the latter carefully noted and copied to Carson. Bonar Law emphasised the dire consequences in Ulster if Home Rule went through. If violence broke out, the Unionists would regard it as civil war, urge the Army not to treat the Liberals as a real government, and to ignore orders.[29] It would not have been characteristic of Churchill to be frightened by this nightmare, but Bonar Law intended, and knew, that it would go straight back to Asquith. The Prime Minister replied to Churchill's account of the discussion by saying, 'I always thought (and said) that, in the end, we should probably have to make some sort of bargain about Ulster as the price of Home Rule.' The key words were *in the end*. But he made clear how much he despised his opponents. He described 'Carsonism' as bluff and blackmail, and Bonar Law's tactics of organised disorder in the House as 'almost puerile in their crudity'.[30]

Bonar Law had an interview with the King on 16 September, of which he made a note.[31] The King was keen on a conference. Bonar Law said that there were only two possible bases for a conference: either a general scheme of devolution applying to the whole of the United Kingdom including

Ireland; or for Ulster to remain part of the United Kingdom with some form of local government for the rest of Ireland. An essential for the latter alternative was approval from the Unionists of the south and west.

The King asked for Bonar Law's opinion on the constitutional position of the Crown. Bonar Law responded that while the sovereign could act only on the advice of Ministers, his action was not automatic. If he had reason to believe that the advice he was given was not in accord with the wishes of his people, and the subject was of vital importance, he had the constitutional right to appoint other Ministers who would accept the responsibility of advising him differently; and he could then dissolve Parliament so that the wishes of his people could be ascertained. This advice was at best dubious, and unhappily also self-serving. The Unionist case rested heavily on the government not having a mandate from the people to grant Home Rule to Ireland. Moreover, an election would stop time running under the Parliament Act, and so defer Home Rule into an indefinite future.

Bonar Law also told the King that if the government tried to use troops in Belfast, it was doubtful whether they would obey orders. And he reminded him that the Unionist leaders had pledged themselves not to encourage or support resistance in Ulster if there were an election and the people decided in favour of Home Rule. The King said that he intended to write a personal letter to his Ministers in the latter part of October pointing out the difficulty in which the Crown would be placed – a difficulty which would be largely avoided if there were an election before the Home Rule Bill became law.

The Leader of the Opposition had gone far to persuade the King that he had to use his influence, if not his power, to procure an election before the Bill became law. This was unscrupulous. An election could not realistically be fought on the single issue of Home Rule – a subject about which the English electorate had already shown its indifference. Nor was it true to say that Unionist leaders would abide by the result of such an election. Carson had been careful to avoid saying anything of the sort.

All this Bonar Law reported to Carson.[32] He was anxious to talk to him before he, Bonar Law, talked to Asquith. 'As you know,' he wrote,

> I have long thought that if it were possible to leave Ulster as she is, and have some form of Home Rule for the rest of Ireland, that is on the whole the only way out ... When do you [Carson was at Craigavon] come back? For it is really not possible to have a proper understanding by letters; and you know that I have not only so strong a personal friendship for you but so much belief in your judgment that I do not think in any case I would go on with a proposal to which you were strongly opposed. I would rather give up the whole thing than do that.

Carson replied from Craigavon on 20 September.[33] His letter gives a very clear insight into his mind at this moment. He considered that the interview with the King was satisfactory, and the letter to be written to the government in October an excellent idea (an idea which incidentally came to nothing). He did not see how a meeting with Asquith could be avoided. 'Now as regards the position here I am of opinion that on the whole things are shaping towards a desire to settle on the terms of leaving "Ulster" out ...' There was a difficulty in defining Ulster, but his own view was that the whole province should be excluded, but the minimum would be 'the six Plantation counties'.* There was also the difficulty of the Unionists of the south and west, and 'it might be that *I* could not agree to their abandonment, tho' I feel certain it would be the best settlement if Home Rule is inevitable'. He thought the Nationalists would not consider leaving Ulster out, and would prefer a general election. Then he said: 'I have such a horror of what may happen if the Bill is passed as it stands and the mischief it will do to the whole Empire that I am fully conscious of the duty there is to try and come to some terms'.

Bonar Law replied that he was 'greatly delighted to find that so far as I can judge you and I take exactly the same view about the present position ...'[34] If Carson felt like that, and Bonar Law felt the same, the time seemed to be propitious for trying to reach an agreed settlement by partition. Churchill and Lloyd George would be likely to support the attempt. But there were a number of questions remaining. Would Asquith feel that now was the moment to settle, and would he show the necessary firmness towards Redmond? Would the southern Unionists, among whom was Lord Lansdowne, the Unionist leader in the Lords and a great landowner in Ireland, accept their abandonment by the north? And would the Diehard wing of the Unionist Party, for whom Home Rule for any part of Ireland struck at the heart of the Empire, even contemplate partition? All these questions appeared to expect the answer 'no'.

Bonar Law sent a copy of Carson's letter to Lansdowne, who was then at his Scottish house in Perthshire. A chill wind from the north was felt at once. Lansdowne warned that he had always felt that 'we have to be extremely careful in our relations with Carson and his friends. They are "running their own show" ...' He did not altogether remove the effect of that by remarking: 'We should indeed be shabby fellows if we allowed Carson to do the rough work for us without helping him so far as help can legitimately be

---

* He was wrong in his definition, for he meant the six predominantly Protestant counties which eventually formed Northern Ireland. They included the two non-Plantation counties of Antrim and Down.

given.' And he was not convinced that Carson's premise for a solution by partition – that Home Rule might become inevitable – was yet right. But he did think that Carson's poor health was a dangerous factor. 'His breakdown would be a serious calamity.'[35] Carson's health and morale at this time gave cause for much concern. Bonar Law was told by an unidentified correspondent that the consumption from which his daughter Gladys was suffering 'hurts and worries him badly ... No one else can run the Irish case in Ireland'.[36]

Lansdowne's attitude was almost completely negative. He wrote to Bonar Law on 23 September to say that he had had visits from Balfour and Curzon, both of whom had been to Balmoral.[37] He gathered that some overture would probably be made to the Unionists for a conference. The assumption would be that the Home Rule Bill held the field and that the only question for discussion was the exclusion of Ulster. That filled Lansdowne with alarm. But he had nothing else to suggest. Bonar Law also had a letter from Balfour.[38] The elder statesman was gloomy, which, as he said, might be due to a day of steady rain in his own Scottish fastness at Whittinghame. The King had spoken to him at great length and given 'very vivid accounts of innumerable conversations'. Balfour thought the best thing would be an election before the Bill passed. But he knew that was unlikely in the last degree. He concluded that 'possibly, the separation of Ulster from Ireland may be the least calamitous of all the calamitous policies which still remain open to us'.

Poor Bonar Law. He wanted a settlement but he was assailed and obstructed on all sides – except by Carson. And he was not impressed by the supposed advantage of a general election. He told Lansdowne that he was doubtful whether it would settle anything – a consideration which made him more willing to try to get a solution by consent.[39] He and Carson seemed to be alone in doubting the idea that consulting the electorate was a panacea.

Bonar Law's troubles were added to by the sudden enthusiasms of F. E. Smith. Having been as intransigent as any of his colleagues, he now let it be known to the Palace that Carson would be ready to agree a settlement on the basis of 'leaving Ulster out'. The admonitory voice from Perthshire was heard again. Lansdowne was 'worried by the knowledge that the King had been led by FE into a kind of fool's paradise ...'[40]

Within a few days, however, there was a development which made Bonar Law more sanguine about the prospects of a settlement. He had had a most interesting conversation with Carson, he told Lansdowne on 8 October.[41] Carson, wrote Bonar Law, was feeling more and more the responsibility of his position as it came nearer the time when there was a likelihood of bloodshed. Not only he, but the leading men in Ulster wanted a settlement on the basis of leaving Ulster out of Home Rule. Having seen a deputation of Unionists from Dublin, Carson now thought that such an arrangement could be made without any serious attack from the southern Unionists. Bonar Law gave Lansdowne an account of the conversation between Carson and the Dublin Unionists:

He [Carson] said to them [the deputation from Dublin]: 'Tell me exactly what you want me to do, and so far as possible I shall do it. Do you want us in Ulster to say that we will resist Home Rule by force of arms, even though the government offer to exclude Ulster [from Home Rule]; or do you wish us to say that, if there is to be Home Rule, Ulster will agree to form part of the new government?' They [the Dublin Unionists], of course, replied that they could not expect the Ulster people to do either of these things. Then [Carson] said to them 'Why is it that there has been nothing this time of the organised opposition to Home Rule, which was shown by the Unionists in the south on the two previous occasions [1886 and 1893]? There has been no resolution of the Dublin Chamber of Commerce; there has been no committee of business men'; and he [Carson] said, further, 'can you undertake now that when you go back to Dublin such opposition will be organised and come into the open?' They had to reply to him that they could not give such an undertaking, for the Unionists dreaded the effect of it on their businesses.

'If this really represents the position', wrote Bonar Law to Lansdowne, 'it seems to me obvious that we are not justified in risking civil war for the sake of people who will take no risks even of a financial kind for themselves ...' To Bonar Law, whose sympathies were naturally with the North, this showed that southern Unionists were more or less reconciled to Home Rule, and had no stomach for the fight. It showed also how effective was Carson's way of dealing with those who spoke but would not act. Lansdowne agreed that the southern Unionists were 'feeble folk'; but he thought Carson's interview showed that 'he means to fight on his inner lines', and he was glad that Bonar Law 'would not agree to a settlement unless it commanded a large measure of support amongst the Unionists of the south of Ireland'.[42] This was ominous. Bonar Law was too optimistic about the acquiescence of the southern Unionists. Lansdowne and those who thought like him would continue to obstruct a settlement by partition, but would not put forward any practical alternative. They were not going to give much help to Carson and Bonar Law to avoid a smash.

Carson himself was not as optimistic as Bonar Law. He was much more discreet now in his letters to Lady Londonderry and did not disclose any detail of the negotiations. But on 10 October he described the situation as difficult: 'the less said about it the better. I fear an entanglement which might make us weaker'.[43] He was more and more oppressed by the threat of civil conflict, and consequently the more inclined to partition as the only way of averting it. He explained himself to Lord Lansdowne.[44] The Unionists in the south and west, he wrote, did not realise that 'we have no power to stop the Bill, and that even if we refuse separate treatment for Ulster the Bill will probably become law all the same'. He was openly contemptuous of the southern Unionists who talked only in generalities. The stronger we are, he said, the more we are backed up in Britain, and the less likely it is that resistance in Ulster will degenerate into chaos. He appealed to Lansdowne for support for this eminently reasonable point of view; but the appeal fell on deaf ears. The triumph of disorder was Edward Carson's final nightmare. This fear goes far to explain his bitterness and frustration at the end, as his native island descended into darkness.

Asquith now wrote to Bonar Law and suggested a private meeting. It took place at Max Aitken's house at Cherkley in Surrey on 14 October. When Asquith arrived, Bonar Law was playing double dummy with his host, 'the need for secrecy precluding a four'.[45] The two leaders had never met privately before and the atmosphere was not easy. It was the first of three meetings at Cherkley. They achieved nothing. Asquith attempted to extract from Bonar Law the minimum he would settle for, but was unsuccessful. Bonar Law was wary of an entanglement. He was also becoming irritated and told Lansdowne that he really did not understand why Asquith took the trouble to see him at all. He concluded that the Prime Minister was playing for time and hoping that, if they refused an offer of special treatment for Ulster falling short of exclusion, the Unionists would not get much sympathy from the British electorate.[46]

Finally, Asquith tried a meeting with Carson. He preferred to deal with Carson rather than Bonar Law, as he told Redmond.[47] But it is difficult to see what Asquith hoped from such a meeting, for he had also promised Redmond that he would make no proposal or offer at that stage.[48] The two meetings between himself and Carson were a failure. After getting nowhere at the first encounter, Asquith sent Carson some 'few rough suggestions ... without prejudice on either side'. They were not put forward as proposals but as 'opening up the field for practical discussion, and inviting counter-suggestions ...' A 'Statutory Ulster', which remained to be defined, would come under the Dublin Parliament, but certain topics such as the taxation of Ulster would be reserved to the Imperial Parliament. Asquith described this doomed compromise as 'veiled exclusion', something which had the double purpose of giving Ulster the substance of what it claimed, while doing as little violence as possible to Nationalist sentiment.

Such sophistry had no appeal for Carson, as the Prime Minister should by now have realised. Exclusion would have to be naked or nothing. Carson responded that he could not feel justified in putting the proposals before his colleagues as 'however guarded, the basis is the inclusion of "Ulster" in the Irish Parliament'.[49] At Asquith's prompting, however, they met again. According to the Prime Minister's note, he said that Carson should at least present in black and white some suggested method by which 'unveiled' exclusion could be put into effect without mutilating the Home Rule scheme. Carson undertook to think about it.[50] But he was not to be caught. A few days later he wrote to say that he did not see what useful purpose could be served by submitting proposals of his own unless it were agreed as a preliminary that Ulster should be excluded.[51]

This was effectively the end of the negotiations. Asquith reported to the Cabinet on 22 January 1914 that he had had a letter from Sir Edward Carson flatly refusing anything short of the exclusion of Ulster. The Prime Minister's next move was to make public his offer to Ulster of something falling well short of permanent exclusion.

The parties had been pressed throughout with the King's anxiety to promote a compromise. George V peppered Asquith with handwritten letters, indicating that a solution could only be found by excluding Ulster – by this stage surely right. On 11 February 1914 the King wrote that excluding Ulster was a policy which 'I have always maintained is the only means of averting civil war'.[52]

Why had the attempts to settle failed? The first reason is that Asquith could not bring himself to risk putting exclusion forward as a hard proposal. He preferred to elicit if he could the minimum that the Unionists would settle for. In this he failed. The Prime Minister's excuse was the inflexible refusal by Redmond to consider any solution that would divide Ireland. In Limerick on 12 October, Redmond said: 'Irish Nationalists can never be assenting parties to the mutilation of the Irish nation; Ireland is a unit. It is true that within the bosom of a nation there is room for diversities of the treatment of government and of administration, but a unit Ireland is and Ireland must remain ... The two-nation theory is to us an abomination and a blasphemy'.[53] Asquith was not prepared to put to the test the thought which he conveyed to Bonar Law at the first of their meetings, that the Irish Nationalists needed him more than he needed them.[54]

On the other side, Bonar Law was in difficulties with the Diehards like Curzon and the Cecils, and with the Southern Unionists. Lansdowne was in this camp. The Diehards clung to the view that Home Rule for all or any part of Ireland would be a deadly blow aimed at the heart of the

Empire. They felt as well that an independent Ireland could never be made viable without Belfast. So long as Ulster held out Home Rule could never come. They were to be proved wrong. In sum, neither side had sufficient will to settle.

Carson did not contribute to the failure of the negotiations. He was ready to settle on the basis of the exclusion of Ulster, and had been for a number of years. But because of Asquith's tactics, the uncertainty and delay imposed strains. Events moved on and Carson had to retain authority over the Ulster Protestants. As he told Lord Stamfordham, the King's Private Secretary, in February, and Stamfordham reported to Asquith, 'this uncertainty and waiting was becoming unbearable and he questioned whether Ulster would remain quiet much longer ...'[55]

While negotiations for a settlement were failing, dark clouds were gathering in the South. The military preparations in the North had a potent and far-reaching effect outside Ulster that was hardly noticed by the Unionist hierarchy. In August 1913 a group of young Dublin Nationalists decided to form an Irish Volunteer Force. Among the leaders were Patrick Pearse, a schoolmaster, John Devoy, a veteran Fenian and Eoin MacNeill, a Celtic archaeologist and enthusiast for the revival of the Gaelic language. Their object was to advance the demand for Home Rule in the same way as Carson was promoting opposition to it – by the threat of force. They had been impressed by Carson's success in Ulster, and the government's weakness in face of his threats. On 25 November the movement was inaugurated in a crowded meeting in the Rotunda in Dublin. Before the meeting dispersed four thousand volunteers had been enrolled. Recruitment gathered pace. The government responded in December to the menace of opposing volunteer movements in South and North by prohibiting the importation of arms and ammunition into Ireland.

The Irish Volunteer movement cut clean across Redmond's aim of achieving Home Rule by constitutional means. But the future of Irish nationalism lay not at Westminster but with the Volunteer Force. It was this force which evolved into the Irish Republican Army, whose title in Gaelic is 'Óglaich na hÉirann' (Young Warriors or Volunteers of Ireland).[56]

12

The Curragh

Carson and Bonar Law had acted hand in hand during the failed negotiations in the second half of 1913. But they had not succeeded in their attempts to intimidate either Asquith or the King, and so force a dissolution of Parliament or a negotiated agreement. The Unionists would have to try another – extra-parliamentary – method. The Army would have to come into the reckoning.

It was a known fact that the Army's loyalty would be severely tested if it were ordered to go into Ulster to put down a rising. The King recognised it. In September 1913 he had asked Asquith whether he proposed to use the Army to suppress the disorders which would inevitably follow the passing into law of the Home Rule Bill. 'Will it be wise, will it be fair to the Sovereign as head of the Army', he asked, 'to subject the discipline, and indeed the loyalty of his troops, to such a strain?'[1] And in February 1914 he warned the Prime Minister that many officers might resign rather than fight in a civil war.[2] Asquith himself, while never fully accepting that the seditious noises coming from Ulster were not bluff, at least knew there was a doubt.

The Army might yet be the fatal weakness in the campaign for Home Rule. Many officers were Ulstermen. Many were the sons of the Protestant Anglo-Irish gentry whose land had been taken away by the successive Land Acts of the late nineteenth century. To men of this background, the issue was simple. Irish Nationalists were disloyal; the men of Ulster were loyal. How could it be otherwise when all the Protestant Loyalists asked for was to remain under the Union Jack? The very name of the flag was enough to make the point.

The Conservatives were not above heating this Unionist temper in the officers' mess. Carson himself tried to draw a distinction. On one hand, he threatened mass resignations among officers if the government were so foolish as to try to enforce Home Rule in Ulster; on the other, he disclaimed any idea of encouraging mutinous thoughts. It was a fine line. In May 1912, just after the Home Rule Bill had passed its second reading, he told the press at the Hotel Cecil that no army could stand the strain of attacking the soldiers' kith and kin in Belfast. But in December of the following year at Manchester he dismissed the accusation that he and his colleagues were trying to tamper with the Army as a foul lie. 'It would be a bad day for the country that the Army, under any circumstances should refuse to obey the lawful orders of those who are put in command over them. Of course they must ... No one will blame the Army for shooting upon Ulstermen; but the country will hold the government that puts forward the Army responsible.'[3]

The speech drew praise from A. V. Dicey, the constitutional lawyer, who, however, admitted to what he called 'a personal scruple'. He had 'even rather more difficulty than probably you feel as to how an Englishman may, if the Home Rule Act, even without a general election, should be passed into law, rightly supply money and aid to what would be technically a rebellion in Ulster, though I believe it would be a rebellion which, on the part of Ulster, would be morally justifiable'.[4] Carson must have been impatient with anxieties so acute that they could only be expressed in tortured syntax.

As time passed, it became clearer that the Unionists did not possess the scruples to which they pretended. Was it not 'tampering with the Army' to say, as Carson did in September 1913 at Antrim, that he had had pledges and promises from 'some of the greatest generals in the Army', that when the time came they would come over 'to help us keep the old flag flying'?[5] Bonar Law was even more explicit. In a speech in Dublin of all places, he reminded Asquith that, in order to carry out his despotic intention, James II had had the largest paid army that had ever been seen in England. 'What happened? There was no civil war. There was a revolution and the King disappeared. Why? Because his own army refused to fight for him.'[6]

The forthright Lord Milner wrote to Carson at the same time as Dicey had conveyed his doubts – December 1913. The proconsul did not experience doubt. He thought that the government were not serious in their advances for a negotiated settlement, and were just passing the time. And if they were not serious, then there must soon – in less than a year – be a rebellion in Ulster. It would be a disaster of the first magnitude if the rebellion failed. 'But it must fail unless we can *paralyse the arm* which is raised to strike you.' It was an arresting phrase.

The arm was not unwilling to be stayed. Some senior officers were open in their views and ready to give practical help to the Unionist cause. None more so than Major-General Sir Henry Wilson, Director of Military Services at the War Office since 1910, a man reputedly brilliant in his profession but much given to political intrigue. On 4 November 1913 Wilson recorded in his diary that he had had a long talk with Field-Marshal Sir John French, Chief of the Imperial General Staff. French was nervous that it was coming to civil war, and his attitude, as it appeared to Wilson, was that he would obey the King's orders. French asked what Wilson would do. 'I told him that I could not fire on the North at the dictation of Redmond, and this is what the whole thing means.' But, thought Wilson, Asquith would not be so mad as to employ force. 'It will split the army and the colonies, as well as the country and the Empire.'[7] As the crisis developed, Wilson scurried about between the War Office and the Unionist opposition leaders, giving them information about the government's plans.

In January 1914, the Unionists sought to recruit the country's most celebrated soldier, Earl Roberts. On the 27th Bonar Law sent Roberts a draft of a letter for him to write to the press.[8] Bonar Law said that he had had the letter ready for a long time, and suggested that a suitable moment to publish it would be if and when the opposition initiated a debate in the Lords to amend the annual Army Act, a gambit they were then actively considering. There is no doubt that Carson knew and approved of the approach to Roberts. As originally drafted, the letter stated that, although the soldier's duty was to obey, in the event of civil war no ordinary rules would apply, and each soldier had to make up his mind which side he believed to be right. It concluded by saying that if civil war did break out as a result of an attempt being made to coerce Ulster, Roberts himself would fight on the side of Ulster – a sentence about which Bonar Law himself had doubts. There is a version of the draft in the Bonar Law Papers, which is later than that sent to Roberts, heavily amended in Carson's hand.[9] He left standing the passage about the soldier's duty, but he deleted the proposed declaration by Roberts that he would fight on Ulster's side. In the event the letter was not published because the proposed amendment of the Army Act was never moved.

The discipline and funding of the army is regulated for a year at a time by annual Army Acts. This has been so since 1688 when, as part of the settlement of Parliament's dispute with the monarchy, the Crown was expressly prohibited from raising or maintaining a standing army in time of peace, without the consent of Parliament. Parliament therefore controls the Army through an annual vote of funds and a review of its code of discipline. Any attempt to interfere with the Army's mandate or its funding is consequently an interference with both parliamentary liberties and the safety of the state. The Army had not meddled in politics since the seventeenth century. The Unionist Party now thought to repeat the experiment.

In December 1913 the idea was put to Bonar Law that the Army Act might be amended in the House of Lords to preclude the use of the Army to enforce Home Rule in Ulster until after a general election. The Lords could be expected to pass the amendment and they could not be overturned in the Commons until after three separate parliamentary sessions. Bonar Law was attracted. He wrote to Lord Lansdowne on 30 January and canvassed the idea at length.[10] He told Lansdowne that he had written to Sir Robert Finlay (a leading member of the Bar who had been Conservative Attorney-General between 1900 and 1905) asking him to look into the legal side. Finlay obliged and produced a suitable amendment which he sent to Bonar Law on 2 February.[11] Bonar Law's own view was that the step had to be taken, 'and so far everyone to whom I have spoken about it is of the same opinion, including the three Cecils, Selborne, Austen Chamberlain and Carson'. 'If,' thought Bonar Law, 'we take that action we shall compel an election ... If we miss this opportunity, then really no other is left except to put pressure upon the King, and, of the two, I am sure you will agree that the latter would be the greater evil.' He went on to summarise the dire consequences of doing nothing.

The real purpose of the move was to force a general election at a time selected by the opposition. The Conservatives had been out of office since 1905 and were hungry for it. But it was a perilous and reckless expedient. To meddle with military discipline and funding at a time when the threat of a European war was looming was the height of irresponsibility. In any case, the plan had a logical flaw. What would happen if there were to be a dissolution? As Bonar Law acknowledged to Lansdowne, the plan was incomplete unless the Ulster leaders agreed to abide by the decision of the electorate. This Carson had carefully refrained from doing. He was content to go along with the plan, but he had never committed his followers to any precise arrangement for the protection of Ulster. As Asquith had told the King during the autumn of 1913, 'Sir E. Carson and his friends have told the world, with obvious sincerity, that their objections to Home Rule have nothing to do with the question of whether it is approved or disapproved by the British electorate.'[12]

That was still the situation when the Shadow Cabinet met on 4 February. The question of the Army Act was discussed and, like many a thorny problem, it was shunted off to a committee. The members were Sir Robert Finlay, Lord Robert Cecil, George Cave, Lord Halsbury and Carson. Four out of the five were leaders of the legal profession. Few were better qualified to understand the constitutional importance of the annual Army Acts and the peril of tampering with them. In the event, the committee never formulated a detailed scheme. The Army itself decided to do their work for them and to put the use of force in Ulster out of the question.

In the early months of 1914 the Home Rule Bill began its third wearisome passage through Parliament. It would become law if passed once again by the Commons, having now twice been rejected by the Lords. The climax approached at last. On 8 February, Asquith made a conciliatory speech on the King's Address, saying only that he would bring forward proposals for Ulster as the price of peace. Carson responded in the same tone, inviting the government now to put on the table a plan for excluding Ulster. 'If the exclusion for that purpose is proposed, it will be my duty to go to Ulster at once and take counsel with the people there.' But, he said, 'if your suggestions try to compel these people to come into a Dublin Parliament, I tell you I shall, regardless of personal consequences, go on with these people to the end with their policy of resistance.'[13] He was now openly inviting partition.

Asquith admired the speech. He wrote to congratulate Carson, saying in a friendly note that it had impressed him more than anything he had heard in Parliament for many a long day.[14] Better certainly than Bonar Law's effort, of which Asquith wrote to Venetia Stanley: 'Bonar Lisa was rather spitfire last night.'[15] Asquith in any case preferred Carson to Bonar Law, whose melancholy Presbyterian outlook and utter indifference to the good things of life he found antipathetic. Carson too was a melancholic, but he had the theatrical style of the courtroom, and the soft Dublin accent with it. With his sardonic manner and lowering presence, he cut a formidable figure. Between Asquith and Carson there was also the enduring camaraderie of the Bar, and Asquith never applied to Carson that favourite pastime of his, the giving of a nickname.

The Prime Minister's view was that, in sum, the debate on the King's Address had gone rather well; but the calm did not last. Asquith had begun by thinking to offer what became known as 'Home Rule within Home Rule', that is giving Ulster a Parliament subordinate to Dublin or giving veto powers in a Dublin Parliament to the Ulster delegates on issues affecting the province. Under pressure from the King, who rightly thought that Carson would not be satisfied with this, he abandoned the idea. Next he proposed that each Ulster county could, by plebiscite, exclude itself from Home Rule for three years, later extended to six. This idea was the product of Lloyd George's ingenious mind. Any offer to the Unionists, he considered, would have to observe two essentials: if rejected it must put the other side in the wrong as far as the public was concerned; and it must not involve any alteration in the scheme of the Home Rule Bill.[16] The proposal was therefore conceived more as a tactical gambit than in the belief that it might be acceptable. But it had no ghost of a chance of attracting Carson, as would be demonstrated soon enough, although agreement to it had been wrung from Redmond only with difficulty. When Asquith unveiled the six-year exclusion on the second reading of the Bill, Carson dismissed it out of hand: 'be exclusion good or bad, Ulster wants this question settled now and for ever. We do not want sentence of death with a stay of execution for six years'.[17] The season was no longer one of goodwill.

At this point the Cabinet began to become anxious that the Ulster Volunteers, who by now numbered some ninety thousand, might make a move to seize the arms depots in the province. This force was known to be one to be reckoned with. Sir Henry Wilson had paid a visit to Belfast in January and was impressed by the discipline and spirit of men and officers and, as he noted in his diary, 'Many remarkable stories of Carson's power were told me'.[18] Wilson's account is corroborated by police reports returned to Dublin Castle. Special branch reported that drilling and practice operations continued through February on an almost daily basis. The Ulster Volunteer Force was 'completely organised and enthusiasm is well maintained'. Live ammunition was used on some occasions, and there was good reason to believe that arms were being smuggled into Ulster in breach of Proclamations of December 1913 which prohibited their importation.[19]

It is not easy to identify what information the government had received to make it think that its installations in Ulster were under threat. Although the police reports show that the UVF was formidable, with trained signallers, ambulance crews, nurses, and transport and commissariat contingents, there is no hard evidence that a strike against the depots was in prospect – unless Home Rule became law.

If, however, the government had known what was going on in Ulster in the first weeks of 1914, the hawks among them would have felt justified in their views. On 7 February, Colonel Hacket Pain, Chief of Staff of the UVF, issued a secret instruction giving an outline procedure for full mobilisation.[20] Among the papers of the Ulster Unionist Council there is also an undated and unsigned memorandum.[21] It is headed 'The Coup' and recommends a 'sudden, complete and paralysing blow'. This was to be effected by the severing of all railway links and telegraph, telephone and cable lines; the closure of all roads into Ulster; and the seizure of all depots of arms, ammunition and military equipment, and of all other supply depots for troops and police.

These revolutionary plans were probably, but not certainly, contingent on the passing of the Home Rule Bill, or in the event of the government moving pre-emptively against the insurgents. There can be no serious doubt that Carson knew and approved of them. For on 21 March, while he was staying at Craigavon at the height of the crisis, he gave verbal instructions which were transcribed by Sir William Adair, commanding the Antrim division, on what was to be done on full mobilisation.[22] The instructions were that the Royal Irish Constabulary were to be arrested and their arms seized; firearms were not to be used unless the UVF were fired on first; and, if attempts were made to arrest UVF commanders, they should be forcibly resisted.

The Cabinet set up a committee to assess the danger and recommend precautionary action. Its members were Churchill (Admiralty), Birrell (Chief Secretary), Seely (War Office) and Simon (Attorney-General), with Lord

Crewe in the chair. On 17 March the committee recommended that troops should be moved from the south of Ireland and from England to strengthen the guard on the depots. Churchill informed his colleagues that the forthcoming practice of the 3rd Battle Squadron, then off the Spanish coast, would take place at Lamlash in the Firth of Clyde, within easy reach of Belfast; a cruiser would be stationed in Belfast Lough itself, and destroyers were being ordered to the south of Ireland.[23]

In the meantime Churchill had made a notably bellicose speech at Bradford on 14 March. He described Carson and the Ulster Unionist Council as being engaged in a treasonable conspiracy, and said that there were worse things than bloodshed. Then, in his peroration, he declared: 'If all the loose, wanton and reckless chatter we have been forced to listen to these many months is in the end to disclose a sinister and revolutionary purpose: then I can only say to you, let us go forward together and put these grave matters to the proof.'

On the same day, Seely sent an instruction to the Commander-in-Chief in Ireland, General Sir Arthur Paget, from the Army Council. This stated that reports had been received that 'evil-disposed persons' might try to get possession of arms, ammunition and other stores in Ulster, particularly those at Armagh, Omagh, Carrickfergus and Enniskillen. Paget was to take action 'at once' to safeguard the depots.[24] Seely summoned Paget to London for further discussion on 18th. What took place on that day and the next in the discussions between members of the Cabinet, their military advisers, and Paget, is still not fully known, but it was in these talks that the origins of the Curragh Incident lie.

Paget's original view was that it would be better to evacuate the arms depots than to raise the level of excitement in an already heated atmosphere by drafting in more troops. This sensible advice was overborne by the Ministers, even though it was supported by Sir John French. Wilson noted in his diary entry for 18 March that Sir John had sent for him after lunch to talk about Ulster. French had been with Seely, Churchill, Birrell, Paget and other senior military figures. 'It appears they are contemplating scattering troops all over Ulster, as though it was a Pontypool coal strike. Sir John pointed out that this was opposed to all true strategy, etc., but was told that the political situation necessitated this dispersion. He said that, as far as he could see, the government were determined to see this thing through.'[25]

No written record of the discussions in London on 18 and 19 March was kept. Similarly, Paget's consequent instructions were not reduced to writing. It can be pieced together, however, from the events which followed, and from what the government either published later or admitted in the House of Commons, that the discussions covered the following: the movement of at least two battalions of infantry to places in or near the borders of Ulster, with discretion for Paget to supplement these troops with all the remaining forces in Ireland if he needed them; the promise that further reinforcements could be made available from England; the cooperation of two small cruisers, which were to proceed to Belfast Lough, together with two other cruisers and a destroyer; in addition the movement of six battleships of the 3rd Battle Squadron to Lamlash, sixty miles from Belfast, and eight destroyers then on the south coast. These were indeed warlike preparations with a very substantial combined force.

Two other matters were covered. First, Major-General Sir Nevil Macready, Director of Services at the War Office, was appointed to the command of the Belfast district and given authority over the police in that city. Last, and crucially, Paget urged that 'indulgence might be shown' to officers who were domiciled in Ulster. It was agreed that in the 'few exceptional cases where officers have direct family connection with the disturbed area in Ulster ... they should be permitted to remain behind either on leave or with details ...' Other officers who refused to obey orders to go into Ulster should not be allowed to resign their commissions but would be dismissed the service.[26]

It is no wonder that Carson and his followers, learning of these plans piece by piece, concluded that there was on foot a government plot to put them down or to goad them into pre-emptive action. The existence of such a plot cannot now be proved affirmatively, but there are some straws in the wind, from which it can be deduced that Churchill and Seely were the principal hawks. It was known that the management of the railway company in the north had strong Carsonite sympathies. On 20 March Churchill wrote to Seely about the means of moving troops north, and proposed something which looked very like provocation: 'I think you ought to make the demand for railway transport to the company at the proper moment this afternoon. Their refusal will raise questions which can be pressed severely. Don't use the cruisers except as a second alternative. The question of taking over the police will have to be faced pretty soon. How is Macready?'[27] Churchill's question about Macready may also be significant. Seely wanted the general to go to Belfast with a 'dormant' commission, 'to be used if and when he thinks necessary, appointing him Military Governor of Belfast', but Simon, the Attorney-General, deprecated the phrase, saying that 'nothing could be more unfortunate, as it seems to me, to use the language of civil war'.[28]

Paget returned to Dublin by boat train on the evening of the 19th. Carson too took the night mail from London that evening – to Belfast. Earlier in the day, Bonar Law had moved a vote of censure on the government for their handling of the Irish question. It was the culmination of several days of intemperate rough and tumble in the Commons, and as so often the theatre belonged to Carson. He unleashed a storm of invective against Churchill. Of the government's military preparations, he said: 'Having been all this time a government of cowards, now they are going to entrench themselves behind His Majesty's troops, and they have been discussing over at the War Office for the last two days how many they will require, and whether they will mobilise'. The First Lord, he said, had told them that the government had said their last word in the offers they had made. Very well. If it is the last word, what more have we to do here? His own place was not at Westminster but at the head of his movement in Ulster.[29] He stalked from the Chamber, turning as he left to raise his hand in valediction.

This was not done on impulse. On the evening before the debate, he had dined with Milner, Sir Leander Jameson of the Jameson Raid and Henry Wilson at the house of a friend of Wilson's. Carson had got to know Jameson well when he had defended him in 1896 for his leading part in the Raid, and knew him for being as ardent a Unionist as Milner. Wilson recorded the meeting at dinner in his diary: 'A long and most interesting talk. Carson says his speech tomorrow on the Vote of Censure will be his last in the House of Commons till after the Ulster question is settled. They all agree the Lords must amend the Army Annual Act'.[30] This is unfortunately the only account of this gathering of desperadoes. One would dearly like to know the content of the 'long and most interesting talk'. Wilson was in a position to bring the others up to date on the military talks in London, enough to make Carson conclude that he ought to go to Belfast to make sure that the Ulster Volunteers were not provoked into some act of rashness. But what did Wilson learn in return? There is no record. All those, however, who thought that Carson was going to Belfast to set up his rebel government were wrong. The air was thick with rumour that warrants were out for his arrest and of his colleagues.

Early in the morning of 20 March Paget assembled a group of his senior officers in his office in Dublin. It then became clear that the orders which he had received in London were less than clear, a defect compounded by their never having being confirmed in writing. This was doubly compounded by the ineptitude shown by Paget himself.

The officers present included Major-General Sir Charles Fergusson, commanding one of the two divisions in Ireland and responsible for the centre and northern half of the island, and Brigadier-General Hubert Gough. Gough commanded the 3rd Cavalry Brigade, part of Fergusson's division, with headquarters at the Curragh camp about thirty miles south west of Dublin. He was one of the youngest brigadiers in the army, a dashing cavalry officer and a charismatic leader who was Irish by blood and upbringing, but not an Ulsterman. Paget was in an excited mood and his discourse rambled. According to Fergusson, he told the group that measures would have to be taken in Ulster and that trouble could well result. The place, he thought, would be in a blaze on the following day.

Paget then said that, with Sir John French's help, he had obtained some concessions from Seely. These were that officers who were domiciled in Ulster would be exempted from operations there. They would be permitted to 'disappear', and when it was all over they could resume their places as if nothing had happened. Other officers who were unwilling to serve would be dismissed. There would be another conference in the afternoon, but only those who were prepared to do their duty were to attend. The decision that faced every officer in the division, and that might destroy the livelihood of each of them, had therefore to be taken within hours.

Gough was not himself from Ulster and so could not be permitted to 'disappear'. He was incensed by what he had been told. As he wrote afterwards, 'I was not really a very interested Ulsterman, but I felt the Army was being made a pawn in the political game ...'[31] Returning to the Curragh, he told the cavalry officers under his command of Paget's ultimatum. In the result, fifty-seven out of the sixty in the brigade, including Gough himself, decided for dismissal. He wrote to Paget on behalf of his officers to say that they were all quite willing to do their duty if all that they were asked to do was to preserve property and maintain order. But if their orders involved the initiation of active operations against Ulster they would prefer to be dismissed. Paget at once telegraphed the War Office: 'Regret to report brigadier and fifty-seven officers, 3rd Cavalry Brigade, prefer to accept dismissal if ordered north.' He at any rate believed that active operations against Ulster were imminent.[32] What had begun as incompetence now became farce. Army officers had been given a choice based on a hypothetical case and the authorities were in no position to complain if they chose to answer in their own way. It was not in any conceivable sense a mutiny.

Wilson heard the news on the same day as Paget's wire was received at the War Office, but from another source. General Sir John Gough told him that his brother had been ordered to undertake operations in Ulster, or be dismissed the service. 'We must steady ourselves a bit', Wilson advised his diary.[33] Whether he intended it or not, Brigadier Hubert Gough now symbolised the Army's resistance to coercing Ulster. But there was another view about where an officer's duty lay in these difficult circumstances. Fergusson, the divisional commander, laboured mightily to restrain the rest of his officers from following the cavalry's lead.[34] He was only able to succeed by asserting that the orders came from the King personally. Unfortunately this was not true. The King was outraged when he learned for the first time of the Curragh Incident from his breakfast newspaper. He wrote immediately to the Prime Minister in his own hand, dropping the conventional courtesies of that correspondence and saying that he was 'grieved beyond words at this disastrous and irreparable catastrophe which has befallen my Army'.[35]

The future Field-Marshal Wavell, then a major, wrote to his father on 21 March: 'The idea of officers of the Army going on strike, which is I think what it really amounts to, is to my mind absolutely disastrous. What about the men?' And in another letter written four days later, he said, 'Wilson made no secret of his opinion. He actually said, "The Army have done what the Opposition have failed to do" and "will probably cause the fall of the present Government." What right have the Army to be on the side of the Opposition, what have they to do with the causing the fall of Governments?'[36]

Paget's wire was received with consternation in London. On learning of Churchill's order to the 3rd Battle Fleet to proceed to Lamlash, Asquith immediately countermanded it. Any orders there might have been to attack Ulster were cancelled. It remained to deal with the resigning cavalry officers. Gough was ordered to present himself at the War Office. Paget, too, was ordered to London. They arrived on Sunday 22 March. Gough could hardly have placed the government in a more awkward dilemma. If an example were to be made of him, it would probably provoke wholesale resignations among Army officers. On the other hand, how could the government give way to these recalcitrants and promise them that Ulster would not be coerced?

Appreciating Asquith's dilemma, Bonar Law decided to back the cavalry officers, and Wilson, too, who was inevitably now involved on their behalf in the hectic consultations in London. Bonar Law wrote to Carson in Belfast saying he did not see how Gough could agree to reinstatement unless it were accompanied by an assurance that Ulster would not be coerced into accepting Home Rule.[37] At the same time, he warned Asquith that he intended to raise the whole issue of the Army in the House.

As Bonar Law and Carson had anticipated, Gough refused to move without a written guarantee that the Army would not be used against the Ulster Unionists. Eventually the Cabinet produced a memorandum. This bland document stated that the incident had arisen as a result of a misunderstanding and reiterated that it was every soldier's duty to obey a lawful command. For some reason known only to himself, Seely thought that he was empowered to add words of 'clarification', and in the improbable company of the elder statesman, Lord Morley, he added:

His Majesty's Government must retain the right to use all the forces of the Crown in Ireland or elsewhere to maintain law and order and to support the civil power in the ordinary execution of its duty.

But they have no intention whatever of taking advantage of this right to crush political opposition to the policy or principles of the Home Rule Bill.

Bonar Law was informed by Wilson of every move in this extraordinary negotiation.[38] Of course it was the assiduous Wilson who 'kept whispering to them to "get it in writing" ',[39] and who prompted Gough to seek clarification. He persuaded Gough to enquire whether the amended document relieved him from liability to order his brigade to assist in enforcing submission to a Home Rule Bill. Sir John French, without consulting Seely or any other minister, wrote 'I should so read it'.

With this document in his pocket, Gough returned to a hero's welcome in Ireland, and prudently placed it in trust for his daughter in case its return should be demanded. In this way the government effectively disabled itself from coercing Ulster. On 26 March the editorial of the *Morning Post* stated: 'The Army has killed the Home Rule Bill, and the sooner the government recognises the fact the better.'

13

Craigavon

While a single brigadier was holding the government to ransom for its policy, Edward Carson was at James Craig's house, Craigavon. He played no part in the Curragh Incident which shaped the future course of his campaign for the separation of Ulster from the rest of Ireland. But he was kept fully informed by Bonar Law, who in turn was being briefed several times a day, in breach of his most elementary duty, by Sir Henry Wilson from the War Office.

Belfast was tense but quiet during these days. The government had been moving troops and police all day through the province and from the south, Carson informed Bonar Law on 20 March. 'This place is an armed camp ... it is a strange "message of peace".'[1] Carson made no move to set up his provisional government. There was no reason why he should. The intention was that it would be established only if and when the Home Rule Bill was passed. That had not yet happened. In any case, events were moving in Carson's favour. As a result of the Curragh Incident the government could not now use the Army to enforce the Bill if and when it became law. The Ulster Volunteer Force was numerous and well disciplined. It already had guns and was shortly to have many more. Carson continued to urge his followers to maintain good relations with the police and to give no possible provocation.

The police, who could often get copies of Unionist documents openly and without difficulty, obtained a copy of confidential instructions which had been issued to the Ulster Volunteers in County Fermanagh on the instructions of Carson. These were illuminating. The keynote was caution.

REMEMBER YOUR RESPONSIBILITY, RESTRAIN THE HOTHEADS
Remember we have no quarrel with our Nationalist neighbours. Do not molest them or be offensive to them in any way ... If the Nationalists take aggressive action against us restrain your men to your utmost, and at once report to Company or Battalion Commander. Send a quiet man to interview an influential Nationalist, who will show him these instructions ... Go on training your men quietly. Don't stand still but progress, and prepare for the worst and hope for the best. For God and Ulster! God Save the King![2]

This was not only prudent. It showed once more Carson's desire for peaceful relations between Protestant and Catholic.

On his side, Asquith made no move against the insurgents. No arrests were made, although rumours were rife and the possibility was certainly discussed in Cabinet. It would have been impossible to bring criminal proceedings without including Carson and possibly F. E. Smith as defendants. Nor could Bonar Law easily be left out. The public utterances of the leader of His Majesty's Loyal Opposition were every bit as seditious as Carson's. A prosecution of all these would have taken the government to the point where courage merged into rashness. It surely would have brought the nightmare of civil war closer. Asquith knew that the King would have been alarmed if he had started criminal proceedings. The previous September he had assured George V that he did not intend to arrest Sir Edward Carson for sedition, since that would be 'to throw a lighted match into a powder barrel'. He had not changed his mind. And, more significantly, it was inconsistent with the Prime Minister's inbuilt tendency to wait upon events rather than seize the initiative. There was surely ample ground for prosecuting, but discretion prevailed. Nothing was done.

Craigavon was guarded by two hundred armed men. Maxim guns covered the driveways. General Macready, who had been sent to the Belfast command, visited the house. Carson thought his visitor, being in full uniform, was on a 'state visit', but Macready's impression was that the scene had its comic side:

> As I drove up with my ADC, sentries of the UVF in uniform presented arms, and a small crowd of press photographers, who appeared to be part and parcel of the establishment, snapshotted us as long as we were in view. Mr Craig, as he then was, received me in a small anteroom, and with much solemnity informed me that Sir Edward would see me directly. I did my best to play up to the evident honour that was being done me, but unfortunately, for no reason at all, I suddenly thought of the Dalai Lama, the mysterious priest of Tibet, and with difficulty recovered my wandering senses. What Sir Edward talked about I have quite forgotten but I am sure we avoided all reference to Ulster. A few days later one of his Staff left a card at my hotel, a politeness not imitated by all of his adherents on whom I had left cards, one gentleman, indeed, returning my own to me.[3]

The Ulster leader had with justice become known as King Carson. Macready himself had little time either for the Asquith government or its opponents: Carson was playing with fire and Asquith was drifting. 'It was a dangerous game which [the Ulster leaders] were playing', he wrote, 'and one which the merest accident might have turned into a bloody tragedy ...' Of the government he said: 'So far as the political government of Ireland was concerned I was entirely indifferent, having no interest of any kind in the island. The policy I did advocate, whether applicable to the North or to the South, was "Govern or get out", and that is exactly what in 1914 Mr Asquith would not do.'[4]

Lilian Spender, the wife of Wilfrid Spender who had become one of Carson's most trusted aides, kept a diary during this time which draws a picture quite different from Macready's. She was fervently partisan, agog with excitement, and revered 'Sir Edward'. Amused irony was not her style. On 19 March 'Wolf' (her husband) told her that things were as serious as could be, that arrests were quite possible, and that he had orders not to sleep at home. He went down to the wharf at 6 the following morning to meet Carson and went straight with him to Craigavon. She had heard also that the men of the UVF had turned out as the Dorsets went by, and saluted, many a Dorset returning the salute. 'I'd love to have seen that!' That day (20 March) she learned from her husband over the telephone of 'the resignation of practically all the officers of the Cavalry Brigade at the Curragh, which appeared in the papers the next day [Saturday]. A splendid piece of news'.

Saturday 21 March was a glorious day. Mrs Spender went into town to shop. The city looked much as usual but the streets were fuller and 'there was a tendency among people to gather in knots'. In the evening she climbed Carnmoney Hill to watch the sun set. To the west she could see a corner of Lough Neagh and blue mountains close by. To the north lay the open sea; southwards Belfast muffled in smoke, with the wild outline of the Mountains of Mourne beyond. Larks were singing and the scene was peace itself, save for two things: two warships, grim and black, rode on the smiling lough, and at her feet was a stone with 'No Pope here' scribbled on it.

She too visited Craigavon. The lodge gates were closed and guarded. A crowd was 'flattening its collective nose outside', and a sentry demanded her pass. 'But when I gave my name, his face cleared, he saluted smartly, and flung open the gates, and I sailed through ...' In a field by the house was a huge mess tent and a small hospital tent. Some UVF men off duty were playing football. A vast Union Jack flew from a flagstaff. She saw Sir Edward briefly. 'He was very pleasant to me, and was charming to Wolf. We talked a little, but he was coughing and looking tired, so I wouldn't bother him.'[5]

Carson did not go into Belfast. He called a meeting of UVF commanders at Craigavon. He explained the political situation to them and told them that they were passing through a grave crisis: they might be called upon at any time to mobilise. When he asked for comments, a young major spoke at once in a critical tone. He was Robert McCalmont who commanded the Central Antrim Regiment and had succeeded his father as MP for East Antrim. McCalmont pointed out that, while the Ulster Volunteers were being asked to sacrifice everything for the defence of the province, they were being let down. Their leaders were telling the world that they would fight to the end; but how could they without guns or ammunition? He was warmly applauded. It was not the first time Carson had heard the complaint; but he could not answer frankly. He could not tell the meeting that a large consignment of rifles and ammunition had already been purchased in Germany for the UVF under conditions of the strictest secrecy.

On the Sunday of the crisis, 22 March, when Brigadier Gough arrived in London for his trial of strength with the government, Carson went to church at Belmont, near Craigavon. The Minister preached a fervid sermon on the text, 'Fight the Good Fight of Faith', and closed with a reference to the Scottish Covenanters who 'resisted and overcame the soldiers of the King'. The newspapermen were there in numbers. They included at least one German correspondent who had learned from London that bloody conflict was imminent in Ulster. The reporters bombarded Carson. He declined to comment on the sermon, but he said: 'The conclusion I draw from the action of the government is that in a fit of panic they have made up their minds to attempt two things – one to intimidate, and the other to provoke. They will fail in both.'[6] He wrote to his daughter, Aileen: 'We are all peaceful here and it is the government who have the jumps. Of course, if the government had attempted to interfere with us, it would have been the beginning of the end. They seem to have climbed down and have made a mess of everything.'[7]

Contrary to what he had told Lord Milner and Sir Henry Wilson the night before he left London for Belfast, Carson was back in Westminster by the end of March for the aftermath of the Curragh débâcle. It was bound to be a humiliating experience for the government. Asquith was compelled to deny that the extra two paragraphs in the paper given to Gough had the Cabinet's authority. The paragraphs, however, were not repudiated. Colonel Seely resigned. Sir John French resigned. Seely withdrew his resignation at the behest of the Prime Minister. Then he resigned for a second time. 'What an example for the British proletariat!' was the judgment of the historian Halévy.[8] Asquith became Secretary of State for War in Seely's place and added the War Office to his prime ministerial cares.

Under pressure a White Paper was issued on 25 March.[9] It was plainly inadequate as an explanation of what had gone on. The scenes of bitterness and intemperance in the House became worse. As day followed day, Asquith and Churchill were assailed by questions designed to show that there had been a plot to provoke violence in Ulster and to give a pretext, plausible to the British public, for snuffing out the insurgents for good. The Ulster Unionist Council published a narrative designed to substantiate this theory. The Liberals called it a pack of lies. Another White Paper was issued on 23 April, giving more details.[10] Still no one could tell where the truth really lay.

15. Carson addressing a rally in Ulster. (*Linen Hall Library, Belfast*)

16. Signing the Covenant in City Hall, Belfast. (*Ulster Museum*)

17. Signing the Covenant in the cattle market, Limavady. (*Tessa Hawkes*)

ULSTER'S SOLEMN COVENANT

SIR EDWARD CARSON. PHOTO. RUSSELL.

HEROES OF THE UNION

Behind this gallant Statesman are men who lead the cause,
The glorious cause of Union. Men of Ulster! do not pause.
We have signed the Solemn Covenant, which binds us to defend
Our faith, our flag, our loyalty unflinching to the end.

18. Ulster's Solemn Covenant. A postcard from the time of the Home Rule crisis. (*Tessa Hawkes*)

19. Ruby Carson's first visit to Ulster, 1914. Standing (left to right): Lady London-derry, Edward Carson, Ruby Carson, James Craig. Sitting: Ronald McNeill, Lord Londonderry, unknown girl, Andrew Bonar Law, Mrs James Craig. (*Carson Family*)

20. Carson driving through Belfast with Colonel R. H. Wallace, Grand Master of the Belfast Orangemen. (*Belfast Telegraph*)

21. Sir George Richardson, officers and friends at Umbra Camp, Limavady. (*Tessa Hawkes*)

22. Reviewing a section of the Ulster Volunteer Force at Drenagh, Limavady. (*Tessa Hawkes*)

23. Andrew Bonar Law. (*National Portrait Gallery*)

24. David Lloyd George. (*National Portrait Gallery*)

25. Carson leaving Belfast by train. (*Linen Hall Library, Belfast*)

What orders had been given to Sir Arthur Paget in London on 18 and 19 March? What did certain Ministers hope and intend should happen? A fog lies over these questions to this day. But the circumstantial evidence that Churchill and Seely, perhaps others, were the moving spirits in a plan to put down Ulster remains persuasive.[11]

Carson had long suspected that Asquith's delaying tactics were intended to test Ulster's patience to breaking point. He had some evidence for thinking so. In January he had had an unsolicited letter from a surprising source. It was from a Miss Constance Williams, private secretary to one of the Liberal Under-Secretaries. She urged him to organise police of his own to suppress any rioting that might take place in Belfast. She explained that she had exceptional opportunities of knowing what the government were aiming at in Ireland, because Ministers, including Mr Asquith, met socially at all hours at the house where she worked, and talked freely. 'The plan is to procrastinate until the patience of the hooligan element in Belfast is exhausted and they begin to riot. This is the moment when troops (they have decided which regiments are to be sent) will step in ...' She thought that Asquith himself 'still hankers after compromise and is not much in favour of this policy, but is being overruled ... They have agents in Belfast, some pretending to be friendly to your people, who send regular reports and are to say when is the right moment to stir up riot ...' 'Perhaps my action in writing in this way is mean,' she wrote, 'but the morals of one insignificant woman are of little account, when such crimes are going forward.'[12]

Carson was convinced that there was a plot to achieve just such a result. He wrote to Bonar Law giving him his view of the situation. It was that 'the government had at first intended and made up their minds to put themselves in a position to take such action as would be necessary to destroy our movement ... It is ridiculous to suppose that all these troops are being sent merely to guard buildings and stores ...'[13] Bonar Law agreed. The second reading of the Home Rule Bill would come on before the end of March and he wanted Carson back in London for that.[14] Bonar Law decided that a vote of censure on the government's whole Irish policy should now be moved. It was set down for 28 April. By that time, however, another event had taken place which ratcheted up the tension further, and which, although it may not have been foreseen at the time, ensured that violence would be the final arbiter of Ireland's unhappy fate. Increasing lawlessness had marked the development of Unionist policy since the House of Lords, the natural bulwark of the Union, had been emasculated.

By the spring of 1914, guns had been run into Ulster in quantities for some years. It was not illegal to import guns into Ireland, provided customs formalities were complied with – which of course they were not, by the Ulster gun-runners – until 5 December 1913, when importation was banned by royal proclamation.[15] The man at the centre of the trade was Fred Crawford. He was then in his early fifties, a man fanatical in his beliefs, living by adventure, and utterly determined to carry through whatever he had set his hand to. As a young man, he threw himself into the Unionist cause and formed a secret society called 'Young Ulster', the qualification for membership of which was possession of one of three specially selected types of firearm. From 1911 Crawford was a member of the Ulster Unionist Council. He signed the Covenant in his own blood. As 'Director of Ordnance of the Ulster Volunteers', he was the man charged with finding and buying guns and ammunition.

Crawford knew the arms dealing fraternity well and he made the acquaintance of a German businessman called Bruno Spiro who was willing to sell him rifles. Spiro was a man with whom Crawford could do business. He was to prove his most reliable supplier, and one as adept as Crawford at the game of disguises, aliases and fictitious buyers. Although the gun-runners often managed to evade the attentions of customs and police, the ports were being watched increasingly closely, and only a relatively small number of rifles had been brought into Ulster by the autumn of 1913. The Ulster Volunteers were chafing about drilling and exercising without weapons. Their political leaders were telling the world that they would fight to the finish, but for the most part they had no weapons; and those that were available were of varying design and calibre. It would be a recipe for chaos if equipment and ammunition were not standardised. Crawford realised this as early as anyone and began advocating a single large importation of a uniform type of small arms.

Carson returned to Belfast in January 1914 after his talks with Asquith had failed. At the request of General Richardson, the Commander-in-Chief of the Ulster Volunteers, he called a secret conference at UVF headquarters in the Old Town Hall, Belfast, to fix the future policy on the importation of arms. Colonel Hacket Pain, Richardson's chief of staff, asked Crawford to come to the conference prepared to say whether he would be willing to undertake a large shipment if Carson authorised it; and, if so, what funds and help he would need.[16] Crawford replied that he would much prefer having nothing to do with it 'for business and family reasons'; but if he did take it on, it would have to be for a purchase of at least twenty thousand rifles and two million rounds in one importation. He would get the guns alongside, but someone else would have to deal with their landing and distribution. He was to be the sole importer and there must be no competition.[17]

Crawford's plan, which he outlined at the meeting on 20 January, was to buy the arms in Hamburg, purchase a steamer in a foreign port, and bring the cargo to an Ulster port. Those who were present were divided. Some thought the risks too great and Crawford too impetuous to be trusted. The decision was a difficult one for Carson. It was an act of blatant criminality. If it failed, his leadership would be in question and the whole Ulster cause would be in danger. On the other hand, as he had been plainly told, if the Volunteers were taken short by a surprise attack before they were armed, they would feel that they had been let down by their political leaders. They had Carson's promise that he would see the thing through. And if it were to be done at all, it must be by one sudden coup. He authorised the plan. In fact it was inevitable that the UVF would have to be armed. They would invite derision if they had only wooden rifles or makeshift weapons. Carson must have known this from the time of the inception of the force.

The man who was to take charge of the onshore arrangements, after the arms had been landed, was Wilfrid Spender, the husband of the diarist who left so vivid an account of Belfast in the days of the crisis. Spender was an Englishman and a soldier who in 1911 was the youngest officer on the General Staff. Through his work on Home Defence, he came to realise how vulnerable the country was to an attack on the long, undefended coast of Ireland. Consequently he believed that Home Rule for Ireland was folly. He signed the Ulster Covenant in 1912. He then sought leave to retire from the Army so that he could he could be free to act according to his political conscience. The War Office refused his request, and ordered him back to his regiment in India. He persisted and even petitioned the King. Eventually, in May 1913, he was permitted to retire without stigma. He had been in touch with Carson throughout his argument with the military, and had sought his advice. But Carson scrupulously avoided involvement with individual serving officers, only warning Spender of the sacrifice he would be making by resigning from so promising a career.[18] As soon as Spender was out of the army, however, Carson offered him a place on the staff of the Volunteers as Quartermaster-General. He immediately accepted and made his permanent home in Ulster with his new bride. Spender was a man of great dash and courage, who was later to serve as the first Secretary to the Northern Ireland Cabinet. There could have been no one better to take charge of the landward side of the gun running.

Spender's plan was to bring the guns ashore at Larne in County Antrim, where most of the guns would be unloaded. The rest would then be transferred by sea to Belfast, and to Bangor and Donaghadee in County Down. A fleet of motorised vehicles was to be mobilised to bring the Volunteers to the ports. Roads leading to Larne and the other ports would be cordoned off, and with the help of a senior Post Office official, telephones and cables were to be disconnected while the operation was going on. The guns would be taken off as fast as possible and got away to all corners of Ulster.

In the meantime the British League for the Support of Ulster was offering not only moral but also tangible help under Lord Milner's leadership. English reserve officers of sympathetic viewpoint were recruited to provide expertise and advice on military topics. By early 1914 the UVF had impressive intelligence, signalling, medical and transport resources. On 3 March the press carried an appeal to sign the British Covenant. Among those who responded were Field-Marshal Earl Roberts, Rudyard Kipling, Sir Edward Elgar and assorted professors of law in the ancient universities. By the beginning of April Milner reported that signatures were coming in at the rate of 'something like 30,000 a day'.[19] A monster rally took place in Hyde Park. A great semi-circle of fourteen platforms stretching from the Serpentine to the Bayswater Road was erected for the galaxy of speakers, who included Milner, Balfour and Carson. There were delegations from the City and from the London clubs making a 'sombre and dignified parade of silk hats and black coats'.[20]

As soon as his plan was approved on 20 January, Crawford went to Hamburg to see his contact, Spiro. The 20,000 rifles he was looking for were available. He returned to Belfast to get definite approval for their purchase. On his way back to Hamburg, he called on Carson at Eaton Place to make certain of his leader. It was an encounter straight out of a John Buchan novel. Crawford explained what he proposed to do and asked if Carson would back him. Carson got up from his chair and stared down at the gun-runner. 'Crawford, I'll see you through this business, if I should have to go to prison for it.'[21]

Crawford stipulated that the guns should be wrapped individually with 100 rounds and packed in parcels of five, so that they could be got away easily from the port of discharge and, if necessary, pressed into service immediately. Next he travelled to Bergen with his friend Captain Agnew, a skipper in the service of the Antrim Iron Ore Company, and purchased a Norwegian ship, the *Fanny*, which had recently arrived from Newcastle with a cargo of coal. He took on the Norwegian captain and crew and arranged for the vessel to sail under the Norwegian flag. The guns were to be taken from Hamburg by lighter through the Kiel Canal and then transhipped to the *Fanny* off the island of Langeland in the Baltic.

The plan was now to sail the *Fanny* to a remote inlet on the west coast of Scotland and there transfer the guns to one or more local vessels, whose appearance would be less likely to provoke interest than a foreign steamer. On 30 March the *Fanny* kept her rendezvous with the lighter at Langeland. Loading began and continued during the day. But in the afternoon it was interrupted by the arrival by launch of Danish port officers. They were suspicious of the cargo and took away the ship's papers, promising to return them next day. Crawford spent a tortured night. But, as luck had it, the last day of March broke over the Baltic with a stiff wind and low fog. Knowing that the port officials could not put to sea in their launch in such weather, Crawford decided to sail – without papers. Now a pirate ship, the *Fanny* slid unobserved out of the Baltic into the relative safety of the North Sea.

On the following morning the press had the whole story. Under the heading 'Mystery of an Arms Cargo: Ulster or Mexico?', the Berlin correspondent of *The Times* reported that a large quantity of rifles had been transhipped to the *Fanny* off Langeland. It was presumed that they were intended for Mexican rebels. The paper's Copenhagen correspondent had the report of the Danish port officer who had boarded the vessel. He stated that an Englishman on board had tried to bribe him. He took the ship's papers, but the ship had left for the north without recovering the papers.[22] The next day the port officer gave more detail. He had watched the *Fanny* for two days while she waited for the lighter from Hamburg. There were, he thought, about 30,000 rifles on board. Two English-speaking gentlemen admitted that the transhipment was illegal, and asked whether they could not 'dispose of the whole business by paying a fine'.[23]

It was an appalling setback for those left in Belfast. The enterprise had been conceived and, until now, carried through in perfect secrecy. Now the world knew. According to Spender, 'news somehow reached the UVF Headquarters that Crawford's intentions were known to the British Government, and the Ulster leaders decided that it was necessary to cancel, or at any rate postpone, any attempt to bring arms from the Continent'.[24] Spender attempted to get a message to Crawford with instructions to leave the guns at Hamburg for the time being; but the message never reached him. The leaders in Belfast had lost contact with Crawford and the *Fanny*. She was at sea somewhere with a cargo on which the fate of Ulster's resistance depended.

Spender was despatched to meet Crawford at the spot previously agreed on the Scottish coast with orders from Richardson that on no account should Crawford bring the guns into British waters. He was to arrange, if possible, to sell back the *Fanny* and her cargo. But if he was shadowed and escape was impossible, he was to throw the cargo overboard or scuttle the ship.[25] So Spender set off on the improbable mission of finding Crawford in one of the more remote stretches of the west coast of Scotland, disguised as if for a salmon fishing holiday with an inappropriately dressed Hamburg shipping agent for company.[26] There was no sign of Crawford there. Thinking that the fleet at Lamlash in the Clyde estuary might be out looking for him, Crawford had decided instead to rendezvous at Lundy Island in the Bristol Channel, putting in first at Great Yarmouth – of all hazardous places – to replace a smashed starboard lamp. He reached Lundy on 11 April, the *Fanny* in the meantime having had her funnel repainted and having twice changed the name on her bow and stern.

There he met Agnew, who handed him a paper which was unsigned and unaddressed, but apparently containing instructions for him. The document dumbfounded Crawford.

> Owing to great changes since you left and altered circumstances, the Committee think it would be unwise for you to bring the cargo here at present, and instruct you to proceed to the Baltic and cruise there for three months, keeping in touch with the Committee during that time, or else take the cargo back to Hamburg and store the goods there until required.

Crawford was incensed by 'this cowardly document', telling Agnew that he did not know who had given it to him, as they had not had the courage to put their names to it. But Agnew should take it back and tell them to go to hell. If he did not receive instructions for landing the guns within six days 'he would run the ship aground in Ballyholme Bay at high water and rouse the Volunteers to come and take her cargo off'.[27]

Crawford had been suffering from malaria during the meanderings of the *Fanny*, and he returned to Belfast like a pale avenging spectre. Carson was at Craigavon, however, and immediately mollified him. 'Well done, Crawford', he said, 'I'm proud of you. We are gathered together to hear what you have done and intend to do.' Crawford answered that he would not take the guns back under any circumstance, and neither would Agnew. His proposal was to buy a nondescript British steamer to take a transfer of the arms so that they could be landed in Ulster. The transhipment was to take place under cover of darkness off the Tuskar Light at the south-east corner of Ireland. There was some anxiety about whether the cargo could be transferred in the open waters of the Irish Sea, but Carson decided that all details should be left to Crawford.[28]

Crawford then purchased the *Clydevalley*, which he renamed the *Mountjoy* – after the ship which broke the boom, and so lifted the blockade in the siege of Londonderry in 1689. The two vessels kept their rendezvous near the Tuskar Light and the cargo was transhipped at night, but not without extreme difficulty. The operation is described in Captain Agnew's log, an extract from which is printed in Crawford's book, *Guns for Ulster*. The two ships were made fast together, one showing a masthead and a red port side light, and the other a green starboard side one, making them look like one vessel. 'In this way', the log runs, we steamed through all the traffic transferring guns from *Fanny* to *Clydevalley* till 4 o'clock in the morning ... When the two steamers were fast together you would have heard the noise of them coming together a good distance off ... Captain Falcke [the Norwegian skipper] was in a bad way when the ships were bumping each other, he wanted to cast off. I knew it was only the top works that were getting it, and they would not sink through that. I did not mind what condition they were in if they landed the goods safely.

The transhipment took the two nights of 19 and 20 April. The only casualty was one man from Belfast who lost a finger: 'it was a wonder there were not more men hurt working in the dark with ships rolling'.[29] On 24 April the *Clydevalley* sailed for Belfast Lough under Agnew's command.

Had they known the true state of the government's intelligence about Crawford's movements, those in Belfast who were nervous about the venture might have had their resolve stiffened up. On 3 April, the British Consul-General in Hamburg, Mr Hearn, learned from his Russian opposite number that a large consignment of arms had been brought to Hamburg from Odessa; and then moved by lighter to the *Fanny* in Danish waters. The *Fanny* had then sailed away northwards without papers, so Hearn learned. Various suggestions were made as to her destination – Galveston, Texas, for the Mexican rebels; South America for ex-President Castro of Venezuela; and Iceland, which had its own Home Rule crisis at the time. But the Consul felt sure they were headed for Ireland. This was speculation, however, and no further information was available to His Majesty's Government after the *Fanny* disappeared into the Baltic mist until the arms were landed at the Ulster ports.[30] With the fleet dispersed around the coast of Ireland in readiness for just such an emergency, this was not a triumph of naval intelligence.

The government, however, did get a first-hand account of the gun running given to the Belfast police by a seaman on board the *Clydevalley* who happened to be a Catholic. Unhappily for the authorities, however, it was received only after the event. The seaman told the police that on 16 April he was looking for work at Belfast Quays, and signed on for the *Clydevalley*. The ship left the quay in the small hours on the following morning. She steamed along the Welsh coast until at Llandudno a gentleman came aboard who was spoken of as Major Crawford. The vessel steamed on through the Irish Sea to the Tuskar Light and then dodged about till dark on 18 April. The seaman had a turn at the wheel during the night and saw Crawford signalling by light to various places along the coast. The following night they ran down again to the Light, and another ship was made fast to the *Clydevalley*. The unnamed seaman was put to a winch and saw that cargo was being transferred to his vessel. It was in the form of bales and he saw the contents of several – long rifles, bayonets and cardboard packages of ammunition. He got a couple of rifles and threw them overboard. The next day the *Clydevalley* dodged about again and Captain Agnew, whom the seaman knew, took command. Agnew asked the seaman what he was doing on board. Was he not a Catholic? And as this was a political game, was he not afraid? 'The Captain said that if my own crowd – that is the Roman Catholics – knew anything about this it would be serious for me. I replied I did not care or mind, that if anyone interfered with me I would use one of the sticks on board and open his skull.' Major Crawford came on board again with a large quantity of tobacco which was given out to all hands. Dodging about the channel continued until dusk on the night of 24 April, when the vessel steered for Larne harbour. The day before, the name *Clydevalley* had been painted out and replaced by *Mountjoy*. They entered harbour in time for the crew to go ashore and have a drink. All the bales, save forty tons which they took on to Bangor, were taken off at Larne. He left the ship at Bangor on the morning of 25 April, and was paid off. He got £2 10s. and was 'fed on the best'.[31]

The government learned that the *Mountjoy* had entered Larne harbour at about 10 p. m. on 24 April. All landward approaches to the harbour had been previously blocked by cordons of the UVF under Major McCalmont MP. Telegraph lines had been severed. Later on about six hundred cars arrived and were loaded with cases containing arms from the ship, and sent into the country to various destinations. Police estimates of the number of guns varied from 30,000 to 48,600. The SS *Roma* was in Larne harbour and took about 1800 rifles to a private wharf in Belfast. Customs officers there were prevented by the manager of the shipyard from making a detailed examination of the cases, which had been brought ashore under an armed guard of UVF. It was also understood that a considerable quantity of arms was transhipped to the motor boat *Inishmurray*. The *Mountjoy* left Larne during the night and arrived at Bangor about 4.15 a. m. on 25 April. Very little was known about what was landed at Bangor, as the Ulster Volunteers had taken possession of all approaches to the harbour, and prevented police and coast guards from 'exercising any supervision over the proceedings of the persons present ...' At Donaghadee the District Inspector had reason to believe that an attempt would be made during the night of 24th to land arms. He went to the pier in the evening with some officers, customs men and coast guards. At about 2 a. m. a large body of UVF under the command of Lord Dunleith and Captain Craig MP rushed the pier and took possession of all approaches. The police were held captive on the pier. They took no steps to interfere with the illegal landing of arms from the *Inishmurray*, and did not even warn those present of the illegality of what they were doing.

The *Roma* and the *Inishmurray* were later seized by the customs, but then released. Preparations were also made to prosecute those involved in the gun-running. Informations based on evidence taken by the police, but with all names left blank, were drafted for the High Court on the instructions of the Irish Law Officers. 'Subsequently, however, it was decided not to take any proceedings in the matter.'[32] Thus ended the inglorious attempt by the forces of law and order to prevent or punish these acts of criminal conspiracy.[33]

From the point of view of the insurgents, the landing of the guns and the spiriting of them away into the Ulster countryside was a stunning success. Lieutenant-Colonel McCammon, who was in charge of administration, made a report of the events of the night of 24–25 April.[34] He confirmed that there was no trouble with the police. When told at Bangor that they could not pass, they replied 'all right' and went away. The operations, the Colonel reported, passed off with great smoothness, everyone cooperating with complete good will. 'The utmost enthusiasm prevailed when the ship arrived with the arms, and Major Crawford received a great ovation when she steamed off.' A statement was published in Belfast giving Sir Edward Carson's 'high appreciation' of the operation, and his admiration for the 'magnificent discipline and self-sacrifice of the men'.

Wilfrid Spender had told his wife on the 24th that he would have to be away with General Adair, commander of the Antrim division, that night. He left soon after lunch, taking a latchkey, as it was possible he might not get back until early the next morning. Although her husband had been discreet, Mrs Spender had more than an inkling of what was going on. She knew about the *Fanny* and her husband's adventures in Scotland. She now learned that 'they' were to 'get them in tonight'. Her husband's post was to be at the Musgrave Channel, 'assisting at the hoax which took in the Customs officers, and kept them occupied all night watching the *Balmarino*, which of course contained nothing but coal!' She was naturally anxious, but to her delight at about 6 o'clock next morning her door opened and in came a 'muddy, tousled, disreputable Wolf whose shining eyes told me that all was more than well'. In fact he had been at Larne helping to unload 'the precious goods' and carrying them to the motors waiting by the wharf. 'The whole proceedings', she wrote, 'are almost incredible ... Need I say that for the organisation W himself was mainly responsible, the scheme having been originally drawn up by him.' Spender had bicycled part way to Larne that night, getting a tow for some miles with a motor-cycle despatch rider. He had had one spill and badly grazed his leg. His wife was proud to bandage him up in her best hospital style, which she had learned for the women's medical services.[35]

Two days after the guns had been run in, Asquith described the exploit in the House as a 'grave and unprecedented outrage', and promised that appropriate steps would be taken to vindicate the authority of the law.[36] The promise was unredeemed. Carson immediately accepted responsibility.[37] Bonar Law knew nothing about the gun-running until afterwards. Carson had deliberately refrained from letting him know because he thought that, in his position, Bonar Law should have no responsibility for it. But all this was immaterial, Bonar Law told Ronald McNeill some years later, because he took full responsibility as soon as he knew, and had never thought that he was wrong to do so.[38] The King was perturbed, and wanted to know whether Carson could 'throw any light on what has occurred'. Carson certainly could, and gave the King's private secretary, Lord Stamfordham, a full account.[39]

Asquith was pulled hard in opposing directions. From the Viceregal Lodge in Dublin, Lord Aberdeen strongly advised the arrest of MacCalmont and Adair, the officers in charge of the Larne gun-running.[40] Augustine Birrell, Aberdeen's Chief Secretary, disagreed. Redmond, equally strongly, was of opinion that proceedings would be a serious mistake. It would, he considered, exacerbate feelings in Ulster and have no deterrent effect; proceedings would drag on a long time, during which the defendants would become heroes; and there was 'not the slightest chance' of securing convictions without a packed jury.[41] There were several Cabinet meetings. In the end it was decided to do nothing. The King, at least, was relieved. In the sometimes warped calm of retrospect, Asquith set out his reasons for not taking action.[42] He followed Redmond's reasoning, and added that it was of capital importance that the birth of the new Irish state should take place under the star of peace. He claimed that the failure to prosecute was from neither timidity nor dilatoriness. It was utterly unconvincing.

For Redmond the gun-running was a most serious setback. The situation which he had always dreaded was developing. He had tried to restrain the Nationalists from emulating Carson's warlike preparations in the north; but their impatience could no longer be contained. Both the Curragh Incident and the gun-running gave great impetus to the recruitment of Irish Volunteers in all parts of Ireland including Ulster. With the help of American sympathisers, they would soon arm themselves. The gun was abroad again in Ireland. It had largely disappeared as a result of the beneficent rule of the Unionist Party in pursuit of its policy of killing Home Rule by kindness, and during the years of Liberal government which followed. But now it was back. By inescapable logic, the UVF had armed itself, and its opponents and plagiarisers were attempting to do likewise.

But in the short term an armed UVF had put Carson in a position in which no one could any longer doubt the reality of Ulster resistance. Talk of bluff was absurd. It has sometimes been doubted whether he was fully in control of the Unionist movement in the north; and whether he was not being pressed further and faster than he would have wished. His part in the planning and execution of the gun running should dispose of any such idea. From the start he remained in charge and authorised every step. If any one was hesitant – and Richardson and other senior figures in the UVF wobbled at bad times – it was not Carson.

While these stirring events were in train, Edward Carson was in love at the age of sixty. So was his young inamorata, Ruby Frewen. During the crisis they could hardly be seen out together for fear of a prying press. On 24 April, the day of the gun-running, he wrote to her from Eaton Place that he probably could not join her at her Somerset home. On the 25th, in the early morning, he and Lord Londonderry each received a telegram with the single code word 'Lion', signifying that the arms had been safely landed. Within hours, special editions of the papers carried the news to the world.[43] Carson ended his letter to Ruby: 'RD [Ruby Darling] this is a very stupid letter but I am feeling extra stupid today. But you have always my love'.[44]

In spite of the precautions which the couple were taking, the word was getting about. Asquith had heard of the romance from Birrell, his Chief Secretary, in February. He wrote to Venetia Stanley with wild inaccuracy:

The Siren is a young and beautiful Ulster lady, who was much moved and attracted by his speeches, and his noble and commanding demeanour. Carson hoped, and still hopes, that he has struck a tenderer chord, but apparently she is prepared to yield her homage, but not her heart – not to speak of her hand. It will be curious to see what effect, if any, this little tragi-comedy has upon the political situation.[45]

J. L. Garvin, the editor of the *Observer*, wrote to his proprietor, Waldorf Astor, on 22 April:

Cupid has intervened in this astonishing business. Carson has fallen desperately in love ... I cannot speak to him on that point, but his demeanour and the undoubted state of his affections, make me think the report true. Carson is a tremendously emotional person like many of the strong men, and if he gets the exclusion of the Six Counties, he will have won his fight for Ulster and inflicted a deadly blow on Redmond. What will afterwards become of the Unionist Party in Great Britain is a question about which Carson does not care a brass farthing.[46]

Max Beerbohm, *Cold-Shouldered Yet: Sir Edward Carson and Mr Bonar Law*, 1914. (*Estate of Max Beerbohm*)

14

War and Peace

Ulster was now armed, and the Army and Navy could not be relied upon to disarm it. The citadel in the north-east corner might be impregnable, but the problem was no nearer solution. The quarrel went on, harsh, obsessive and parochial. The House of Commons was continually in a bad temper. Charges and counter-charges were flung across the floor. As the threat of European conflict moved closer, the quarrel, far from abating, intensified from the rancour it fed on.

On 28 April the Unionists moved for an enquiry into the naval and military movements at the time of the Curragh Incident. It was a impudent tactic, as Winston Churchill observed, uncommonly like a vote of censure by the criminal classes on the police.[1] But at the end of a strongly partisan speech he offered Carson an unexpected olive branch, on his own initiative: 'The Right Honourable Gentleman the Member for the University of Dublin', he said,

> is running great risks – and no one can deny it – in strife. Why will he not run some risk for peace? The key is in his hands now ... Why cannot [he] say boldly, 'Give me the Amendments to this Home Rule Bill which I ask for, to safeguard the dignity and the interests of Protestant Ulster, and I in return will use all my influence and good will to make Ireland an integral unit in a federal system?'[2]

Carson responded in the same coin the next day.

> I am not, then, very far away from the Right Hon. Gentleman in what he says ... I would say this: that if Home Rule passes, much as I detest it, and little as I will take any responsibility for the passing of it, my earnest hope, and indeed I would say my earnest prayer, would be that the government of Ireland for the South and West would prove, and might prove, such a success in the future, notwithstanding all our anticipations, that it might be even for the interest of Ulster itself to move towards that government, and come in under it and form one unit in relation to Ireland.[3]

In acknowledging that the Union could not now be saved, and in urging that all Ireland work together, he had travelled a long way. He had also, at last, to show his hand and declare what he would settle for.

He was buoyed up by the unquestioning loyalty of the Ulster Protestants. But he was losing hope for peace. On 5 May he and Bonar Law met Asquith again. The Prime Minister conceded what was now inevitable – that he would be no party to the coercion of Ulster. But he really wanted to talk about procedure. He suggested that the Home Rule Bill finish its course in the Commons and then negotiations could be restarted. He did not seem to realise what would be the effect in Belfast of the Bill's going through. According to Bonar Law's note, Carson repeatedly emphasised that there would be rejoicing among the Belfast Nationalists when the Bill was read for a third and last time; and that it would be next to impossible to prevent a bloody collision between the two factions. Asquith said that it was his intention to introduce an amending Bill to deal with Ulster at the same time as the main Bill. But he did not say what it would contain.[4] On 12 May Asquith told the Commons that he intended to take the third reading of the Bill before the Whitsun recess, and promised that an amending Bill would be introduced. He hoped this announcement would encourage the parties to an agreed settlement, but again he gave no clue what might be in the amending Bill.

An indication of the Prime Minister's insouciance about the subterranean forces at work in Ireland at this time can be gained from his reaction to a secret report on the Irish Nationalist Volunteers in a number of counties in the south and west. The report described increasing lawlessness, much drilling, and a demoralised and discontented police force. It continued ominously: 'The driving power and financial support of the volunteer organisation are being supplied by the Irish American representatives who are reported to have visited Ireland and promised a plentiful supply of arms and ammunition ...' Asquith sent it on to Churchill, with his own annotation: 'I have shown this to Birrell and he agrees that it is an interesting report. The lawlessness in Clare is chronic, and less serious now than for a century past.'[5]

Asquith's announcement that the Home Rule Bill would finish its parliamentary journey before the Whitsun recess acted as a spur to the extreme wing of Unionism, led by Lord Milner. Always one for 'getting forrader', Milner did not possess Carson's patience. He concocted a plan to forestall Asquith by seizing the initiative. The lieutenants and magistrates in Ulster would act as a sort of committee of public safety and call the provisional government into existence for the purpose of keeping the peace. He commended the plan to Carson in a conspiratorial letter, saying that it had better not receive any answer.[6] But Carson had no intention of taking up any such idea.

The Home Rule Bill passed the Commons on 25 May 1914. It awaited only the royal assent to become law. But, contrary to expectations, Belfast and the whole province of Ulster remained calm. The unsettled spring weather gave place to a summer in which the sun shone and the brave old world broke in pieces. As the weather improved, however, a tense situation built up in Belfast. Nationalist and Unionist Volunteers faced each other with guns, across an unbridgeable gulf of religious bigotry and fear. In early May, General Adair of the UVF asked for confirmation from headquarters that he could disarm Nationalists at the first sign of their giving trouble. The answer showed Carson's influence. Adair was told to be tolerant; only in the last resort should his opponents be disarmed.[7]

When the promised amending Bill was introduced in the Lords on 23 June, it was found to go no further than what had been offered in March, and was summarily dismissed by Carson. All it amounted to was a proposal that any county of Ulster could take a poll to decide whether or not it wished to be excluded from Home Rule for six years. Lord Crewe, who introduced the Bill, stated that any amendments from the opposition would receive 'the most careful and respectful consideration with a view to discussion in another place'.[8] The Unionist peers accepted the invitation and, although the gesture was now empty, substituted for the six year county option the permanent exclusion of the whole nine counties of Ulster. In that form it was sent down to the Commons.

Lord Milner continued to agitate. He was keeping in touch with his old co-conspirator, Sir Henry Wilson. The two met at the beginning of July and Wilson found that the proconsul was giving all his time to 'the Ulster business'. Milner was in an impatient mood and wanted to know what the Army would do. Wilson told him that 'if Carson and his government were sitting in the City Hall, and we were ordered down to close the hall, we would not go.'[9] The wonder is that Wilson was kept in post as Director of Military Operations, one of the most important at the War Office.*

Milner's views were shrewd. He considered that time was not on the side of the Unionists, and he wrote to Bonar Law on 15 July to give his reasons.[10] 'We have now reached the most critical stage in the whole game', he said.

---

* Asquith did ponder Wilson's behaviour when he took over the War Office after the Curragh Incident, and he discovered the part Wilson had been playing in 'the inner plottings of the Ulster Party'. Asquith records that he was 'strongly tempted to send him off for a while to cool his head and his heels "Where the remote Bermudas ride, /In ocean's bosom unespied", a disciplinary step he well deserved. But I was anxious to promote a temper of appeasement and I had a genuine appreciation of his military qualities'. H. H. Asquith, *Memories and Reflections, 1852–1927* ii, p. 154 (London, 1928).

Asquith's plan was to drag things on with federal schemes, conferences and other red herrings; and then get his Bill through at the end of the session. The Prime Minister, thought Milner, did not believe that Ulster would do anything; and, even if Ulster did rise, he would not take any serious steps himself. Milner pointed out that the imminent parliamentary recess was crucial. Asquith would not be able to let Ulster stew in its own juice with the Commons in session. On the other hand, if the Prime Minister got his Bill through and then Parliament rose until December, the Ulstermen would be in great difficulty. They would have to carry on 'under great discomfort and in comparative obscurity'. He did not believe the Ulster camp would be any camp at all if it were much longer deferred. This was a perceptive analysis of Asquith's 'game', and Carson probably agreed with it.

Carson's own mood was pessimistic. He went over to Belfast for the Boyne celebrations on 14 July and was greeted once more like a returning prophet by a huge crowd on the quay. On the 10th there was a special meeting of the Ulster Unionist Council. It sat for the first time as the provisional government.[11] But it took no practical step to take over the administration of the province. The next day Carson spoke at Larne. He urged restraint on his listeners. 'Remember that we must have no act committed against any individual or any man's property which would sully the great name which you have already attained.' The tone was sombre. Unless something happened, he said, the evidence for which was not then visible, 'I am bound to tell you that I see no hopes of peace. I see nothing but darkness and shadows'.[12] Unless something happened.

On 28 June 1914, the Archduke Franz Ferdinand, heir to the Austrian throne, was murdered in Sarajevo, the capital of Bosnia, then part of the Austro-Hungarian Empire. The assassins were Bosnians and Austrian subjects, but the murder had been planned in Serbia by a fanatical irredentist group. Although the British Foreign Office had been concerned in the unrest in the Balkans, it seemed to be a faraway incident that could not affect Britain. But Serbia was a thorn on the southern border of the Austrian Empire, and the Austrians decided to use the murder as a pretext for attacking Serbia. On 5 July, the Kaiser promised the Austrian Emperor his full support. On 23 July, the Austrians delivered a harsh forty-eight hour ultimatum that they did not expect to be met. The Serbians did their best to comply but the Austrians rejected the response. Russia and France were drawn in. The intricate network of alliances and guarantees which were designed to ensure the security of Europe were not so much unravelling as proving that, if called upon, they would precipitate a major conflict.

Asquith edged nearer to a compromise on Ulster in the middle of July.

He kept his young correspondent, Venetia Stanley, up to date.[13] He had had a talk with Bonar Law, he wrote, who had reported that the Master of Elibank and Lord Rothermere had been 'in confabulation with Carson' with a large supply of maps.

> They had had long discussions and arguments with Carson, and in the end I asked them to find out whether C and his friends would *definitely* treat, if I made them an offer to exclude Antrim, Derry, Down (except the Catholic parts of the South), Armagh (except South), North Fermanagh, with the possibility of a split Tyrone: provision to he made on both sides for the migration at State expense of Protestants and Catholics into and out of the excluded area. They have gone to see what his reply is. Of course I said I could not *guarantee* that Redmond would assent, but if C falls in, I shall have to put on the screw to R.

At this perilously late hour it seemed that the Prime Minister was at last ready to make an offer. The idea was to abandon county boundaries and try to form a solid block along the religious divide. He was even willing to pay for migration to smooth the rough edges of partition. But Carson and his friends were not ready to deal on that basis. They would get little more than the four counties of the north east, and splitting the county of Tyrone ('that most damnable creation of the perverted ingenuity of man', as Asquith called it) was not acceptable.

Asquith was expected to introduce the amending Bill to the Commons on 20 July. But instead he announced that the King had called an all-party conference at Buckingham Palace for the next day. Asquith and Lloyd George were to represent the government, Bonar Law and Lansdowne the Opposition, Carson and Craig the Ulster Unionists, and Redmond and Dillon the Nationalists.

The auguries were not favourable. Bonar Law thought the conference useless and Carson agreed.[14] He considered that it was just another gambit by which Asquith could buy time. He might well think so. But whether the Prime Minister's inactivity was masterly or not, he left the Irish question unanswered at the outbreak of war. And he left his ally, John Redmond, high and dry as power moved to the men of violence in the South.

'I wish you well out of the Buckingham Palace trap', Milner wrote to Carson on the opening day of the conference, advising him not to give an inch of ground.[15] The King's opening statement warned the participants that the cry of civil war was on the lips of the most responsible and sober-minded of his people. He then withdrew, leaving the Speaker to chair the sessions. The Unionists wanted to discuss time limits, the Nationalists the area of the excluded zone. Bonar Law and Carson gave way.

Carson then proposed that the whole province of Ulster should be excluded. According to Bonar Law's note,[16] Carson's opinion was that, if this were done generously, it would be likely that within a reasonable time Ulster would be willing to come into a united Ireland, 'whereas if any attempt to coerce any part of Ulster were made, a united Ireland within the lifetime of any one now living would be out of the question'. It was a characteristically practical idea, and it showed Carson's continuing sympathy with the aim of a united Ireland. Paradoxical though it was, unity might have come more readily through the exclusion for a time of the whole province. It contained a substantial Catholic minority. In some counties they were in a majority. There was therefore a good chance that in the foreseeable future Ulster would come in. Redmond and Dillon certainly read it that way. They admitted that if they had been free agents they would have adopted Carson's plan; but they said it was absolutely out of the question, for if they were to propose it, they would be without a party either in Ireland or anywhere else.[17] So the proposal foundered.

The idea came too late to bear fruit, but it was far-sighted. Carson foresaw, as eventually happened, that a smaller Protestant-dominated block in the north east, if split off, would have less and less in common with the rest of Ireland and would eventually become an alien redoubt. Here perhaps were the first signs of divergence between him and his followers. The conference then lost itself, in Churchill's phrase, in the muddy byways of Fermanagh and Tyrone. It struggled on for three days and then broke down. 'Nothing', said Asquith, 'could have been more amicable in tone, or more desperately fruitless in result.'[18]

There were other indications of divergence between Carson and Craig. On the day the conference collapsed Craig had a private conversation with the King. George V was profoundly disappointed by the failure at Buckingham Palace and worried that a provisional government might be set up in Belfast at any moment. He was beset by conflicting advice from all sides. Carson was telling him that if the Home Rule Bill became law, Ulster would look on it as a betrayal and would rise. Craig told the King frankly that he and Carson did not see eye to eye on that. Craig's view was that a general election might still save the situation. His advice was to 'abide by your constitutional advisers', sign the Home Rule Bill, 'if your Majesty's constitutional advisers present it', and hold an election immediately afterwards. 'I believe', said Craig, 'it is not only the right action, but the really courageous course ...' 'But what about your people in Ulster?' asked the King. 'I can only say that some risks must be run somewhere in so grave a crisis', Craig replied. If the election resulted in an overwhelming majority for Unionism, that would be a mandate to repeal Home Rule. If there were a small majority, it would justify the exclusion of Ulster. If the

Unionists were defeated at the polls, then Craig believed that Ulster was strong enough to secure single-handed from any government as good terms as were being offered by the present administration.[19] Here was a split not only in tactics but in strategic aims. Craig believed that north-east Ulster could go its own way. Carson still hoped that a way could be found to save the Union.

As the European powers squared up for the fight for which Germany and Austria were openly spoiling, the British imbroglio in Ireland occupied the diplomats of her friends and enemies. The French were anxious about their ally. In April, Sir Henry Wilson had had to cross to France to explain what had happened at the Curragh.[20] The Belgian Minister at Berlin told his government on 26 July that Britain, one of the guarantors of his country's neutrality, was thought by German officials to be paralysed by internal dissensions and its Irish quarrels. And the American Ambassador to Germany, James Gerard, reported that Prince Lichnowsky, the German Ambassador in London, had told his government that Great Britain did not wish to enter the war. Gerard reported that the Germans believed Ireland would rise in rebellion the moment war was declared.[21]

The reports which the diplomats sent home were understandable. They had watched the fury of the two sides in the House of Commons, the one accusing the other of plotting a massacre of the Ulster Protestants, the other charging the first with sedition and treason. 'Was it astonishing', asked Winston Churchill, 'that German agents reported, and German statesmen believed, that England was paralysed by faction and drifting into civil war, and need not be taken into account as a factor in the European situation? How could they discern or measure the deep unspoken understandings which lay far beneath the froth and foam and fury of the storm?'[22]

There was one group, however, who did not share any such unspoken understanding. This was the Nationalist Volunteer movement. Although Redmond reluctantly took steps to become its leader, its effective driving force was increasingly alienated from his own aim of Home Rule within the Empire. In 1919 the Volunteers were to become the Irish Republican Army. Now in 1914 they were moving towards Sinn Fein, the Radical Nationalist party led by Arthur Griffith, and the Irish Republican Brotherhood, both of which had as their objective an Irish Republic independent of Britain. These men of growing influence were ready to use force to get it.

Unknown to Redmond, the Nationalist Volunteers sought to emulate the Larne gun-running. A small committee led by the Protestant Home Ruler, Roger Casement, had since April been planning to run guns into the South. Casement was the son of an Ulster Protestant father and a Catholic mother.

Knighted in 1911 for his fearless reporting of brutality in the rubber industry in the Congo and in the Amazon basin, he later became a passionate devotee of Irish Nationalism and developed an equally passionate hatred of Britain and its Empire.

A small but significant quantity of arms was landed from a yacht in broad daylight at Howth in Dublin Bay almost as soon as the Buckingham Palace conference broke down, on 26 July. The yacht was owned by Erskine Childers, the author of *The Riddle of the Sands*. The Volunteers marched back towards Dublin with their new rifles. They were met by a mixed force of police and troops, who demanded that they surrender the arms. The Volunteers refused and broke away. The troops were ordered to march back to Dublin, but before they reached the city they met an angry crowd who pelted them with stones. A fracas took place and at Bachelor's Walk, alongside the Liffey, the troops fired on the crowd, killing three and wounding thirty-eight. It was a bad blunder by the military, who, as a judicial enquiry found, should never have been called out in aid of the police. Amid the anger which the incident provoked, many pointed to the glaring contrast between the government's responses to the Larne and the Howth gun runnings.

As July ended, the two crises, that in Ireland and the immeasurably more important German threat, converged. At the same time as Craig was making the final precautionary preparations for taking over control of Belfast and the rest of Ulster, he urged Carson to offer to postpone the Home Rule question. It would be a patriotic and generous gesture, he wired to Carson in London on 30 July, and it would greatly disconcert the Liberals and Nationalists, who would find it awkward to follow on with a similar offer. 'Surely the country would be able to read between the lines and store up that much to our credit when the issue is finally fought out.'[23] Carson evidently took up the suggestion or had the same thought.

On the same day as Craig made his suggestion, Asquith received a surprising message from Bonar Law asking him to go round to Bonar Law's house to see him and Carson. On the Prime Minister's arrival, Bonar Law suggested that the amending Bill should be postponed, saying that to advertise domestic tensions at that critical moment would weaken Britain's influence for peace. Carson added that, while he had first thought the idea of postponement impossible, he now saw it as a patriotic duty. Asquith welcomed the proposal. Later in the day, he saw Redmond, who also agreed. Redmond also made the 'really useful suggestion' that, if the amending Bill were postponed, he would agree that the main Bill 'to be put of course on the statute book now' should itself be suspended until the amending Bill became law.[24]

As the European crisis approached its climax, the Cabinet was deeply divided on Britain's obligations to France. Churchill was the most vocal advocate of supporting France, but there was a large peace party in the government and it seemed likely that there would be several resignations. Churchill asked his friend F. E. Smith to sound out the Unionist leaders on the possibilities of a coalition. An opportunity soon presented itself. Bonar Law was staying at Edward Goulding's house at Wargrave for the week-end of 1 and 2 August, as were Carson, FE, and Max Aitken. All were strongly in favour of supporting France. But Bonar Law disliked this type of indirect approach: if there were to be an invitation to join the government, it must come from the Prime Minister. In any case, like many Conservatives, he distrusted Churchill.

Between Carson and Churchill, in contrast, cordiality now bloomed. Carson admired Churchill's stance over France. On 5 August, the day after the declaration of war, he wrote to Churchill:

> I know too well what a strain you are going through and at such a moment a friendly line from an opponent may be a little help. Whatever bitterness has existed in the past believe me I desire to show to you my appreciation of the patriotic and courageous way you have acted in the present crisis ... my present admiration for what you have done will not be transitory and I wish you any comfort and assurance in your present anxieties that your most devoted friends could desire for you.[25]

This was a warm gesture of friendship indeed, and Churchill replied equally warmly. Each recognised in the other the spirit of audacity.

On 3 August Sir Edward Grey made his statement in the House on the darkening European situation. He spoke of the awful responsibility resting on the government in deciding what to advise the House to do; and remarked that the one bright spot was the changed feeling in Ireland. When Redmond spoke he took up that theme. 'I say to the Government that they may tomorrow withdraw every one of their troops from Ireland. I say that the coast of Ireland will be defended from foreign invasion by her armed sons, and for this purpose armed Nationalist Catholics will be only too glad to join arms with the armed Protestant Ulstermen in the North.'[26] Two days earlier, Carson had told *The Times* that a body of Ulster Volunteers were ready to give their services for home defence and many would be willing to serve anywhere they were required.

With this brave display, it was hoped that the Irish problem had been pushed into the future so that a unified country could face the menace of European war. The day after Grey made his statement, Germany violated

Belgian neutrality, the Cabinet was at one again, and Britain was at war. But hope about Ireland was sadly short-lived.

Any hope that the war would submerge the Irish quarrel was dashed within hours. The trouble was about whether the Home Rule Bill should be put on the statute book at once. It was Asquith's intention to do so. Redmond assumed it would be done in return for his brave decision to support the war by offering that the North and South together defend the Irish coast. Carson and Bonar Law assumed the opposite. They had volunteered that the amending Bill should not be proceeded with for the duration of the war, and thought it a matter of course that the main Bill would be treated in the same way.

On 5 August there was a meeting between Carson and Redmond under Speaker Lowther's auspices. Carson was in a black mood and, according to Redmond's account, it was impossible to discuss anything calmly with him.[27] That night Carson wrote to Ruby Frewen. He was very much depressed, he told her. The government meant, if they could, to betray the Unionists and pass the Home Rule Bill 'over our heads and whilst it is impossible to resist in Ulster ... They are such a lot of scoundrels I believe they are quite capable of anything.'[28]

As so often, Asquith was dragged in opposing directions. He was assailed by long memoranda from Redmond and a 'rather threatening' letter from Carson. This on the opening days of a world war. The Prime Minister might well sometimes wish, as he told Venetia Stanley, 'we could submerge the whole lot of them and their island for, say ten years, under the waves of the Atlantic'.[29] He adjourned Parliament for a fortnight and then for ten days more. Eventually he decided to put the Home Rule Bill on the statute book, but to suspend its operation during the war. In his statement on 15 September he assured the House that the employment of any kind of force to coerce 'was an absolutely unthinkable thing'.[30] He gave the further assurance that the operation of the Bill would be suspended for the duration of the war.

Although on the face of it Asquith's solution might have been thought a reasonable compromise, it satisfied no one. The Nationalists thought it a complete victory for their opponents. It was greeted with the cry of broken pledge from Bonar Law. He told Asquith that he had taken advantage of the Unionists' patriotism to betray them. His was the Opposition's only speech. When it was over, he and his party marched out. Asquith thought it an unimpressive spectacle, 'a lot of prosaic and for the most part middle-aged gentlemen, trying to look like early French revolutionists in the tennis court'.[31] In Belfast there was a revulsion against the King for giving the royal assent. Pictures of George V were booed and members of the congregations in some Protestant churches walked out when the national anthem was played.[32]

Did it matter whether the Bill was enacted or not if it was not to have any effect until the war was over? Carson emphatically thought it did. Once on the statute book, he thought Home Rule could never be repealed. And, as the war went on, the choice for Ulster Unionists would become more stark: either come under some scheme for Home Rule; or be faced once more with the prospect of violence and bloodshed at the war's end. To an extent the anger was due to impotence. The Unionists had called a truce to party politics and promised support to the government. They had either to be silent or join a coalition. And the prospect of joining hands with the Liberals was made more remote by this quarrel.

The Bill became law on 18 September 1914. The Union for which Carson had fought for the greater part of his life was formally broken. Although it was not then obvious, Home Rule became unattainable as well. Redmond's vision of a self-governing Ireland with Dominion status and standing with Britain against a common enemy was not the objective of the new Nationalist movement. For them England's difficulties were Ireland's opportunity.

The Ulster Volunteer Force was now 100,000 strong and the most efficient infantry force outside the regular army. The instinct of its officers and men was that it should volunteer for service on the Western Front or anywhere it might be needed. But by doing so Ulster would leave itself vulnerable to Asquith's trickery, as it was perceived. 'Can we assure men before giving names for United Kingdom or foreign service no danger of Home Rule Bill passing while they are away?' ran one telegram sent to Carson on 8 August.[33] There must have been many like it. Wilfrid Spender had written to Carson about the same dilemma just before the outbreak of war.[34] 'I have been ordered to join the staff of the eastern coast defences at once, and am now on my way with the General's [Richardson] approval. If the government use the mobilisation as a means of advancing Home Rule, I shall have no hesitation in returning to Belfast with or without leave ... I know I am acting on the lines you would wish.'

Carson and Craig saw Lord Kitchener, the new War Minister, to seek approval for the UVF staying together in its own army group. It was a difficult meeting. Kitchener disliked the intrusion of politics into the organisation of the Army, and he did not much care for politicians anyway. It was not until 3 September that Carson was ready to go to Belfast to announce the formation of an Ulster Division. He had also to bring the news to the Ulster Unionist Council that the amending Bill was to be postponed indefinitely, while the fate of the main Bill was then still unknown.

But he had no doubt how the Ulster Unionists' dilemma should be resolved. 'England's difficulty is not Ulster's opportunity', he said.

> England's difficulty is our difficulty ... I have seen it stated that the Germans thought they had hit on an opportune moment, owing to our domestic difficulties, to make their bullying demand against our country. They little understand for what we were fighting. We were not fighting to get away from England: we were fighting to stay with England ... I say to our Volunteers without hesitation, go and help save our country.[35]

The marriage of Edward Carson and Ruby Frewen took place on 17 September in the little Somerset church of Charlton Musgrove. Lord Londonderry was best man and Andrew Bonar Law was there. No one else from public life attended. They took their short honeymoon in Minehead on the Bristol Channel coast. There were miles of seashore and a good hotel, but the weather was stormy. Every day brought sad news as the horrifying character of the war emerged from the killing fields of Flanders. The bridegroom's solace was his young bride. He was her hero and she took up his every cause with schoolgirl enthusiasm. 'Ruby is a very loving and affectionate girl', he told Lady Londonderry six months later, 'and so I am comparatively happy.'[36] It was a strangely grudging tribute to the young woman who was to give him contentment at home for the rest of his life. Perhaps it was the character of his formidable correspondent which made him write in that way.

But it is abundantly clear from the letters he wrote to Ruby that he was much more than comparatively happy, though his pessimistic obsession with Ireland never lifted. The letters lay bare a side of Edward Carson that few would have guessed at. Everyone who knew him socially felt the charm of his personality. But who knew him, as Ruby did, capable of a loving and warm relationship and as a gentle suitor? His daughter Aileen did. She wrote to him when she knew he was to marry again.[37]

> Pater darlingest, Your news was *not* unexpected. I have been wondering about it for quite a long time ... and dear old thing I'm *glad* 'cause I know you will be happy and I always hate to think of you being alone at Eaton Place – of course just somewhere inside me there is a little ache at the thought of sharing you with anybody – I can't help it just yet, but it has to be squashed – and I feel sure Ruby and I will be the best of pals. I'm so glad she is jolly and young. I don't think I could have borne to let any of Lady L's 'choosings' steal you from me ... you will be ever so happy and of *course* it couldn't make any difference between you and me – we shall always be 'sweethearts' – yes?

The rivals for his affections were much of an age. Aileen, although married, was looking after her father, and during the last stages of Annette's life and afterwards, acted as his housekeeper and companion. She relieved him of much tedious detail by running the house in Eaton Place smoothly and efficiently. Carson's younger daughter, Gladys, continued to make her father anxious. She was constantly ill. In 1910, she had been in a sanitorium for tubercular patients in Switzerland, where she met and fell in love with an American. Carson was displeased. 'I do not relish foreign relations' he confided to Lady Londonderry. 'Gladys's "young man" is a terror. I think she must be quite topsy turvy to think of him'.[38]

The progress of the friendship between Edward Carson and Ruby Frewen until they knew they were in love can be traced through his letters to her. None from her to him survive. It seems that she made the first move after they met in the summer of 1912 at Homburg by sending him a Christmas present of her own manufacture. 'My dear Miss Frewen', he wrote on Boxing Day, 'You are a very nice friend to knit me such a pretty tie', thanking her in German to remind her of their meeting. She wanted to come and see him in court, and in the following June he arranged for his clerk to get a seat for her in the 'holy precincts'. She was still then Miss Frewen, but by September she had become 'Ruby Darling' or just 'RD'. The pace was quickening, and he wanted her to understand the implications of his being thirty years older and in the thick of a political crisis. 'Be quite sure – won't you RD?' He told her that he was amused at the attacks on him in the 'Radical Papers'. 'How such a scoundrel is allowed to be at large it is difficult to understand, but how anyone, and especially the darlingest in the world could love him is almost inconceivable!' Ruby was a keen rider to hounds, and in the same letter he wrote that it must be 'interesting work hunting the stag – but Ruby D I could not bear to see it die.'

As time went on he told her more of what he was doing, although always discreetly. He told her too how lonely he was, and – not once – how depressed and worn out he felt. He told her (too often) that he was old, but added 'I will feel young again all right when I am with you – won't I?' It was impossible for her to see as much of him as she wanted. Sometimes her patience was tried, but always he gave her reassurance. 'RD, you were very sweet to me today so thank you and good night.' By February they had pledged themselves. A little strain appeared. Ruby's father protested that it reflected on 'the girl who is our daughter and is to be your wife' that the engagement had not been made public. If, said Colonel Frewen, Carson had wanted it to be kept secret, Ruby should not have been seen about with him in London. Carson was irritated and wrote to Ruby, quoting her father's letter. 'RD we really must be allowed to manage our own matters in our way.' Ruby apparently did manage her father, for two days later (on 26 February) Carson wrote again that he was glad everything had settled down at home. 'Fuss never does any good ... How good and sweet and trusting you have been to me RD. But it is all right.'

Within days of the wedding Carson was ill again. He had been made anxious by Asquith's delaying tactics and the burden of what lead to give to the Ulster Unionists. He was confined to bed and from there he scribbled a note in pencil to Ruby: 'so much depends on my judgment and RD you will understand how I am prepared to lose everything over this – I can have no real happiness whilst all this is pending ... I know you will not think you have wasted your life in giving love and brightness and help to me'.

The marriage was happier even than it promised to be. In the first letter to Ruby as his wife, when she was staying at Craigavon in December 1914, he told her that he was longing for her return. In an undated letter of about 1920, he wrote: 'I will desire all sorts of extra love when you come back – I am longing for you every minute and nothing makes me happy when you are away ...' He was sixty-six and experiencing that special elation of spirit which comes from the love of a young woman.

Immediately after their honeymoon Carson took Ruby to be introduced to Belfast. She was thoroughly approved of. On 28 September (Ulster Day) during the visit, Carson made an uncompromising speech, describing the Home Rule Bill in an unfortunate phrase as a scrap of paper which 'so far as concerns us, we will repeal in ten minutes'.* But the defiant front Carson showed concealed a continuing pragmatism. On 13 March 1915 he had a visit from a supporter of John Redmond, Alfred Graves, who put before him a scheme for a Home Rule government in Ulster with proportional representation to protect the Catholic minority. Carson was interested and suggested it be 'ventilated privately in the right quarters'. Graves reported to Redmond that Carson thought that if the Catholics assisted in the government of Ulster, 'six years might see either a fusion between the two Home Rule governments, or in the case of a financial breakdown of the Home Rule system, a reversion to the Union'.[39] Carson had not given up hope that, with generosity of treatment, there might still be some way of saving the Union, or at any rate preserving Ireland's unity.

While gestures of intransigence were being made in Belfast, the war was going badly. Britain's unpreparedness was plain. After early reverses, the Western Front had become the stalemate which was to characterise it

---

* The phrase 'scrap of paper' had been used by Bethmann Hollweg, the German Chancellor, to describe the treaty of 1839 by which Belgium's neutrality was guaranteed.

for four long years. In September 1914 three cruisers were sunk by a single U-boat, an ominous precursor of the later war at sea. The next month one of the newest battleships, HMS *Audacious*, was mined and sank. And in November a German squadron commanded by Admiral von Spee destroyed a weaker British force off Coronel in Chile. These defeats shocked a nation accustomed to unchallenged superiority at sea. Churchill's unhappy tenure of the Admiralty was made worse by the failure of a rash amphibious expedition to Antwerp in October.

At the end of that month, Prince Louis of Battenberg had to give way to a wave of anti-German feeling and resigned as First Sea Lord. Churchill appointed the seventy-four year old Lord Fisher in his place. Fisher was a legend, irascible, mercurial, emotionally unstable, but still a national hero. He was also a friend of Bonar Law and had the support of the Unionist Party. A clash between Fisher and his equally headstrong political chief was a high probability.

The Unionists sat impotent, with deep misgivings about the three men most responsible for the direction of the war: Asquith, the procrastinator; Kitchener, the patriotic symbol and immobile titan; and most of all, Winston Churchill, disloyal, unreliable and, as it seemed, hungry for power. Carson may not have shared his colleagues' distrust of Churchill (although Ruby did), but his sense of frustration was acute. On 13 March 1915 he wrote to Lady Londonderry: 'I work away daily in the courts as it is a waste of time to go the House or try any politics. It is no use being half hot and half cold and pin pricks only give an idea of a desire to oppose without having any courage to do so.'[40]

In February, Lord Londonderry died. Carson's consistent supporter, genial friend and host, and the best man at his wedding seemed suddenly to have given up hope. He left Carson's long-time correspondent a widow and dowager, more and more reminiscent of the Duchess in *Alice*.

It was now accepted on all sides that the war would not be a short one. Various projects were floated to break the deadlock on the Western Front. Churchill's idea was to attack the Dardanelles and so open up Constantinople. This, he argued, would knock Turkey out of the war and lead to an assault on the Central Powers from the south east. His advocacy persuaded the Cabinet, and the expedition arrived in the straits in the middle of March, 1915. Unfortunately, the enterprise was ill thought out and ill provided for. It was to prove the worst single disaster of the war, and it sent Churchill into the wilderness.

Fisher had a rival scheme for breaking into the Baltic and attacking Berlin from the north. Competition between the two plans sharpened the antagonism between Churchill and his First Sea Lord. By the beginning of

May it was already apparent that the Dardanelles would not be the quick brilliant victory its sponsors had hoped. It was more likely that it would become a dangerous battle of attrition, soaking up troops and resources that could not be spared. Then Fisher suddenly resigned and precipitated a major political crisis.

For the opposition nothing could have been worse than the prospect of Fisher going and Churchill staying. Bonar Law made clear that, if that happened, there would have to be a public debate and he would attack the policy which had led to the situation. The party truce would be over. Fisher stoked up the fire by writing to Bonar Law and giving his – heavily underlined – opinion that 'WC is a bigger danger than the Germans by a long way in what is just now imminent in the Dardanelles. *Concentrate on the Dardanelles!'*[41] Asquith bowed to the storm and agreed to a coalition. Churchill was unceremoniously informed that there would be no debate on Fisher's resignation, and that he himself was to leave the Admiralty.

When the reconstructed government was announced on 26 May it was found that the Liberals held most of the important places. Asquith remained Prime Minister and Lloyd George became Minister of Munitions, McKenna taking his place at the Treasury. Simon went to the Home Office. Balfour took the Admiralty. Bonar Law accepted the (in wartime) second-line Colonial Office and Lansdowne became Minister without Portfolio. Churchill was demoted to the Duchy of Lancaster. The size of the Cabinet remained at twenty-two.

Carson became Attorney-General with a seat in the cabinet. Although he had excellent credentials, the appointment was pregnant with irony. 'Was it only a year ago that you were nearly arrested for treachery?' asked his friend the Duchess of Abercorn. Redmond wrote to Asquith to protest. But his case was weakened by his refusal to accept office himself. His difficulties were growing daily, among them Kitchener's discriminatory treatment of recruits from the South as compared with those from Ulster. There was strong antipathy towards Carson in the Liberal ranks. Augustine Birrell, the Chief Secretary, wrote to Redmond with whom he was on terms of close friendship: 'you cannot imagine how I *loathe* the idea of sitting cheek by jowl with these fellows who either believed or pretended to believe (the one is as bad as the other) that we organised a *pogrom* of Ulster *men* and, I suppose, *women* too'.[42]

As Birrell acknowledged, however, Carson was reluctant to come in. Ruby took a straightforward view of her husband's duty. 'They are pressing Edward very hard to come into the Cabinet,' she reported to Lady Londonderry, 'and he will have to, which I think is quite right as he must stand by Mr Bonar Law who stood by him so well over Ulster.'[43] Carson conceded and accepted office. He quickly found that it was a divided coalition. 'We are a strange lot of bedfellows in the Cabinet', he told the same correspondent in June.[44] But he employed his experience of cross-examination to good effect, particularly against Kitchener, who, it was suspected, did not read his telegrams. 'Edward is being worked much too hard', Ruby wrote, again to Lady Londonderry, 'but I hear he is the terror of the Cabinet which is good, but I still think most of them are a shifty disgusting lot and I am sure Winston Churchill means to talk himself into the most powerful place he can again.'[45] Lady Carson was a good hater. Her husband was not happy in the Cabinet. It was unwieldy and ineffective under Asquith's tergiversating leadership. In August Carson told James Craig that he was 'tired, tired, always tired'. The work was irksome, the numbers were too large and it was hard to do anything one would like to do.[46]

Everything, however, was dwarfed by the disaster of the Dardanelles. The original plan was for the Navy to force the straits by itself. When this failed the Army was sucked in. Soldiers were landed on Gallipoli, a peninsula running along the western shore of the narrows like a bony finger. The mountainous landscape was easy to defend by well-equipped and determined troops dug into trenches, as the Turks were. Larger and larger numbers of British, Australians and New Zealanders, who could not be spared from France, were left clinging to precarious beaches and ledges with no room to manoeuvre or turn the Turkish defences.

Carson was kept informed at first hand by friends in the Irish regiments who were trapped on the peninsula. His cousin and school friend, General Sir Bryan Mahon, wrote to him from there in July 1915 and confirmed Carson's fears. Mahon's view was that the adventure was bound to end in disaster and should 'at all costs' be abandoned.[47] In October Carson was told by another friend that temperatures were over 100 degrees, there was no water, and that the men were delirious with thirst and drinking their own urine.[48] It had become more than a possibility that the expedition would be destroyed by disease.

On 8 October Carson had a letter from Sir Henry Craik, a Unionist MP. Craik believed that the understanding among Members on both sides of the House to support the government had been strained to breaking point, and he was convinced that only Carson and perhaps one or two others could give a rallying cry.[49] On the 10th, the Germans and Austrians invaded Serbia, and then Bulgaria joined the assault. Bulgaria's opportunistic entry into the war on the side of the Central Powers had opened up a land route between Germany and Turkey, allowing German supplies to bolster the defence of Gallipoli. Kitchener did not know of the attack until nearly twenty-four hours later. Carson passed a note to Lloyd George in cabinet: 'K does not read the telegrams – and we don't see them – it is intolerable. EC'[50]

On the 12th, Carson, whose patience with the ineffectual direction of the war was exhausted, sent a brief note to Asquith saying that he had decided to resign and that he would give his reasons later. Asquith appealed to him to stay, but his mind was made up. He made a short statement in the House basing his action on the failure to come to the aid of Serbia, the original victim of pan-German aggression. On 2 November Asquith made a long statement on the state of the war. It was coolly received. He said that he did not propose to reduce the size of the Cabinet. The War Committee would number between three and five, but the Cabinet would retain ultimate authority. Carson took the opportunity to deploy his criticisms. It was really his resignation speech.[51] He attacked the Dardanelles expedition outright. The losses, he said, should have been cut far earlier. Even now, the government had not made up its mind whether to go on, or whether boldly to withdraw so as to save suffering and loss. There was absolutely no hope of any satisfactory result. It was impossible, he continued, to carry on the war through a Cabinet of twenty-two meeting spasmodically or once a week. It would not help one bit to have a small War Committee accountable to the Cabinet. The problems would still go back to the twenty-two. What was needed was a small number – the smaller the better – of competent men with full powers of decision sitting from day to day with the best expert advisers. *The Times* reported that Carson's speech was a remarkable proof of his position in the House. 'By comparison with Mr Asquith's it was unpolished and almost unprepared. But it was full of force, contained some striking phrases, and was punctuated by cheers which seemed to come impartially from both sides of the House.'[52]

Although others, notably Lloyd George, were unhappy about the government's grip on the war, Carson resigned alone. Some of his friends were saddened. Archbishop Crozier of Armagh implored him to stay in the Cabinet.[53] Bonar Law thought it was not an opportune moment to go. There were other disapproving voices. J. L. Garvin wrote to Churchill: 'Carson's resignation, much as I like him, does not satisfy judgment at all. Single resignations are merely disappointing in their effect on public opinion and bad for the country since they only weaken the actual War Cabinet without bringing about a thorough change.'[54] Max Aitken, later Lord Beaverbrook, was severe. Carson, he thought, could have been of the greatest assistance to Bonar Law if he had stayed on, and had moved in concert with his leader to force the Prime Minister's hand. 'Resignations in echelon, like attacks, are always a mistake.'[55]

Another view is, however, possible. Carson's departure shook up the old system of governing and showed its inadequacy in wartime. It would take another year to accomplish the changes that were necessary, but the point was taken. By the act of resigning, he made himself a formidable opposition leader in war. And he showed once more his contempt for mere solidarity if there were greater issues at stake.

15

Opposition

In the Second World War there was no organised parliamentary opposition to the coalition government led by Winston Churchill, but rumbling discontent about Asquith's methods and policies in the First War gathered around the figure of Edward Carson as soon as he resigned. *The Times* remarked that his restrained statement on leaving the government had greatly strengthened his position in the House of Commons. 'He is by far the most commanding figure there, outside the swollen ranks of the government.'[1] In the following January a back-bench committee of Unionist MPs was formed under his leadership. It soon made itself felt, growing rapidly to a membership of 150, and collaborating with Sir Frederick Cawley's smaller Liberal War Committee. These groups formed a credible opposition. Their purpose was to put some ginger into the direction of the war.

Carson himself was burning. On New Year's Eve 1915 he wrote to Lady Londonderry to say that the Dardanelles should have been abandoned long since. 'I believe any twenty-two men would do just as well – the whole machine is as rotten as possible and I cannot see when we are to begin to win until both sides are exhausted – I don't think the country will ever again trust what is euphemistically called "The Governing Classes" with their everlasting playing for office and votes!'[2] Some even doubted whether Asquith took the life and death struggle with Germany and the bloody stalemate in Flanders seriously enough. The Prime Minister continued to indulge himself in lengthy personal correspondence in the midst of official business. He 'thus sits dreaming of his Peace in War', Lord Beaverbrook summed up.[3]

With Carson's resignation there was a new alignment in the Cabinet. Churchill had resigned too in November, to go to France and command a battalion of the Royal Scots Fusiliers. Lloyd George, the one remaining restless spirit, bided his time at the new Ministry of Munitions. Bonar Law held the key to the maintenance of the coalition. He had undergone a transformation. Although he had threatened to resign over the failure to cut losses in the Dardanelles, loyalty towards and indeed admiration of Asquith had become his ruling principle. This led to a marked coolness between Carson and his old friend and leader.

Carson's Unionist War Committee attacked the government on the issue of conscription. Until the autumn of 1915 recruitment was entirely voluntary. Moral pressure was applied by the poster of Kitchener's pointing finger and the fear of the white feather, a symbol of cowardice. Conscription was contrary to the traditional British practice. It had never been used. It was opposed by the trade unions and by the old peace party in the Cabinet – Simon, Runciman, McKenna. But the appalling losses in France and Gallipoli called up a surge of feeling in the country. Something had to be done. Able-bodied young men were still walking the streets at home. Let them be conscripted.

Carson was strongly in favour of conscription on the simple ground that it shared the burden evenly. In January 1916, Asquith brought in a Military Service Bill which imposed conscription on unmarried men between the ages of eighteen and forty-one. Only Simon resigned. Tribunals were established to deal with cases of conscientious objection. The measure did not achieve much in the way of recruitment and the clamour was renewed. Asquith produced a further and feeble Bill extending the service of time-expired men. Carson made a powerful speech and forced the government to withdraw the Bill. 'Edward made them throw it out, he must have made the most splendid speech', Ruby proudly recorded in her diary. 'He says that no Prime Minister has ever been placed in such a humiliating position.'[4] The exaggeration was pardonable. A new Bill was brought forward providing for universal male military service up to the age of forty-one.

None of these measures applied to Ireland. Carson argued that to exempt the Irish was morally wrong. The voluntary system was draining Ireland of Loyalists, and leaving the field to those Republicans who treated the war as England's problem. The Ulster Unionist Council had passed a resolution in January recording their 'deep sense of the wrong that will be done to the loyal manhood of Ireland if the Compulsory Service Bill be not applied to every portion of the United Kingdom'.[5] Carson appealed to Redmond to take the same view as his own.[6] But Redmond would not, could not. He relied on the voluntary system which, as he fairly said, had produced an impressive number of recruits and some very brave Irishmen.

The issue of conscription carried a high emotional charge. Why, it was asked, should the Irish be exempt? They were citizens of the United Kingdom. But that was just the point. Conscription showed that the Union was repudiated in Irish Catholic minds. In October 1918, H. A. L. Fisher, the distinguished historian and then President of the Board of Education, visited Ireland and reported to the Prime Minister. 'To the Irishman', he wrote, 'there is a vital connection between Home Rule and conscription. To fight for a free Ireland is one thing, to fight for a subject Ireland is another thing.'[7]

It was only a month before the Armistice, but it could have been written at any time in the war.

The Carsons' home at Eaton Place became a centre for opposition to the government. The old conspirators, Jameson, Milner and Wilson, gathered there on Monday evenings, with others – Leo Amery, F. S. Oliver, a protégé of Milner and proponent of federalism, Geoffrey Robinson (Dawson) of *The Times*, as well as members of Carson's ginger group in Parliament. Ruby described them as 'his men' and often left them to their own devices, but she was proud that her husband was their leader. 'Lord Milner and Mr Geoffrey Robinson came over to tea, they all made plans that Asquith must be forced to go and say if not we shall lose the war ... Lord Milner is splendid.'[8] She evidently got on well with Wilson. He wrote to her in April: 'Will you tell that Edward of yours that the Army is looking to him as the only man who can rid them of Squiff' (his detractors' nickname for Asquith).[9] Bonar Law baffled her. 'I really believe he is hypnotised by Asquith, he thinks it would be difficult to find anyone to do better.'[10] Then she met Lloyd George. 'Edward and I dined with the McNeills to meet Lloyd George as he wanted to see Edward quietly. I thought him quite attractive but quite the most dishonest looking face I have seen.'[11] That quiet meeting was the first of many as each of the two felt his way towards a joint venture to encompass the fall of Asquith.

After his resignation from the government, Carson resumed his practice at the Bar. Like many barrister politicians, it was a relief to him to get back to the collegiate atmosphere of the Temple, away from the frustrations and, as he saw it, the rottenness of politics. He found no shortage of briefs, but at the beginning of February 1916, in the middle of a long case, he fell ill. There was concern about his heart. He was ordered to rest and visitors were forbidden. Ruby was solicitous. She recorded in her diary that Lady Londonderry got very excited with her and said that she was making an invalid of her husband. 'She talked all the time at the pitch of her lungs and was quite difficult and yet I can't help liking her.'[12] It was just as well. The Dowager knew all about Carson's hypochondria but had no notion of tact.

In March the Carsons borrowed a bungalow at Birchington in the Isle of Thanet where Edward could complete his convalescence. On the 13th they had a visit from Mrs Winston Churchill. She brought some letters from her husband who was in France. Churchill and Carson had been corresponding since January. Churchill had decided to return to Parliament and wanted Carson's advice on timing. 'I am naturally anxious', he wrote, 'to act in sympathy and accord with you, and should welcome a frank expression of your views.'[13] Mrs Churchill was at the time acting as her husband's eyes and ears, and as an intermediary for messages and letters. 'I have no one but you to act for me', he wrote to her[14] He told her that the group he wanted to work with were 'LG, FE, BL, Carson and Curzon. Keep that steadily in mind. It is the alternative Government when "wait and see" is over.'[15] Mrs Churchill thought that Winston should be at home, but she knew his impulsive nature better than anyone. This had been dramatically demonstrated by his sudden descent on the House to speak in a debate on the Navy on 7 March. He spoke with great force and was listened to respectfully. But he then astonished the House by calling for the return as First Sea Lord of Fisher, whose earlier resignation had precipitated the crisis in 1915 which led to the coalition government. It was almost beyond belief and destroyed the effect of his speech.

Churchill had obtained a promise from Asquith that his return to Parliament would not be impeded by military obstacles. On 13 March he asked Asquith to redeem his promise, and then withdrew his request by telegram. He wanted to talk to Carson, and possibly others, before making his mind up. But on his way to Birchington, his car broke down, and he was not able to see Carson before catching the boat from Dover. It was in these circumstances that Mrs Churchill called on the Carsons on his behalf. She had to find her way in driving rain, and understandably was overwrought when she arrived. Ruby recorded that 'she seems very upset and really cried to me as she explained Winston had tried to do as he thought right ... I really liked her, she is so pretty'.[16]

On the following day Mrs Churchill sent her husband an account of the visit.[17] At first she could not see Carson as he was sleeping. She noticed as she waited that there were no daily papers in the bungalow, 'only several Irish and (particularly) Ulster periodicals'. Eventually she was admitted to the bedroom.

> There on a narrow little bed looking very weak, but very intelligent lay poor Carson (do not repeat anything about his health as they are both very sensitive about it). He was very pale and one eye was slightly larger than the other ... He spoke with great admiration of your qualities and said that when he was in the government you seemed to him the only man with imagination and 'go' (he included LG in this). He first enquired if your letter to the PM (asking to be relieved) had actually been sent and when I said 'yes' he looked grave and said it was a very serious step and he hoped you had not made a mistake ... if you returned in these not very favourable circumstances he feared that for the present your position would not be a good one and that therefore your usefulness would be temporarily impaired ... He asked me when I thought you would be returning and I said I thought about a week and he said he would *very* much like to see you then. He cannot write to you as this is not yet allowed ... He told me that on three separate occasions since he left the Government he had been put in possession of

facts by which he could have overthrown the Government, but that he had not felt justified. I wish so much that we had planned things better and that you had seen him before sending the PM your letter ... I hope I have not given the impression that Carson does not think you would be an asset here. He does but would like the asset in an undamaged condition.

Mrs Churchill described Ruby: 'She has beautiful eyes and is I feel a true good cat but with a very violent disposition! I think we have a good friend in her.'

On 23 March Carson was able to write a pencil note to Churchill to confirm his views.[18] Having announced that he was going on active service, he said, Churchill might be criticised if he came back without being able to show grave necessity: 'it would be very bad for your career and usefulness if the country got the impression you acted spasmodically or without sound and deliberate judgment'. Carson had put his finger on the weakness of the younger man. Churchill replied, saying that he felt acutely the force of what Carson had said: these reflections had caused him embarrassment. However, he still had the conviction that he had some power to avert the dangers of the war. 'But upon the question of time and occasion I value immensely your opinion ... I do not think that this is the moment to terminate the life of this ill-starred coalition. But the formation and development of an effective and resolute opposition is now required urgently ... Asquith's failing is not lack of *decision*, but lack of *design*. On that all turns, and the helplessness of gallant effort at the front is pathetic.'[19] In the event, Carson's response to Churchill's plea for help disappointed Mrs Churchill. She thought that Carson should have mobilised the support of his influential back-bench committee. But she surely underestimated the depth of Unionist hostility to her husband.

On 24 April Ruby recorded (with two exclamation marks) that she and Edward had dined with the Churchills in London. 'Who would have thought that could ever have happened.' She still wondered how honest Winston was. 'He talks an awful lot and gave me the impression his tongue worked faster than his brain though it goes pretty fast.'[20] On 5 May Churchill wrote to Carson again. 'Any arrangement which succeeded the Asquith regime must be between you and Lloyd George. I trust you will keep in touch with one another.'[21]

It is interesting to compare Churchill's appraisal with that of Bonar Law, who gave it in a private conversation with, surprisingly, John Redmond. Bonar Law thought that the government might be beaten at any time in the House. If, he said, Sir Edward Carson had the health and desire, he could lead an opposition, and drive the government from office in no time. Redmond then asked who could possibly take Asquith's place. Was it Carson?

Bonar Law said no, that would be impossible, even if Carson's health were good. Redmond asked, was it Bonar Law himself? No, said Bonar Law again, and added that he had become 'to some extent' unpopular in his own party. Bonar Law then said Lloyd George. Redmond asked what he thought of that. Bonar Law made an expressive gesture and said, 'You know George as well as I do'.[22]

By Spring 1916 Carson had nevertheless established a strong position in the House and in the country. The disaffected Tory back benches looked to him for leadership rather than Bonar Law, who lacked charisma, was somewhat depressed and, above all, was shackled to a failing coalition. Carson had many supporters outside his own party and outside Parliament. His straightforward and consistent approach to the paramount need to win the war was seen to advantage in opposition, where there was no need either to manage a department or to trim in order to keep government together. Nor was he fearful in the slightest degree of promoting disunity in the country by vocal assaults in the House. Was he not therefore in a good position to succeed Asquith if the Prime Minister fell? The reason why that question was to be answered in the negative was sensed by Bonar Law, as he explained it to Redmond, but perhaps more discerningly by Mrs Spender, who was now a close friend of Ruby Carson. Spender, who was in France, asked his wife for her views about Sir Edward. She told him that there was much that she wanted to say but dared not put into a letter; but she wrote: 'I think he is beginning to realise that he really is needed, and once he grasps that *fully*, I think his body will obey his mind, and all will be well. But he *must* give up the law, and that is a terrible wrench, as he hates politics and loves law. He hasn't a spark of political ambition, and is incurably modest, most astonishingly so ...'[23]

On Easter Monday 1916, a dissident splinter of the Irish Volunteers seized the General Post Office in Dublin and raised the green flag with golden harp and the green, white and orange tricolour. Patrick Pearse, a schoolmaster and revolutionary, proclaimed an independent Irish Republic with himself as President. Pearse's words fell among a largely uninterested crowd. The principal sounds to be heard were not cheers but the crash of breaking glass as a Dublin mob, taking advantage of the absence of the police, began to loot the fashionable shops in O'Connell Street (then Sackville Street).[24] Another group took possession of the Four Courts. Another, led by Eamon De Valera, occupied Boland's Flour Mills, while another, including the flamboyantly romantic Countess Markiewicz (formerly Constance Gore-Booth), set itself up on St Stephen's Green. On Good Friday Roger Casement had been put ashore by a German submarine and was promptly arrested.[25] On the same day, a German arms ship flying the Norwegian flag was intercepted and scuttled in Irish waters.

It took a week to put down the insurrection. It attracted very little support and some derision. Pearse's sister, arriving at the Post Office on Easter Monday, ordered him to 'Come home, Pat, and leave all this foolishness'.[26] It had been prepared in complete secrecy and took Ireland unawares. The great majority, who supported Britain's cause in the war (unlike their kin in the United States), were shocked. Those that heard thought it ludicrous when Pearse referred to Germany as a 'gallant ally'. John Redmond heard the news of the rising with 'horror, discouragement, almost despair'; and thought the insurgents had tried to make Ireland the catspaw of Germany.[27]

But the rising was far from ludicrous. It was hopeless as an effective rising from the start, but the rebels wanted to make a blood sacrifice that would change the course of Irish history. In that they succeeded. The immediate cause of a change in Irish attitudes to the rising was the reaction of the British authorities. Martial law was declared throughout the island. Fifteen leaders of the insurrection were court martialled and shot by firing squad: not at once but apparently randomly, singly or in twos and threes over a period of nine days. James Connolly, a labour leader and commandant of the Irish Citizen Army who had agreed to join the insurrection, was injured in the fighting and was shot propped in a chair. Another who was shot was Sheehy Skeffington, a Dublin journalist who had nothing to do with the rising. The officer responsible was found to be insane.

The shootings inflamed American opinion. The United States were still neutral. Sir Cecil Spring-Rice, the British Ambassador, sent a telelgram on 19 May which was deciphered for the Cabinet. 'Movement received little real sympathy at first but executions have greatly changed situation and I fear if they continue effect will be very serious.'[28]

The poet Yeats marked the change. His first reaction was that it was a piece of foolishness, and that its leaders were misguided ideologues flirting with the gallows. But as the violence continued through Easter week he was shaken. The courts martial and the shootings turned him. In May he began to write his poem, *Easter 1916* with its repeated refrain, 'a terrible beauty is born'. The poem raised the leaders to a martyred nobility.

> Was it needless death after all?
> For England may keep faith
> For all she had done and said.
> We know their dream; enough
> To know they dreamed and are dead.

The faith which England might or might not keep was the promise to grant

Home Rule. From the time of the rising more and more Catholic Irishmen believed that the promise would not be kept. More and more were drawn into the orbit of the violent revolutionaries from whom the IRA was born. The rising sealed the fate of Redmond's constitutional Nationalism. It deepened sectarian hatred. Protestants, in turn, were appalled that Irish Catholics could strike England in its time of need.

The Carsons first heard of the insurrection from Colonel Sharman Crawford, a member of the commission that had drafted the constitution for the provisional government of Ulster. He had crossed from Dublin the night of Easter Monday and arrived at Eaton Place with the news. He told them that Dublin was in the hands of the Sinn Feiners, and that they had taken over the stations, blown up railway lines and cut the cable: the city was in an uproar. Ruby Carson recorded Sharman Crawford's account in her diary for 25 April, the Tuesday of Easter week, and added, 'In Ulster all is quiet, what a contrast!!' The news realised Carson's worst fears. A feeble administration in Dublin led by the complaisant Chief Secretary, Augustine Birrell, had ignored the warning signs. The Royal Commission on the insurrection reported soberly, but damningly, that lawlessness had been allowed to grow unchecked, and that Ireland had been governed for several years past 'on the principle that it was safer and more expedient ... to leave law in abeyance if collision with any faction of the Irish people could thereby be avoided'.[29]

Carson's first thought was that Easter week had put paid to Home Rule.[30] He might well have thought so, but he was soon disillusioned. Birrell resigned and Asquith, for once, moved quickly. On 11 May he crossed to Ireland to see for himself. He went to Dublin, Cork and (for the first time) Belfast. On his return he told the Commons that the machinery of Irish government had broken down, but there was a unique opportunity for a new departure. He had therefore asked Lloyd George to try to promote a settlement. Carson and Redmond both said that they would cooperate.[31]

The atmosphere was tense in London as well as in Dublin. Carson was getting a lot of threatening letters, his wife recorded, and at some times police and detectives were outside the house.[32] All but a group of obdurate Unionists realised that Ireland must not be allowed to distract the country from the war, whose outcome looked far from certain. A series of shocking events occurred at the beginning of June. The greatest naval battle of the war off Jutland resulted, at best, in an honourable draw. The Somme offensive was about to begin, of all the conflicts on the Western Front the most senseless and the most terrible.

HMS *Hampshire*, on its way to Russia with Kitchener on board, was sunk – although it was not clear how effective a War Minister he had been, except as a recruiting sergeant. Ruby Carson was not among his admirers. 'He seemed to me a grand looking sham, just medals and an uniform', she wrote in her diary after the memorial service on 11 June. Lloyd George wrote to Carson and gave a terse summary of the situation as he saw it. 'This terrible disaster in the North Sea [the loss of Kitchener] makes it more necessary than ever that we should get Ireland out of the way in order to press on with the war ... I must have a talk with you on Monday, not only about Ireland but about the whole position, before you leave for Belfast. Let us settle Ireland promptly ...'[33]

Asquith's view was that the only way to prevent the Sinn Fein extremists from wresting all popular support in Ireland from Redmond was to concede Home Rule, or some measure of it, at once. The Prime Minister wanted Lloyd George to take over as Chief Secretary to pilot the changes through, but that was not welcome to the proposed beneficiary. Lloyd George had no wish to be stuck in Dublin while there was a war to fight, on which he had his own ideas. He was, however, willing to try once more for an agreed settlement. The Commons gave him a great ovation when his mission was announced. He was recognised as the best possible choice, not least because of his extraordinary optimism. When his Parliamentary Secretary, Arthur Lee, asked him if he thought he would pull it off, he replied, 'You know, I am that kind of beggar. I always do think beforehand that I am going to bring things off'.[34] But he was under no illusions about the vital character of his task. 'Nothing would have induced me to intervene in this unfortunate Irish business at this stage', he wrote to a friend, 'except the urgent conviction that it has a direct and important bearing on the conduct of the war. It has already aggravated our relations with America, and we cannot afford a hostile America at a time when victory is still in the mist.'[35]

He decided to see each of the parties separately: Carson and Craig for the Ulster Unionists; Redmond, Dillon, Joseph Devlin, the Ulster Nationalist leader, and T. P. O' Connor for the Nationalists. No Unionists from the south and west were consulted. Against all odds and all experience, Lloyd George rapidly achieved agreement in principle. The negotiators on each side were to seek approval for the proposals from those they represented.

Home Rule was to be put into effect immediately in twenty-six counties in the south and west. The six remaining north-eastern counties of Antrim, Armagh, Down, Fermanagh, Londonderry and Tyrone were to be excluded from Home Rule and remain part of the United Kingdom, together with the parliamentary boroughs of Belfast, Londonderry and Newry. The division was thus the same as rules today. The MPs from the twenty-six counties, who were to sit in the new Dublin Parliament, would also continue to sit at Westminster. The Act embodying these proposals would remain in force until twelve months after the end of the war, but if Parliament had not by then 'made further and permanent provision for the Government of Ireland', the life of the Act was to be extended by Order in Council 'for as long as might be necessary'.

Carson realised that he would have to do his best to get approval for these proposals. The alternative was unattractive in the extreme: another weak executive in Dublin, challenged at every turn by hostile, disappointed Nationalists. To run these risks for the sake of putting off Home Rule until the end of the war, and then see it come into force automatically, was, as he told Sir Horace Plunkett, neither a sound nor a statesmanlike policy. He viewed with real horror the prospect of active hostilities in Ulster after the war – and for what? Surely to get no more than was now on offer.[36] In any case, he agreed with Lloyd George that Ireland must give place to the war effort. He had to make the best bargain he could, when he could. There would never be a better time.

But it was essential that the cut between the six and the twenty-six counties must be a clean one, and that it be neither temporary nor provisional. Lloyd George accepted that. On 29 May, sending his proposals to Carson, he wrote: 'We must make it clear that at the end of the provisional period Ulster does not, whether she wills it or not, merge in the rest of Ireland.'[37] Carson wrote out a copy and sent it to Bonar Law. He understood Lloyd George to mean that the six counties were not to be included within Home Rule unless the Imperial Parliament passed an Act to that effect. He made a memorandum of his understanding;[38] and, when the Prime Minister made a statement in the House about the negotiations, he obtained explicit confirmation. 'They', said Asquith in reference to the six excluded counties and in answer to Carson, 'could not be included without a Bill.'[39]

It seemed plain enough, but, as emerged later, Redmond had been given the impression that the arrangements proposed were provisional only. He and his colleagues, said Redmond in the House, never for one moment contemplated the idea that this great question was to be foreclosed and settled now.[40] Lloyd George was attacked for duplicity. Carson had a letter from a Dublin solicitor warning him that Asquith and Lloyd George were deep tricksters. 'For you the exclusion is to be permanent, for Redmond temporary.'[41] Lloyd George was indeed a master of creative ambiguity. But he was only the most gifted exponent of a device which has been used many times since, in an attempt to reconcile the opposing stone-cast certitudes of warring Irishmen. However that may be, it was not the question of whether exclusion was to be permanent or temporary which, in the event, scuppered the settlement.

On 5 June Carson left London for Belfast to lay the Lloyd George proposals before the Ulster Unionist Council. They were, Ruby recorded, a great party going over: the Londonderrys, Lord Farnham who had come home from France to take part, Mr and Mrs Ronald McNeill, and the Duke of Abercorn. 'Will there be a settlement – I wonder if Ulster will consent to take six counties.'[42] It was to be one of the most uncomfortable episodes in Carson's life. He addressed the Council on the 6th. The meeting was private. According to McNeill, who was there, Carson spoke for almost two hours and was a model of lucidity and conviction.[43] But the proposition he had to put forward was a repugnant necessity: repugnant to his audience because of the abandonment of the three remaining Ulster counties of Cavan, Donegal and Monaghan; and a necessity because, as he said, he had no desire to show a dissentient Ireland to the Germans.

The meeting adjourned for a week so that delegates could consult their constituents. 'The three left out counties are not satisfied', Ruby recorded, 'Not surprising ... Edward is very worried ...' But when the delegates returned on 12 June, they gave their reluctant consent to Carson continuing negotiations on the basis of Lloyd George's proposals. McNeill described it as the saddest hour the Council ever spent, and the most poignant ordeal that their leader ever passed through.[44] For the first time, the Ulster Unionists accepted that the excluded area should be six counties.

It cannot be doubted that Carson was right about the urgency of reaching agreement. As Lloyd George advised Asquith, Ireland had to be governed; and, if Home Rule were impossible, coercion was the only alternative. 'The country is one seething mass of discontent. Sinn Feinism is for the moment right on top.'[45] But Carson's own feelings were very mixed. His course was clear, but it was not one he would have chosen had he been free. He wrote to Bonar Law just after the Ulster Unionists' decision. 'For my own part I have had a very painful and difficult task in trying to induce the Six Counties to accept the terms the Government have offered ... I feel very lonely in the whole matter, but I have found confidence reposed in me in the North of Ireland which was, to say the least of it, refreshing.'[46] He went on: 'I have heard rumours today that the Cabinet have known nothing about the negotiations or the terms, but that I do not credit ...'

Unfortunately the rumours were true. Lloyd George and Asquith had not kept the Cabinet informed. Carson was sharply attacked from Cavan, one of the Ulster counties left out, and from the intransigent wing of the Unionist party. Major Somerset Saunderson was the son of the first leader of the Ulster Unionists, one of the Cavan delegates and a close associate of Walter Long. He wrote to Carson within days of the decision of the Ulster Unionists. His impression, he said, was that 'we have been sold and betrayed by our leaders in the Coalition by reopening the Home Rule question'. He had been to see Walter Long and had been told that Lloyd George's proposals had never been before the Cabinet (of which Long was a member).[47] Saunderson's attacks continued into July, when he argued that the Ulster Unionist Council's decision was based on a misconception and could not stand, a view which Carson indignantly repudiated.[48]

A storm was rising in the Unionist Party. For the Diehard element, Home Rule during the war was a betrayal and a reward for the lawless violence of Easter. Its leaders were Lords Lansdowne and Selborne, and Walter Long. But Long led the pack. He stirred up the southern Unionists and bombarded Carson with what Mrs Spender called 'reams of fury'.[49] Long had been Carson's predecessor as leader of the Irish Unionists, a disappointed contender for the leadership when Balfour resigned, and a former Chief Secretary. He looked like a benign Wiltshire squire, but beneath was an ambitious and jealous spirit. Lloyd George described the situation in the Unionist Party in a letter to Asquith on 20 June: 'I have seen Bonar Law and Carson. Bonar is frightened and timid, but willing to stand by Carson. Carson says he must stand by the agreement. He was very angry with Long who has actually been telling his Ulster people to throw Carson over.'[50]

Ruby's views were predictable and plain. 'The whole Cabinet is now at daggers over the Ulster settlement and pretend they knew nothing', she wrote in her diary on 19 June. 'Walter Long is going to resign [he thought better of it] and says Lloyd George has tricked Edward. They are all playing a low game except Lloyd George. WL says he is an honest gentleman. He would be much better hoeing turnips than in the Cabinet ... I think the real truth is that a good many of them would have liked to have thrown over Edward and have failed.'

Asquith and Lloyd George had kept the Cabinet in the dark and misled their colleagues. As Austen Chamberlain courteously insisted in a letter to the Prime Minister of 23 June, the Cabinet had authorised Lloyd George to act on the basis that Home Rule would not come into operation until the end of the war.[51] Asquith's own cabinet memorandum of 21 May had stated it in such terms.[52] But this condition had been abandoned in the negotiations, and the Cabinet had not been informed of the change until 21 June, that is after the Irish parties had conferred with their constituents. Tricky dealings of this sort were unlikely to achieve their purpose. In the event they proved fatal. On 29 June Lord Lansdowne effectively sank the negotiations by stating in the Lords that the basis on which they had been conducted had not been authorised by the government.[53]

These events shook Carson's personal position in Belfast but he still remained dominant. There was no alternative leader. Bonar Law called a meeting of the whole Unionist Parliamentary Party on 7 July. He told them they would make a terrible mistake if they went back on the negotiations.

Carson, Bonar Law and Balfour fought hard for the settlement, but their opponents were too numerous. The meeting adjourned without reaching a conclusion. Ruby noted that all the party was 'on the quarrel'. She thought the Unionist ministers were 'more despicable than the Radicals'.[54] Long continued to snipe; Selborne resigned. The chances of holding the agreement were slipping away. The Liberals tried to meet objections by tinkering with the Bill – which was already in circulation. But the squirming failed. By the end of July the settlement was dead.

Of all the attempts to settle the Irish imbroglio this was the most promising. The stress of war gave it an impetus which earlier attempts lacked. The exclusion of six rather than nine counties was painful, but it had an important advantage. There was a Protestant majority in the six counties taken as a block, whereas the other three each had large Catholic majorities.* Was partition inevitable if the negotiations were to succeed? The Bishop of Down certainly thought so. 'All this talk about the partition of Ireland is nonsense,' he wrote to Carson, 'Ireland is partitioned already.'[55] The Bishop's view was that if ever unity was to be achieved by cooperation, it would come through a frank recognition of the real facts, and not through forcing warring elements into an artificial combination. It was precisely Carson's opinion.

It is arguable that the settlement could have been rammed through if Asquith and Lloyd George had had the necessary determination. They made a serious mistake by not keeping the Cabinet informed. If, however, the Prime Minister had made the issue one of confidence, the Diehard Unionists might possibly have been overridden, and at worst the expendable Lansdowne and Long could have gone their own way.[56] But the feeling in the Unionist Party against Home Rule being brought into operation during the war was strong and widespread, as the meeting on 7 July had demonstrated, and the strength of the coalition would have been tested at a bad time in the war.

Carson and Lloyd George had shown that they could work together. There was to be more for them to do in cooperation before the end of the year – as Lloyd George foreshadowed when urging Carson to get Ireland out of the way so as to press on with the war. 'The management of the war on the part of the Allies', he wrote to Carson at the beginning of the negotiations, 'is fortuitous and flabby, and unless something is done immediately the British Empire and civilisation will sustain the greatest disaster since the

---

* The 1911 census showed that of the individual counties of Ulster, there were Protestant majorities in only Antrim, Armagh, Down and Londonderry; and there were narrow Catholic majorities in Fermanagh and Tyrone. (Cmd. 5691).

days of Attila. I must therefore have a talk with you with a view to taking immediate action to force a decisive change in the control of the war.'[57]

While the settlement was being sunk by Unionists who had never made a constructive suggestion for resolving the Ulster crisis, the 36th (Ulster) Division attacked the German lines. It was the battle for which the UVF had been waiting. It began early in the morning on 1 July 1916, the opening day of the battle of the Somme. The division held a sector of the front opposite Thiepval wood.[58] Carson received an account from Wilfrid Spender who was serving on the Staff and saw the opening of the assault.[59] The Ulstermen began at a slow walk across no man's land, then suddenly let loose as they charged at the trenches, shouting 'No Surrender'. Gunfire raked them from left and right. They came out of the shattered Thiepval wood quite steadily, their numbers reducing all the time, until they reached their final objective, the fifth line of trenches. The division was now in a narrow salient which could not be held. The order to retire was given. It was symbolic of the whole futile Somme offensive. The Ulster Division had won four Victoria Crosses and lost more than half its men.

16

The Fall of Asquith

When he resigned at the end of 1916, Asquith had been Prime Minister for almost nine years, the longest continuous period for any First Minister for nearly one hundred years. There were many who could hardly imagine public affairs in the hands of anyone else. Although his origins were humble, there was an air of the patrician about him. As was said of him by General John Charteris, Sir Douglas Haig's Chief of Intelligence: 'Asquith was a Sahib: he may have been a tired-out Sahib, but he was, and is, and always will be, a Sahib ...'[1] His political skills were of a high order and his command of the House of Commons was unquestionable. No contemporary had his experience in government. But there were weaknesses, and they were beginning to matter as the war entered its third year. Whatever the circumstances, Asquith's guiding principle was to 'wait and see'. It may have been a workable approach in peacetime, but it would not do in a war leader. Asquith was like the chess player who forgets that his opponent has a move too. Moreover, he ran the government through a large and unwieldy Cabinet which was not adapted to despatch wartime business. As Lloyd George told Carson, the management was 'flabby'. The Prime Minister insisted on retaining authority over everything – except, it seemed, military strategy.

By a pact made at the end of 1915, Lord Kitchener had handed over control of strategy to Sir William Robertson, Chief of the Imperial General Staff. Robertson reigned supreme at the War Office in London and Haig in France. When Lloyd George became War Minister, after Kitchener's death, he found he had little power. He told Max Aitken: 'I am the butcher's boy who leads in the animals to be slaughtered – when I have delivered the men my task in the war is over.'[2] The essential of civilian control of the military had gone by default. It must at least be open to question whether, if Lloyd George had had effective control of the War Office, 450,000 British casualties would have been sustained, for the gain of a few miles of ground, in the four and a half months of pointless bloodshed which was the battle of the Somme.

To compound these failings, an infirmity of judgement began to appear in the Prime Minister. After some wavering, he bowed to a noisy demand, led by Carson, and ordered enquiries into the expeditions to Gallipoli and

Mesopotamia.[3] In doing so, he exposed the performance of his government to international scrutiny, appearing to many to be conceding at least the possibility of mismanagement. Neither Lloyd George nor Churchill would have done that in wartime.

The origins of the crisis which led to Asquith's fall lay in the way the war was being managed from Westminster. The winding and sometimes bewildering course of the intrigue which brought him down has often been described. Some incidents are still cloudy. But what is clear is that three men were responsible: Lloyd George, Bonar Law and Carson. Lloyd George was the principal actor and the only one of the three who could command popular support as Asquith's successor. Bonar Law wavered until the very end. As he said himself, he was a friend to both sides. Carson, the only one who was not in the government, was the least prominent. But his command of a credible opposition in the House and his influential circle outside made him indispensable. Moreover he was the prime mover. He had been the first to advocate a small War Council with absolute authority to run the war, and he never wavered in his view that Asquith would have to go.

Throughout the crisis, the relations between Carson and Lloyd George were good. But Bonar Law did not trust Lloyd George and was unfailingly loyal to Asquith. Indeed, if he were not, the government would lose its coalition partner and it would inevitably fall. He felt a special responsibility to prevent that. But he knew that the machinery of government had to change, and that Asquith was unlikely to be the man to reform it. The dilemma pressed on Bonar Law's melancholy disposition. It also tended to widen a difference between himself and Carson.

The rift was revealed in an apparently insignificant incident. A liquidator appointed to wind up Nigerian enemy property proposed to put it up for sale in London. On 8 November 1916 Mr Leslie Scott, a Tory back bencher and member of Carson's ginger group, moved that the property should be sold only to British subjects.[4] The government considered the restriction impracticable and unwise. Bonar Law defended the official policy. Nearly every Tory speaker was against the government. Carson heckled Bonar Law's speech. He goaded him into saying that he was sure that Carson realised the seriousness of what he was doing and was prepared to take the consequences if he succeeded in the division: in effect, let him bring the government down if he dare. On the vote, Bonar Law was sustained by only a small majority of his own party, although by a large majority of the whole House. The diminishing numbers of Bonar Law's followers among the Unionists was thus clear for all to see.

Carson's guerillas were endangering Bonar Law's leadership of the Unionists and, through this, the life of the government. After the Nigerian debate, Bonar Law felt that the Unionist Party in the House was not only hostile to the government, but, as he put it, 'was fast reaching a point when their hostility would make it impossible for me to continue in the Cabinet'. His political friends, both inside the House and out, were complaining that it was he alone who was keeping up a government which had lost the power of effectively prosecuting the war.[5] In attacking Bonar Law, Carson knew exactly what he was doing. It was the weak point in the Ministry's armour. If Bonar Law had to resign under pressure from Carson, there would be little alternative for him but to make an alliance with Lloyd George and Carson. It was to this alliance that Sir Max Aitken bent his efforts. Aitken was a Conservative back-bencher still in his thirties, who by dint of energy and shrewd judgment was able to move events. He was the impresario of the coup; and as Lord Beaverbrook he left, in his *Politicians and the War*, the most vivid and compelling account of the crisis which has been written.

Bonar Law was reluctant to join hands with Lloyd George. He thought that the latter considered no interests but his own, and was ambitious for power. It took much time and effort by Aitken and Lloyd George to persuade him otherwise. In the process Aitken found that Bonar Law could be 'desperately sticky'.[6] Relations between Carson and Bonar Law were also fragile. Carson thought that Bonar Law must take his share of the blame for the failures of the government. He was impatient about what he took to be Bonar Law's weakness. In Carson's eyes nothing mattered except winning the war, an objective to which even personal loyalties must yield. This was reflected by Ruby Carson, who nearly always took colour from her husband's views. At the climax of the crisis she wrote: 'Bonar Law can't make up his mind but is slowly realising he wants to pull himself out of this mess by Edward'.[7] And damningly on the following day: 'Mr Maxse [the owner and editor of the *National Review*] came in to tea with me. He says Bonar Law is finished. I think he will now stick to Edward and Lloyd George and then he may recover. He is not a real man'.[8] This was a crude misjudgment, but it showed the strength of feeling in the Carson household.

It took all Aitken's skill and tenacity to bring 'the triumvirs', as he called them, together. During the crisis that determined Britain's fate in the war, he saw them constantly and formed his own judgment of their characters. Of Carson he wrote: 'He had set the game on foot and seemed prepared to hunt it down. The popular view of him, though it struck home on the vital point of his courage, was in other respects almost absurdly inaccurate.'[9] It was wrong, Aitken judged, to identify him with his Ulster followers. He was neither dour nor narrowly fanatical. There was indeed something romantic both in his appearance and in his eloquence. 'He thought the matter out carefully, and where his mind stayed, it fixed.' Nonetheless, in Aitken's view, he was capable of great breadth and moderation.

The triumvirate met for the first time in Aitken's rooms in the Hyde Park Hotel, his then London home, on 20 November. The atmosphere was strained. Lloyd George put the case for a small War Council to Bonar Law. It was exactly what Carson had consistently advocated from the autumn of 1915. But Bonar Law was mistrustful and thought that Lloyd George's object was to put Asquith out and himself in. They met again on the following day, and Lloyd George made it clear that Asquith could not be a member of the War Council – although he could, he thought, continue to be Prime Minister. Bonar Law reacted adversely. Discussions continued and Bonar Law's position inched closer to that of the other two.

On 25 November there was another meeting at Bonar Law's house. The views of the three were now sufficiently aligned for Aitken to be able to present a memorandum which he had drawn up for submission to Asquith.[10] It proposed a small War Council with complete authority, subject to the Prime Minister. The Council would meet every day and so could not have as its members Ministers with departmental responsibilities. The Prime Minister would be president and would attend when he could. The chairman was to be Lloyd George; but the questions of who should be the other members, and what should be the Council's relation with the Prime Minister were left blank. It was approved (although Carson frankly wanted Asquith out) and agreed that Bonar Law should take it to Asquith.

Bonar Law saw Asquith that evening and the latter took a copy of the memorandum. He promised to respond and indicated that he might agree if he could be sure it represented Lloyd George's final demand, not just a first instalment. On Monday, 27 November Bonar Law received Asquith's response. It was a complete rejection. According to Aitken, in its original form Asquith had made some disagreeable comments on Carson. He had been vacillating in the Cabinet, Asquith had writtten, and far from capable in general affairs: he was perpetually striving after strength until this constituted a weakness.[11] On being told by Bonar Law that he would have to show the letter to Lloyd George and Carson, and that it was undesirable that Carson should read these reflections on his capacity, Asquith took out the offending passage and put in its place the following innocuous formulation:

As regards Carson, for whom, as you know, I have the greatest personal regard, I do not see how it would be possible, in order to secure his services, to pass over Balfour, or Curzon, or McKenna, all of whom have the advantage of intimate knowledge of the secret history of the last twelve months ... It would be universally believed to be the price paid for shutting the mouth of our most formidable Parliamentary critic.[12]

The triumvirate were not yet at one. Carson was determined that Asquith should not be in a position to control the War Council. The other two were more flexible, and Bonar Law still hoped it might be possible to run Lloyd George and Asquith in double harness. There was also another development. Carson was using his influence with the press. He was seeing a lot of H. A. Gwynne, the editor of the *Morning Post*, and it was significant that the paper now reversed its former hostility to Lloyd George and portrayed him as a saviour. This, said Aitken, who was in a good position to know, was clearly Carson's work.[13] The charge of 'trafficking' with the press was to assume some significance in the crisis, and Carson's name was associated with it. Was this discreditable? In an age before sound and television broadcasting, the daily press was the only medium by which public opinion could be reached and formed. It might be better if politicians did not attempt to influence the media, but that is hardly realistic.

It was now time for Bonar Law to report to the Conservative Cabinet Ministers. This took place on 30 November. Bonar Law explained with complete candour what had transpired. He was met with a wall of opposition. His colleagues saw the War Council as no more than a plan for the aggrandisement of Lloyd George. Their animosity against him went back to the People's Budget and the castration of the House of Lords – if not earlier. Their leader, they felt, was being used as Lloyd George's tool because he was frightened of Carson. And they smarted under Carson's attacks on themselves as members of the coalition. Ruby despised the lot of them. 'One true thing,' she wrote in her diary on 3 December, 'the Unionists in the Cabinet want Edward kept out at all costs. They are a public disgrace. Each for themselves, not one for the country.' Bonar Law received an unpleasant letter from Lansdowne, the day after the meeting, which began, 'The meeting in your room yesterday left "a nasty taste in my mouth".'[14] Lansdowne's attitude sprung from his feeling that the war could not now be won, and a growing belief in peace by negotiation. It is fair to say, however, that none of his Unionist colleagues had been infected by this virus.

Matters were approaching their crux. On Friday 1 December, Lloyd George wrote another memorandum to the Prime Minister. He proposed a War Council of three, consisting of a chairman, the First Lord of the Admiralty and the War Minister. It would have full powers, subject to the supreme control of the Prime Minister, who could refer any matter to the Cabinet. He saw the Prime Minister and not only pressed the formation of the War Council, but urged that it should consist of Lloyd George, Carson and Bonar Law.[15] Asquith rejected the proposals, saying that the Prime Minister could not be relegated to the position of 'an arbiter in the background or a referee to the Cabinet'.[16] Lloyd George felt that the initiative must now lie with Bonar Law. He sent Asquith's letter on to him on the Saturday (2 December), saying simply: 'I enclose a copy of PM's letter. The life of the country depends on resolute action by you now'.[17]

But Bonar Law had not yet brought his mind to the sticking place. Carson's view was unchanged. His instinct, wrote Aitken, had penetrated to the belief that the country was faced by a menace which might be described as respectable defeatism.[18] It was a memorable phrase which deserved to be remembered in the thirties in the days of appeasement.

On Sunday 3 December, *Reynolds's News* carried an article saying that Lloyd George was ready to resign if his demands were not met, and he would then appeal to the country. Carson, the paper said, was in alliance with him, and Bonar Law would probably resign as well. Bonar Law called another meeting of the Tory Cabinet Ministers. His colleagues were sure that Lloyd George was behind the *Reynolds's* article. Their conclusion was that the only thing to be done was the immediate resignation of the whole government. Bonar Law was to carry this message to the Prime Minister. If Asquith would not follow this advice, then the Unionists would all resign from the Cabinet. The object of this dramatic tactic was to see off Lloyd George's challenge; or, as Bonar Law put it, the Unionist Ministers 'did not wish to seem to have their position forced by the action of Lloyd George'.[19] The Unionist Ministers were convinced that, if he went to the country, Asquith would score a resounding victory and crush Lloyd George. Foremost in advancing this proposal were Lord Curzon, Lord Robert Cecil and Austen Chamberlain (dubbed by Aitken as 'the three C's') with Walter Long. Although he was not in favour of this idea, Bonar Law agreed to take the message to Asquith.

This he did on Sunday afternoon. He did not show Asquith the memorandum the Unionist Ministers had drawn up, but he gave him the gist of it. Asquith was understandably alarmed by talk of his resigning and may not have understood the object of the tactic.[20] He thought he could finesse Lloyd George's proposal and remain in overall charge; so he summoned Lloyd George. They came to terms. Asquith would remain Prime Minister and Lloyd George would have his War Council. Only the members of that body remained to be settled. A press statement was issued at a quarter to midnight on Sunday 3 December: 'The Prime Minister, with a view to the most active prosecution of the war, has decided to advise His Majesty the King to consent to a reconstruction of the Government'.

Asquith was relieved that the storm had apparently passed overhead. That night he wrote a personal letter to Pamela McKenna. He had driven down to Walmer, he wrote, hoping to find sunshine and peace. But it had been bitterly cold, and he had had to drive back soon after 11 in the morning to grapple with a crisis -'this time with a very big C. The result is that I have spent much of the afternoon in colloguing with Messrs Ll. George and Bonar Law, and one or two minor worthies. The "Crisis" shows every sign of following its many predecessors to an early and unhonoured grave. But there were many wigs very nearly on the green'.[21] The carefree tone, which was a characteristic of his letters to women, was misplaced.

On the following day, Monday 4 December, Asquith performed a *volte-face*. The immediate reason seems to have been a leading article in *The Times* that day devoted to the announcement that the government was to be reconstructed. In view of its content and tone, Asquith assumed, wrongly, that it had been inspired by Lloyd George. The leader described the Lloyd George proposals accurately. Mr Bonar Law was 'believed' to support Mr Lloyd George, and Sir Edward Carson was 'believed to form an essential part of Mr Lloyd George's scheme'. The War Council, announced *The Times*, was to be fully charged with the supreme direction of the war; and it added in its most infuriatingly patronising tone, 'of this Council Mr Asquith himself is not to be a member – the assumption being that the Prime Minister has sufficient cares of a more general character ... The testimony of his closest supporters ... must have convinced him ... that his own qualities are fitted better, as they are fond of saying, to "preserve the unity of the nation" (although we have never doubted its unity) than to force the pace of a War Council'.

The leader was written by Geoffrey Dawson, the editor, and a member of the close group centred around Carson and Milner.[22] The first part of the article was written on Saturday, which Dawson had spent with Waldorf Astor at Cliveden. The rest was written after Dawson had returned to London and had stopped on his way to Printing House Square to talk to Carson. According to *The History of The Times*, after his resignation in 1915, 'Carson was quick to see the desirability, value, and importance of a destructive leading article in *The Times*, and Dawson's visit gave him the opportunity to put the issue beyond misrepresentation'.[23] Aitken rightly concluded that it was not 'those dreadful people, Lloyd George and Northcliffe' [then owner of *The Times*] who were responsible, but the 'highly respectable' Dawson and Carson who were behind the article.[24]

Asquith was annoyed by the editorial, and took the view that, if the press were being tampered with, all negotiations must be at an end. He sent a sharp note to Lloyd George; but his letter did set out the arrangements agreed the previous day. Lloyd George replied at once. He said that he had not seen the article, and he hoped that Asquith would not attach undue importance to 'these effusions'. Lloyd George genuinely wanted to carry out what had been agreed, even though it was less than he hoped for and gave the Prime Minister final authority. His letter ended: 'I fully accept in letter and spirit your summary of the suggested arrangement – subject of course to personnel'.[25]

The announcement of a reconstruction in the Monday morning papers brought all the Prime Minister's Liberal colleagues 'buzzing like flies'. They objected to Lloyd George's scheme as vehemently as had the Unionist Ministers. They told Asquith that his office would be reduced to a shadow if he allowed himself to be manipulated. They swore by all that was solemn to stand by the Prime Minister. Then Asquith saw a delegation of Unionist Ministers.[26] They made it clear why they had recommended resignation. Lloyd George, they explained, would then be given an opportunity to form a government. He would fail; and Asquith would be returned immeasurably strengthened to reform his administration without the revolters. The Prime Minister was made aware for the first time of the apparently overwhelming strength of his battalions.

It was then that Asquith resolved to stand and fight. Bonar Law had also made up his mind at last. Unless Asquith were willing to honour the agreement he had made with Lloyd George on Sunday, Bonar Law would break with him. 'Up to this point,' he noted, 'I had been in a very difficult position – of being friends with both sides, and I was greatly worried by the fear that each side might in the end think that I had proved false to it. After reading the Prime Minister's letter, however, I came definitely to the conclusion that I had no longer any choice, and that I must back Lloyd George in his further action.'[27] The letter to which Bonar Law referred had been written by Asquith late on Monday and was received by Lloyd George the next morning, Tuesday 5 December. It completely repudiated the understanding Asquith had reached with Lloyd George and stated that the Prime Minister must chair the War Council. It ruled out Carson's membership. Lloyd George's reply, sent on Tuesday, was in the circumstances, the only possible one. 'As all delay is fatal in war, I place my office without further parley at your disposal.' 'I am fully conscious of the need for national unity,' he said, 'but unity without action is nothing but futile carnage, and I cannot be responsible for that. Vigour and vision are the supreme need at this hour.'[28]

The endgame had now been reached. Its brief course belongs more to the lives of Asquith, Lloyd George and Bonar Law than to that of Carson, because it was played out within the government. However, Carson wrote to Bonar Law on the Monday (4 December) to advise him to drop any idea of Asquith and Lloyd George becoming colleagues in a new administration.[29] His view at this point, characteristically straightforward, is of some significance.

I am convinced after our talk this evening that no patchwork is possible – It would be unreal and could not last – a system founded on mistrust and jealousy and dislike is doomed to failure and in a crisis like the present it would really be disastrous on this account to the country. The only solution I can see is for the PM to resign and for Lloyd George to form a Government – a very small one. If the House won't support it he should go to the country and we would know where we are ... If the country is sound everything will come right – if not (and I think every day under the present regime is producing pacifists) we will save further sacrifice.

On Tuesday (5 December) the three C's waited on Asquith. They told him that if Bonar Law and Lloyd George both resigned, they would not be willing to remain in the government. Asquith was shaken. He thought he had had their pledge of allegiance the previous day. Now they seemed to think that they were somehow released. If so, they deserved Ruby's summary that what they wanted was 'their little red boxes'.[30] The Tory Ministers then sent Long to summon Bonar Law to a meeting to explain himself. With every justification, Bonar Law lost his temper. He thought his colleagues were trying to oust him, and told Long bluntly that if that were so, he would appeal to the party over their heads. He would summon his own meeting later that day. Cooler judgments then prevailed and Bonar Law was acquitted of ever having misrepresented his colleagues' views to Asquith. Bonar Law wrote to the Prime Minister to tell him that, unless he were willing to stand by the agreement he had made with Lloyd George on the previous Sunday, all the Unionist Ministers would resign.[31]

That evening Asquith tendered his resignation at Buckingham Palace. It was clear that he would advise the King to send for Bonar Law. Bonar Law, however, thought that the right man was Lloyd George. But Lloyd George was not keen. He preferred to chair a small War Council with Bonar Law as Prime Minister. In the end they agreed that if Asquith would join a Bonar Law government, Bonar Law should accept the task of trying to form one. If not, Lloyd George should make the attempt.[32]

Bonar Law was duly summoned to the Palace. George V was perturbed by the prospect of Asquith's demise. The King wrote in his diary: 'I fear it will cause a panic in the City and in America and do harm to the Allies. It is a great blow to me and will I fear buck up the Germans.'[33] Nothing could have demonstrated so devastatingly how out of touch with reality the monarchy was. Bonar Law told the King that Lloyd George was the best choice, but he would not decline until he had seen Asquith. The latter refused to help his rivals by agreeing to serve under them. He may have still nourished some hope that both Bonar Law and Lloyd George would prove unable to form a government.

On the following morning, Wednesday 6 December, Bonar Law, Lloyd George, Carson and Aitken met at Bonar Law's house. They decided to consult Balfour, who had been ill in bed during the crisis. He advised that a conference be called at the Palace to see if a National Government could be formed. It was held that afternoon. Balfour, Bonar Law, Lloyd George, Asquith and Arthur Henderson, the Labour leader, were present. It was soon apparent that Asquith was not willing to serve under anyone else. After consulting his Liberal colleagues, Asquith wrote to Bonar Law to say that he and they were of the opinion that they could give more effective support from outside the government – the time-honoured way of declining to help at all.

In the evening, Bonar Law and Lloyd George went to the Palace together. Bonar Law had his audience first. He told the King that he must give up his attempt to form a government. The King then saw Lloyd George. His government, for which he was by no means unprepared, was composed without difficulty and was found to be heavily weighted in favour of Unionists. The change was decisive for the war. Under Lloyd George it was going to be fought to a finish. It also spelt the end of the old Liberal Party.

Lloyd George was the principal actor in the enterprise of bringing Asquith down. He played his part with great resource and coolness. As he had said on an earlier occasion, he always did think that he was going to bring things off – an invaluable gift in politics. The coup could not have succeeded without Bonar Law. He was the key to the life and death of Asquith's coalition. But after all allowance has been made for his loyalty and fair-mindedness, he showed a want of resolution which sorely tried his friend Aitken, and the other two triumvirs. What then was Carson's contribution? He added political strength by his control of 150 dissident Unionist back-benchers, and through his influence on powerful figures outside the House, including an important segment of the press. He was the first to realise the peril of a tide of 'respectable defeatism', and the way it was being allowed to rise as a result of Asquith's limp direction of the war. He never deviated from his conviction that the war had to be run by a small dedicated group of Ministers, and that that would never be achieved while Asquith was at the head of affairs. He was at no time willing to compromise on that. His most distinct contribution was the clarity and consistency of his judgment.

The new Prime Minister decided to have a War Cabinet of five. This eliminated the old unwieldy peacetime Cabinet, and solved at a stroke the problem which had plagued the negotiations with Asquith: the relationship between the War Council and the full Cabinet. Lloyd George's answer was to merge the two in a small Cabinet. It was an immediate success. On 9 December Ruby recorded in her diary that Edward had attended his first meeting, and told her that more was done in a few hours than used to be done in a year. It was expected that Carson would be a permanent member. Lloyd George's solution had grown out of Carson's idea of a small all-powerful committee, and he had been Lloyd George's closest ally in the campaign to reform the political direction of the war.

But there was both confusion and mystery about what job Carson was to have. Ruby understood first that her husband was to go to the Admiralty. On 7 December, however, she wrote in her diary, 'E went to see Bonar Law and now he isn't going to the Admiralty but to be on the War Council alone. I am a tiny bit disappointed and yet I am not really'. On the following day she wrote, 'Edward came back to dinner. He is going to the Admiralty after all with a seat on the War Council'. On the same day, her friend Lilian Spender wrote to her husband that Carson had been offered the Lord Chancellorship, but had refused, partly because there was not enough to do, and partly because the big pension would embarrass him in the future, 'if he wanted to cut loose over Ulster'.[34] Carson told Dawson of *The Times* about the offer. Dawson recorded the conversation between Lloyd George and Carson in a contemporary note. Of course, said the new Prime Minister, you will be Chancellor. Carson replied characteristically that nothing would induce him to be anything of the kind. 'He did not want to have any cares of any sort or kind outside the prosecution of the war, and, if he must take office at all, he would take it without portfolio.'[35]

The original members of the War Cabinet were Lloyd George, Bonar Law (Chancellor of the Exchequer and Leader of the House), Arthur Henderson, Curzon (Lord President) and Milner. Only Bonar Law had a portfolio. Curzon was perhaps fortunate in view of his wavering loyalties during the crisis, but he possessed a great deal of administrative experience. The appointment of Milner was a bold and successful stroke. He was brought in from the outside, never having been in government in Britain. But he, like Curzon, had a long history of administrative service, in his case in Egypt and South Africa. Although a friend to the generals, he could to be relied upon to take the Prime Minister's side in his struggle to take control of military affairs. It was between Milner and Carson who should have the last seat in the Cabinet. The other was to take the Admiralty.

Lloyd George himself wrote that it was his original intention to bring Carson into the Cabinet without portfolio. 'He had no administrative experience and I thought that his great talents could be better utilised in a consultative capacity than in an executive position. Conservative Ministers, however, resented his promotion to the Cabinet that directed the war, and I had reluctantly to give way.'[36] Whether or not the reason he gave – yielding to the Tories' wishes – was the whole truth, it is a pity that the Prime

Minister's first thought did not prevail. For it proved to be right. Milner was better qualified to run a service department. There is, however, another story. When Lloyd George went to the Palace with his list of proposed Ministers, still then intending to have Carson in the War Cabinet and to appoint Milner to the Admiralty, the King was firmly in favour of sending Carson to the Navy. The royal reasoning remains obscure; but Lloyd George deferred. It was odd that he gave way on a matter of such consequence, because he did not generally have a high regard for the King's judgment.[37]

The subject of these manoeuvres gave the impression of being quite indifferent to his fate in government. As Lord Beaverbrook remarked: 'The moment Asquith's fall was accomplished a kind of incuriousness seemed to descend upon him. He was like a man whose task was accomplished. He made no claim for himself. He gave up the War Council readily and took the Admiralty, which he really did not want. Nor did he make any claim for office on behalf of friends and allies in the House of Commons.'[38]

So, perhaps against his better judgment, Carson went to the Admiralty. It was a vital, possibly the most vital, of all offices at this critical juncture. Unless the stalemate on the Western Front could be broken, the outcome of the war would depend on whether Britain or Germany could first starve the other into submission. Success in the land war looked unlikely. The commanders' minds were locked in the past. The tank was in its infancy and had not yet taken the field. The future lay with mobility and armour, but that was hidden from the mind of the professional soldier. So too was the reality of trench warfare. A truce at Christmas 1914, during which the troops of both sides celebrated together and then went back to killing, demonstrated the humbug and false panache which had infected not only the military mind. Nor was the Navy immune. It suffered from a debilitating nostalgia for the Nelson Touch. When the German High Seas Fleet at last ventured out into the North Sea in May 1916, the British Grand Fleet failed to destroy it, and then allowed it to slip home. The Germans did not come out again after Jutland, but the issue of the war at sea lay elsewhere: under the surface where the U-boat went about its sinister business.

Churchill justly described the submarine war as being in scale and stake the greatest conflict ever decided at sea. 150 German U-boats prowled the Western Approaches, invisible except for a broomstick-thin periscope, each capable of destroying four or five merchant ships in a single day. Some thousands of potential victims passed this way every week. 'Of all the tasks ever set to a Navy,' Churchill wrote, 'none could have appeared more baffling than that of sheltering this enormous traffic and groping deep below the surface of the sea for the deadly elusive foe. It was in fact a game of blind man's buff in an unlimited space of three dimensions.'[39] The removal of this danger was Carson's task at the Admiralty. As in the Second World War, Britain's fate depended upon it.

Until 1917, most German U-boats observed the rules of maritime warfare. They would bring their prey to, by actual or threatened gunfire, and then, having ascertained that they were enemy ships, would close in for the kill. The merchantman, if armed, would have some opportunity to protect itself and perhaps escape. But the economic effects of the British blockade had made the German government and High Command come to doubt whether this relatively gentlemanly submarine warfare was sufficiently effective. Like the Allies, they considered it unlikely that the military stalemate in France could be broken; and they believed the war would have to won by blockade. They decided to start an unrestricted submarine campaign from 1 February 1917. The U-boats would attack without warning and sink any vessel approaching British or French waters at sight, regardless of nationality. It was a last card. The Germans realised that it would bring the United States into the war, but they hoped to knock Britain out before American power could be made to count.[40]

The campaign was appallingly successful. In January U-boats sank nearly 300,000 tons of British, Allied and neutral shipping; in February nearly five hundred thousand tons; and in April, 834,000 tons.[41] To put those figures in perspective: in December 1916 the Germans reckoned that Britain was supplied by only ten and three-quarter million tons of shipping. Three million of that tonnage represented neutral shipping, which might be expected to be frightened away by unrestricted submarine warfare. The Germans were making U-boats at the rate of at least three a week – more than were being destroyed by the Allies. Only half a million tons of new British merchant shipping had been built during the whole of 1916. Efforts made in the first half of 1917 to increase the rate of shipbuilding were dismal.[42]

No wonder that Carson and his First Sea Lord, Admiral Sir John Jellicoe, were pessimistic about combating the submarine.* C. P. Scott of the

---

* When Jellicoe met Admiral Sims of the US Navy for the first time in April 1917, just after America had entered the war, he gave Sims the details of shipping which had been lost in the last months. Sims expressed consternation. 'Yes', Jellicoe said as quietly as if he had been discussing the weather and not the future of the British Empire, 'it is impossible for us to go on with the war if losses like this continue.' Sims asked if there no solution. Absolutely none that we can see now, said Jellicoe. Quoted in Arthur Marder, *From the Dreadnought to Scapa Flow*, iv, p. 148 (Oxford, 1969). Jellicoe later maintained that he meant that there was no *immediate* solution.

Manchester Guardian, saw Carson in the middle of April, the blackest month of all, and found that he was not encouraging. 'We were not destroying them more rapidly', he reported Carson in his diary, 'and no means of countering them had been found. People had urged adoption of system of convoys. They had tried it and convoyed four Norwegian ships by destroyers. Two were sunk.'[43] The scepticism about convoys which seemed to pervade the Admiralty was the gravamen of the complaint against the Navy; for it was the convoy which eventually reduced the submarine menace to manageable proportions, and which in the Second World War was treated as the primary method of getting the merchant vessels through.

The Navy warmed to Carson. He had none of the aloofness of Balfour, his predecessor. He admired sailors, enjoyed talking to them, and loved their traditions. He toured the naval bases and made monthly visits to the Grand Fleet. He made no claim to technical knowledge that he did not possess; and he told a friend that he had no intention of becoming an amateur in naval tactics and strategy. At a lunch at the Aldwych Club on 8 March, he announced the policy he would follow. 'As long as I am at the Admiralty the sailors will have full scope. They will not be interfered with by me, and I will not let anyone interfere with them.'[44] It was, and was intended to be, a warning to the Prime Minister. Carson did not believe in the political control of naval – or military – commanders. His self-imposed restraint and lack of assertiveness, taken with his lack of administrative gifts, largely nullified his powerful assets of energy, courage, independence and intolerance of complacency.[45] The issue which would test these qualities was the protection of merchantmen, and specifically the idea of the convoy.

Sailing in organised groups of ships under armed escort was a practice which went back at least to the middle ages. In the First World War battle fleets did so as a matter of course, with destroyers acting as a defensive screen. But the Navy was reluctant to adopt the idea for merchant shipping. It was a defensive role with which the service felt uncomfortable. Patrolling the high seas and hunting down the U-boat, even though it bore resemblance to searching for a needle in a haystack, was, by contrast, an offensive activity and more congenial.

The story of how the convoy came to be adopted in spite of professional naval scepticism has provoked angry controversy. Lloyd George claims the credit in his *War Memoirs* for forcing a change in the attitude of the 'palsied and muddle-headed' Admiralty. At the other extreme, those who are concerned to exculpate Carson, claim that the Admiralty introduced the convoy of its own accord as soon as it could.[46] Neither is true.

Jellicoe was a considerable improvement as First Sea Lord over his predecessor, Admiral Sir Henry Jackson. Within days of his appointment, in

December 1916, Jellicoe set up the anti-submarine division under Rear-Admiral A. L. Duff. Much innovative work was done. Merchantmen were armed. Decoy ships and improved depth charges were developed. But the key to success was the convoy. The Navy's objections to it were not obscurantist but principled. Its reasons, apart from the probably unconscious preference for an attacking role, were that there were not enough armed escorts available; that a convoy would present an easier target for a U-boat than single vessels; that convoys would cause 'bunching' and congestion in the ports; and that the masters of the merchantmen would not be able to keep station, particularly when taking evasive action under attack. These were not arguments without substance, but on close examination or fair trial, they all proved to be either false or outweighed by the advantages of moving goods in convoy.[47]

So much for the attitude of the Admiralty. What of its First Lord? There was a meeting on 13 February 1917, attended by Lloyd George, Sir Maurice Hankey, the Cabinet Secretary, Carson, and Admirals Jellicoe and Duff. The purpose was to discuss a paper by Hankey strongly advocating convoys. Carson was more open-minded than the Admirals. He promised to take the views of a group of merchant captains, and to be guided by the results of a study of the escorted sailings to France and Scandinavia. Carson did not agree limply with the Admiralty point of view, and was always in favour of giving convoy a proper trial. But, in accord with the policy he had announced, he was not prepared to overrule expert naval opinion.[48] This is curious. For, although he was a wholehearted admirer of Jellicoe, he knew that Admiral Sir David Beatty, the Commander-in-Chief of the Grand Fleet and a man of celebrated dash, was an adherent of the system of convoys. Moreover, as an experienced advocate, Carson had many times tested expert opinion in court by cross-examination. It is strange that he did not test the Admiralty view in the same way and more rigorously.

Lloyd George decided that, in face of appalling losses in the Western Approaches, he must act. His patience finally snapped when Jellicoe submitted a paper to the Cabinet on 23 April.[49] It showed that losses of 420,000 tons of shipping had been sustained during the black fortnight between 1 and 18 April. Almost all was due to submarine, but the paper did not even mention convoy as a possible remedy. On 25 April the Prime Minister secured Cabinet approval for his making a personal visit to the Admiralty. It was an unusual step. According to the Cabinet minute,[50] the visit was to investigate all the means available to combat the submarine, but Lloyd George described its object more dramatically, as 'to take peremptory action on the question of convoy'.[51] On the following day he wrote to Carson. 'Since we met this morning I have received the enclosed [a notification that fifty-five merchant ships had been sunk in seven days]. There seems to me to be no doubt that it is vital to this country that we should settle this infernal question. Otherwise we might sink.'[52]

Lord Beaverbrook's vivid account of the Prime Minister's descent on the Admiralty on 30 April owes more to the author's sense of theatre than strict veracity. He says that Lloyd George sat in the First Lord's chair and humiliated Carson.[53] It seems unlikely, but in any event, five days before Lloyd George visited the Admiralty, Admiral Duff had convinced himself that the convoy system had to be started without delay. The immediate reasons for the change of heart were the steeply rising shipping losses, and the assurance that American escort vessels would be provided to help.[54] The United States had at last entered the war on 6 April.

There was another reason. The Admiralty used returns from the Customs giving the number of merchant vessels entering and leaving UK ports each week. The total figure was running at some five thousand vessels per week, and included every small coastal and cross-channel craft, some calling more than once in a single week at a British port. The information was published and was intended to keep up morale, particularly among neutrals. The published figures of shipping movements made the losses, which were also announced, look less serious than they in fact were.

On 24 March, Reginald McKenna, a former First Lord, showed Carson a question he was proposing to ask in the House about the weekly returns. If the Admiralty were willing to give the information, McKenna would ask that the returns should distinguish between ships of over and under 1600 tons. Carson wrote to him on 27 March[55] and said that the returns had given him and Jellicoe a good deal of trouble. 'The reason', he said, 'why total figures are given for sailings and arrivals is that, as you know, the German submarine campaign throughout February succeeded in frightening neutrals into keeping their ships in port, and we were particularly anxious not to advertise this fact more than we could help.' Moreover, Britain's allies would have preferred that no figures of losses should be published. 'The Admiralty would therefore certainly prefer that you did not put your question.' McKenna did not ask his question.

If McKenna had not quite put his finger on the point, then Admiral Lord Charles Beresford, the irascible Tory MP who had stood on the platform in Belfast City Hall with Carson when the Covenant was being signed, certainly did. On 15 April he wrote: 'My Dear Edward Carson, Will you please let me know whether your weekly list of arrivals and departures includes the coastal distributing vessels. Some of these touch at several ports on their way to their destination, and, if these are included, it may produce a false impression, as the public think that the list is made out for oversea ships.'[56]

Did the Admiralty itself know the true rate of losses? It is far from clear that Carson and his Admirals had found out how many of the five thousand sailings and arrivals were ocean-going merchantmen. If the First Lord knew that, for reasons of propaganda, the published figures inflated sailings and so diminished apparent losses, how could it be that his department did not know the true rate of loss? If they had known, they would have learned that only between 120 and 140 per week were ocean-going; and they would thus have discovered that the problem of providing adequate escort vessels was much less serious than they thought. The discovery was made early in April by a relatively junior officer. It had a dramatic effect on Admiralty policy on convoy.*

By the end of April there were rumours in the press that Carson's position at the Admiralty was not secure. There was fire beneath this smoke. Lloyd George was dissatisfied with the administration of the department. He brought into the Admiralty as controller of shipbuilding Sir Eric Geddes, a forceful Scot with a railway background and a tight administrator. Lloyd George wanted to dismiss Jellicoe. He considered that under his regime the Navy would never take the aggressive initiatives that its superior strength justified. But it was going to be difficult to get rid of Jellicoe. He enjoyed great public prestige. And Carson stood in the way. If Jellicoe were forced out, Carson would probably resign. Lloyd George feared the prospect of Carson resuming his position of back-bench critic of the government, and the bad press he and his government would get.

Then Field Marshal Sir Douglas Haig, Commander-in-Chief in France, took a hand. His opinion of Jellicoe was that he was an old woman.[57] He described Carson as 'recently married, he is very tired and leaves everything to a number of incompetent sailors'.[58] He launched an orchestrated campaign to get rid of both. Haig had friends in high places, beginning at Buckingham Palace. He visited London in June. In the space of a few days he saw Lloyd George, Curzon, Balfour, Asquith and Geddes. On 26 June he

---

*   The blandness of the official account is breathtaking. '[A] careful investigator', it reads, 'well acquainted with shipping was bound to find that the published return had no real significance as regards the essential trades. The Ministry of Shipping had produced figures showing the actual arrivals and departures in the ocean trades to be between 120 and 140 each week. This revision of figures, carried out mainly by Commander R. G. Henderson, was now in Admiral Duff's hands, and no doubt assisted in some degree towards the approaching settlement.' Henry Newbolt, *Naval Operations. (Official History of the War)*, v, p. 18.

breakfasted with the Prime Minister, Milner and Geddes.[59] In all these machinations he preached the inefficiency of the Admiralty and the urgent necessity for change – from the top downwards. He promoted Geddes's claim to the Admiralty. It seems that his audience was impressed.

In September 1917, Carson visited Haig in France and stayed two nights. Haig found him straightforward and the two got on well. The discussions showed the strength of Carson's conviction that politicians ought to keep out of military matters. He assured the Field Marshal that the War Cabinet would not interfere with him, and told him that he was opposed to all meddling by the Prime Minister and other politicians. They discussed Lloyd George's shortcomings, one of which was that he had no knowledge whatever of military operations.[60] This disloyalty reflected badly on Carson. He did not know that he was talking to the man who three months earlier had done so much to drive him from the Admiralty.

It was Milner who supplied the solution to Lloyd George's dilemma. This was to make Geddes First Lord and kick Carson upstairs to the War Cabinet. In that way there would be no danger of political strife with Carson. Bonar Law and Curzon agreed. The King was informed and had no objection. He too probably heard Haig's trumpet call. On 6 July Lloyd George wrote to Carson.[61] He told him that he had wanted him in the War Cabinet from the start; but his plans had been thwarted 'for reasons you know'. 'We need your insight, courage and judgment ... I tried to see you today to get your views about your successor at the Admiralty.' He sent the letter by messenger down to Birchington, where the Carsons were staying. They were asleep, and having been woken, they had to find a bed for the messenger. The Prime Minister was now in a hurry, but Carson was distrustful of him. He replied the following day.[62] Of course, he said, he was ready to fall in with Lloyd George's views that a change should be made at the Admiralty if he considered it in the public interest. As to the War Cabinet, he would prefer not to give an answer that day: he was suffering from neuralgia. Lloyd George faltered in face of this evidently cool response. He wrote back the same day that he feared Carson had misunderstood. If Carson wanted to stay at the Admiralty, his suggestion fell to the ground. The changes he wanted at the Admiralty Board could be effected under Carson's leadership.[63]

It was an extraordinary retreat, but Milner stiffened him up and advised him on 16 July that the 'Carson-Geddes business' must be settled right away. The changes were announced in the press the next day. Carson was to go to the War Cabinet, Geddes to the Admiralty and Churchill to Munitions. Carson knew of course that he had been sacked and was sick about it.[64] He had been First Lord for only seven months.

It was not until the turn of the year that Jellicoe was dismissed. 'A great row on at the Admiralty', Ruby wrote in her diary, 'Sir Eric Geddes has dismissed Jellicoe as one might a dishonest butler.'[65] Carson wrote to Lloyd George to complain about it, and about the way his own name had been brought into the matter. He asked for a private interview with the Prime Minister. There was an unseemly dispute between Carson and Geddes about whether the latter had consulted Carson before deciding to dismiss Jellicoe. The argument niggled on into the Spring of 1918. But, as Lord Beaverbrook remarked, Carson's objection to the removal of Jellicoe was really a notice of intention to resign from the War Cabinet.[66] He was not happy and was justified in thinking that he had been marginalised. He left the government in January, giving as his reason the incompatibility of his leading the Ulster Party and remaining in the Cabinet.

Carson's tenure of the Admiralty, although short, took place at the war's most anxious juncture. Churchill wrote to him in 1927, 'you actually had to live through the worst period during which the great remedial decisions were taken'.[67] But there can be little doubt that Carson's attitude to his experts was too uncritical and too deferential for the good of the country. While Lloyd George was absorbing information from any source he could, including junior naval officers, and convincing himself that the convoy must be adopted, Carson was listening to his Admirals and becoming 'house-trained' by them, as one commentator put it.[68] When the task of defeating Asquith was over and he had executive authority at last, Beaverbrook wrote, a change came over Carson. 'He became at once the orthodox Minister, trusted by his permanent officials and ready to defend their errors loyally. In counsel he showed indecisiveness or even weakness. He seemed to throw away in power every single quality which had given him his authority in opposition and placed him in the Government.'[69] There was truth in this. It was indeed strange that as a rebel he was visionary, resolute, positive, tactically adroit; as a Cabinet Minister, rather run of the mill. The adoption of convoy, the critical issue which faced Carson while he was at the Admiralty, owed nothing to his personal efforts, and showed him up for the poor administrator that he was. He declined to press his own view, which was that convoy should at least be given a fair trial. The change of policy came from a change of heart in the Admiralty, which itself was stimulated by the entry of the United States into the war, and by the merciless promptings of Lloyd George.

17

Final Attempt

The Irish quarrel lay like a poisonous fog across the years of war. Now, as the submarine threatened to strangle Britain's sea lifeline in the first months of 1917, it rose again, insistently demanding attention. Frances Stevenson, Lloyd George's long-time personal secretary and mistress, and ultimately his wife, recorded a conversation the Prime Minister had with Carson in late April. At every stage, Lloyd George said, the Irish question was a stumbling-block. 'It ought to have been settled last year. I feel that I was a coward not to insist upon a settlement then.' Now he was being pushed by America and Australia to give Ireland self-government. He had so far refrained from pressing the question, knowing Carson's difficulties; but, he said, he could leave it in abeyance no longer. 'If we do not settle it now, this government will not be able to continue.'[1]

The Americans were a special difficulty. There was a strong lobby in the United States in favour of Home Rule, and Irish Catholics there were providing funds and fomenting rebellion. President Woodrow Wilson had stood out from the war in the hope of brokering peace, but the unrestricted submarine campaign had brought him down at last against Germany in April 1917. He told Walter Page, his Ambassador to Britain, that only one thing was still in the way of perfect cooperation: Britain's failure to give self-government to Ireland. Wilson was a Presbyterian, but he was not in sympathy with his co-religionists in Ulster. He had many of the qualities of a missionary, and dreamed of a new era in history with himself in the role of the giver of peace and good government. He wanted to remake Europe in the American image. The Ambassador was his willing instrument. Page wrote to a colleague in the State Department on 3 May that 'the United States can play a part bigger than we have yet dreamed of if we prove big enough to lead the British and the French instead of listening to Irish and Germans'. Page considered that neither England nor France was a democracy. 'We can make them both democracies and develop their whole people instead of about 10 per cent of their people.'[2] It was part of this discomforting evangelism that Britain, which claimed to support the right of small countries to self-determination, should be brought to practise what it preached and give Ireland its own government.

In Ireland itself there were urgent reasons to try again. Redmond was a drowning man, trying to keep his party afloat in the rapidly rising tide of Sinn Fein. Dublin Castle had again lost its grip on law and order. Although the difficulties were great, Edward Carson was willing to negotiate once more. He was horrified by the prospect of renewed conflict in the North as soon as the war ended and the Home Rule Bill automatically became law. He told C. P. Scott of the *Manchester Guardian* that his object was to bring North and South together; but there were strict limits to his powers. The moment he went beyond them his people in Ulster would throw him over and choose another leader.[3]

On 7 March 1917, T. P. O'Connor moved an amendment to the Address that Ireland be given the self-governing institutions which had for so long been promised. Major William Redmond, the Irish leader's brother, returned from France to make one of the most moving appeals ever heard in the House. He prayed for a new start and called on Carson to shake hands with his fellow countrymen. 'In the name of God,' he said, 'we here who are about to die, perhaps ask you to do that which largely induced us to leave our homes.'[4] He was killed that June on the Messines Ridge. When Lloyd George spoke,[5] he acknowledged that the Irish grievance was not a material one, but one which came from pride and self-respect. But, he said, it would be as glaring an outrage to put Ulstermen under a Dublin government as to deny the rest of Ireland their own institutions. It was a clear indication of partition, and it bitterly disappointed Redmond. From his point of view it would be futile to continue the debate.[6] He led his party out of the Chamber. Neither he nor the party would have any further effective role to play.

Immediately after the debate, Carson set about preparing a scheme with the long-range objective, as he had told C. P. Scott, of bringing North and South together. It would, he hoped, tempt Ulster into a devolved Irish government by demonstrating that there was nothing to fear. A heavily amended nine-page draft of the scheme is among his papers.[7] Ulster would be left out of Home Rule, but the central feature of the plan was an All-Ireland Council composed of representatives of the Irish Home Rule Parliament and the Ulster Members in the Westminster Parliament. The Council would consider legislative proposals for the whole of Ireland, and frame a procedure by which, if agreement were reached between the two delegations, the proposals could be enacted simultaneously in Dublin and in the excluded counties. It was the forerunner of the 'Irish Dimension' of more recent times.

Carson did not know whether this idea would be acceptable to Ulster, but he was prepared to press it on his own supporters. Nothing could be worse, he wrote, than starting off Ireland with a Parliament in which everyone took sides according to his religious views – which would certainly happen if the Home Rule Act as it stood were put into force. He hoped that under his plan Ireland might still be unified within the Empire. But surely Carson could not have believed that any such idea, involving as it did the exclusion of Ulster, could possibly be acceptable to the Nationalists. It was in any case too late. He reckoned without the now dominant power of Sinn Fein, whose members were not interested in anything except the severance of the English connection and an independent Irish republic. For his own survival, Redmond had to reject any settlement which involved the division of Ireland, even for a temporary period.

Lloyd George obtained Cabinet approval to Carson's scheme. He prepared a letter to write to Redmond about it.[8] The letter contained, almost as an afterthought, the alternative of an Irish Convention, in which all shades of political opinion in Ireland would come together to try to agree among themselves a scheme for the government of Ireland. If there were substantial agreement, the Westminster government would legislate. The origins of this idea are not clear. Jan Christian Smuts, the former Boer general and South African member of the Imperial War Cabinet from 1917, may have suggested it.[9] He had had successful experience of it in South Africa. Or it may have been first suggested casually by Redmond.[10] Whatever its provenance, the idea of a Convention had some appeal to the Prime Minister. It should satisfy the annoying Americans, and it would buy time. Redmond naturally accepted the alternative. No more was heard of Carson's initiative.

The Prime Minister announced the setting up of the Convention to the House on 21 May 1917.[11] Its purpose, he said, was to submit to the British government a constitution for the future government of Ireland within the Empire. It would consist of representatives not only of the Irish political parties, but also of local government, trade unions, churches and commercial and educational bodies. Its deliberations would take place behind closed doors, Lloyd George remarking *en passant* that the American States had framed their constitution in secret. Unfortunately the parallel ended there.

The Convention met for the first time at Trinity College, Dublin on 25 July 1917. Its chairman was Sir Horace Plunkett, a well-meaning but ineffective figure, more apt in devising schemes of agrarian reform than in politics. The Ulster Unionists reluctantly sent a delegation, headed by H. T. Barrie, the Member for North Derry, but there were only nineteen out of ninety-five delegates who could be reckoned as sympathisers with the Ulster point of view.[12] Sinn Fein boycotted the whole of the proceedings, riding a swell of

Irish opinion against the Convention. On 10 July a by-election in East Clare caused by the death of William Redmond had been won by Eamon De Valera, lately released from prison. There was another contest at Kilkenny shortly afterwards, when William Cosgrave, another hero of the Easter Rebellion, was returned in triumph. These were unmistakable pointers. The Convention continued its discussions until the spring of 1918, when it finally admitted failure. It therefore realised at least one of the hopes the Prime Minister had for it, that of passing time.

It was doomed before ever it sat. Apart from the Sinn Fein boycott, the Ulster Unionists refused to budge from the exclusion of the six counties. The Convention took up its time discussing proposals for a separate constitution for the whole of Ireland, including Ulster. No such proposal had any hope of being adopted so long as the government upheld its pledge that Ulster was not to be coerced. Edward Carson played no part in the discussions. As a member of the Cabinet he could not lead the Ulster delegation and could only offer guidance behind the scenes. Nonetheless the Convention gave him much anxiety. He said later that it gave him more trouble than almost anything he ever had to do with in relation to Home Rule. 'In point of fact,' he said, 'it eventually drove me out of the Cabinet in the middle of the war. And why? Never was Ulster in a more dangerous position when the Convention was drawing to a close ...'[13]

Carson resigned on 22 January 1918, telling Lloyd George that his position in the Cabinet was now untenable.[14] He could no longer accept responsibility as a member of the Cabinet for a decision which might endanger Ulster's position. The imminent danger was Redmond's attempt to join hands with Lord Midleton's Southern Unionists and so isolate Ulster. This was done with the Prime Minister's encouragement. On 31 December 1917 Curzon had given a pledge to Redmond that if a scheme put forward by the Southern Unionists, for Home Rule for the whole of Ireland with Customs reserved to the Imperial Parliament, were carried by the Convention with 'substantial agreement – i.e. with the opposition of Ulster alone', the Prime Minister would use his personal influence to accept it and to bring it into law. The pledge was initialled by Lloyd George. This was in flat contradiction to the assurance which Bonar Law had given to Ronald McNeill in the Commons on 24 May that there could be no such 'substantial agreement' without the concurrence of Ulster.[15]

It was for this good and sufficient reason that Carson feared that Ulster might be coerced after all, in defiance of repeated assurances by Asquith, Lloyd George and Bonar Law that this was unthinkable. And for this reason he felt compelled to regain his freedom of action. He had only contempt for Midleton and his followers. 'The Southern Unionists lost their courage', he said later. 'They gave their case away. I do not believe they represented anybody but themselves. They said we were traitors, whereas as a matter of fact it was they, under the leadership of Lord Midleton, who were prepared to say: "If we go down, Ulster must come down too."' [16]

As it happened, Midleton's alliance with Redmond came to nothing. The Roman Catholic Bishop of Raphoe blew it apart. He and others of the hierarchy did not want Home Rule. It did not go far enough. The Bishop refused to endorse the proposal to leave control of the Customs with Westminster. So the Convention collapsed. Redmond had put his all into it, but he was a sick man. He died on 6 March 1918.

John Redmond had been Edward Carson's adversary throughout the Ulster crisis. He had always been true to his objective of Home Rule within the Empire. He was as loyal to Britain's cause in the war as the Australians, New Zealanders and Canadians, all of whom sympathised with his aims. He had lost a brother on the Western Front. His son, a captain in the Irish Guards, had been wounded and awarded the DSO. In the end he was defeated by Asquith's want of resolution, Carson's obduracy and the polarising effect of the war on Irish sentiment. He is indeed a tragic figure. Almost alone among Carson's contemporaries, he never felt the lash of that wounding tongue upon his character. When tributes were paid in the House, Carson recalled that he had first known Redmond on his own circuit at the Irish Bar. 'I cannot recall to mind', he said, 'one single bitter personal word that ever passed between John Redmond and myself.' [17]

During the spring, the Germans launched successful offensives which threatened the whole outcome of the war. Manpower was urgently needed to staunch the flow. In its desperation the government proposed to link compulsory military service in Ireland with immediate Home Rule. Carson was shocked and wrote to Bonar Law on 8 April. [18] The idea, he said, would simply result in the Nationalists raising their demands. In any case it would be impossible to enforce conscription in Ireland. He enclosed a letter from Henry Shannon, the senior Resident Magistrate, saying that the attempt to do so could plunge the south and west into conditions 'hardly distinguishable from civil war'.

The government might think, Carson wrote, that the Irish would fight for a free country but not for a subject nation; but, if so, it could not have been more wrong. Sinn Fein had no intention of joining the war against Germany, and were in contact with the authorities in that country with a view to the exact opposite. On 16 April Carson made a bitter attack in the House on the whole futile notion. [19]

A rift between Carson and Bonar Law now opened. Ruby noted in her diary for 26 April 1918, 'Bonar Law and Co. are behaving too badly over Ulster, they have quite gone for Home Rule and are altogether beneath contempt'. On the following day, her husband wrote an angry letter to Bonar Law.[20] Sinn Fein were cooperating with Germany, he said; the Catholic prelates were claiming to tell the people when they could ignore the Imperial Parliament; the very slightest provocation would precipitate religious war in the North. It was obvious it would be impossible to enforce conscription in Ireland after Home Rule had been set up. 'Can you imprison ... a Government which you have just set up ... Surely you and the Unionist Party are not under these circumstances going to be party to a Bill imposing Home Rule in Ulster.' He threatened to publish the letter. Bonar Law replied that if Carson published, it must be the beginning of conflict between them. Carson did not publish and the storm blew over.

Early in May, General Smuts analysed the problem of Ireland and the war in a letter to Lloyd George.[21] His views, which were always listened to with respect, agreed with Carson's and he poured a douche of cold water on the idea of Irish conscription coupled with Home Rule. 'At a time of supreme crisis in our military fortunes', he wrote, 'I do not think the government are justified in throwing this apple of discord in front of the people and undermining their confidence in the judgment and wisdom of their rulers.' Smuts considered that it would be both indecent and impossible to pass Home Rule against the wishes of Ulster when the Ulster Volunteers were at the front fighting the enemy. A Home Rule Bill now would fail and bring down the government with it. He reminded Lloyd George that the existence of the Empire was at stake. 'Home Rule in such a crisis leaves me stone cold, and I daresay all prudent citizens of this Empire, whatever their origin or party.' He advised the government to withdraw the Bill and not to try to enforce conscription in Ireland – which would in any case be futile. Let the Americans produce the men and make good the failure of the Irish.

The government did precisely as Smuts – and Carson – advised. Treasonable connections between Sinn Fein and Germany were uncovered which put Home Rule out of the question while the war lasted. And the government blenched when the Roman Catholic hierarchy sanctified defiance by advising their flock, under penalty of eternal damnation, to resist conscription. 'I am inclined to think that the action which the government have taken is probably right,' Carson remarked acidly, 'because in the midst of a war such as we are waging, it is not worth bothering about Ireland, if you have to go through all this indignity and all this humiliation.'[22]

Retirement from Government had its consolations. After leaving the Admiralty he had felt side-lined, being assigned to a job in propaganda. A jaundice was spreading across his view of his colleagues which would turn into bitterness. The strain of maintaining the struggle and keeping his followers loyal to his leadership was telling. He turned to the companionship of his wife and the Bar. They spent more time at their bungalow at Birchington. Their pleasures were simple ones. He took walks with his old barrister friend, Charles Gill, who had a bungalow nearby. Ruby worked in the garden and kept chicken and ducks to eke out the wartime rations. One day they went into Margate by bus to try to find matches and jam. They went on the pier and watched the fishermen. It was at this time that Ruby Carson first thought she might be pregnant. Her doctor confirmed it, but she lost the child. 'I have got to see him again so I hope for better luck next time.' [23]

The diary shows a growing distrust of the Prime Minister. As early as May 1917, she noted that 'Edward finds Lloyd George rather trying, I think. He is always off at a tangent.' By the following February, he was 'that coward'. On 24 February, a bare month after Carson had left the Cabinet, a portentous delegation arrived for tea at the Beach Hotel, Littlehampton, where the Carsons were staying. It consisted of the Prime Minister, Lord Milner, Sir Henry Wilson and Colonel Hankey, the Cabinet Secretary. 'The PM said he wanted Edward back as soon as possible. I said, "Then you must give Ulster all she wants." He is a little thief really.' Her husband greatly enjoyed these sallies.

The diary also recorded visits to Belfast. In February 1918, Ruby accompanied her husband and saw the adulation for herself. The working men carried him out of the railway station on their shoulders and made him make a speech. She was much moved. 'It's so splendid the way the people here do things, they carry them through and do them with all their minds. I am more and more Ulster every time I come over.' [24] When she returned to London, Mrs Spender wrote to her husband that she thought Ruby was rather pale after her strenuous week. She had been crushed by enthusiastic crowds, slapped on the back and showered with presents 'Once Ruby had to wait outside the Reform Club for Sir Edward, and the crowd took it in turns to jump on the step of the car and take a look ... Said one woman on the step, gazing fixedly at Ruby, "She looks very young." Another pushed her away, thrust her own face through the window and had a good look for herself, then remarked, "She's none so young!" ' [25]

It was an exhilarating experience for them both to know that the loyalty of the Ulster Protestants was as strong as ever. In October 1918, the last month of the war, H. A. L. Fisher, the distinguished historian and President of the Board of Education, went to Ireland for a week's visit, and reported

to the Prime Minister.[26] He thought that a general election at that moment
would result in a sweeping Sinn Fein victory. 'Sinn Fein' was a name
covering a number of groups having nothing much in common but a
hatred of England and a general desire to secure liberty for Ireland. Few
Irish schoolchildren knew who the King of England was, and apart from
Lloyd George himself, the only other British statesman they could name
was Sir Edward Carson.

The war neither changed nor resolved the Irish question. When it was over
the landscape was found to be unaltered. Winston Churchill described it in
a famous passage.

> Then came the Great War. Every institution, almost, in the world, was strained.
> Great Empires have been overturned. The whole map of Europe has been
> changed. The position of countries has been violently altered. The modes of
> thought of men, the whole outlook on affairs, the grouping of parties, all have
> encountered violent and tremendous changes in the deluge of the world, but as
> the deluge subsides and the waters fall we see the dreary steeples of Fermanagh
> and Tyrone emerging once again. The integrity of their quarrel is one of the few
> institutions that have been unaltered in the cataclysm which has swept the
> world.[27]

This same quarrel had forced Carson from the War Cabinet in January
1918, and from that time his power to move events began to wane. Mrs
Spender asked her husband at the time of the resignation whether he would
not write to his old leader. 'He is very unhappy, I think,' she wrote, 'and
will probably go away with her for a fortnight to make a break, as it will
feel so strange and horrible being out of everything. It has revived all my
old feelings of passionate loyalty to him.'[28] The real source of his unhap-
piness lay in the inconstancy of his former colleagues. He wrote to his
long-time confidante Lady Londonderry in May: 'somehow I feel I am
growing stupid and cannot follow the evolution of intrigue and insincerity
which is all round in the atmosphere'.[29] There was talk of his leading a
new party, but he lacked the ambition and, so Mrs Spender thought, the
self-confidence to do it.[30] She noted too that Lloyd George had turned
against him and wanted to isolate him: he was not answering his letters
about Ireland.[31]

In this time of disappointed hopes, he turned for solace to his wife. 'It
is lovely having Edward to myself the whole day long and it so seldom
happens', she wrote in her diary while they were on holiday in Littlehampton.[32] Ruby liked to have breakfast in bed and occasionally could
inveigle her husband into joining her. 'Edward and I had breakfast in

bed and were most comfortable. It is very nice being alone!'[33] She continued to make cutting – but sometimes naïve – observations about those who were less than faithful to her husband. Sir Henry Wilson, who was about to succeed Sir William Robertson as Chief of the Imperial Staff, 'is only an intriguer and all out for himself.' Lord Beaverbrook, who had just been made Minister of Propaganda, was 'distrusted and disliked by all decent Canadians, but he is a friend of Bonar Law's and has him so completely under his thumb that I expect he had to get it [the ministerial post] for him'.[34]

In July 1918 the tide began to turn in France, and victory soon became inevitable. Ruby described the coming of the end. She was strongly against negotiating with 'the Hun'. On 5 October she recorded that they had asked for an armistice, 'which of course is the last thing anyone would think of giving them. Now is the time to hammer them.' On 9 November she wrote that there was revolution in Germany, the Kaiser had abdicated and fled, there was a naval mutiny and fighting was going on in the streets. 'What an end.' On 10 November, the eve of the armistice, 'Everyone is just waiting quietly no excitement but everyone has a sort of holiday look'. On Armistice Day itself she was out and about all day: at Buckingham Palace at eleven to see the King and Queen on the balcony. 'There was an enormous crowd and we sang and cheered and cried with joy.' At lunchtime her husband made a speech at the Cannon Street Hotel. Then she went to the House to hear Lloyd George's statement, then to St Margaret's, Westminster, both Houses in procession. 'Early dinner with Mrs Spender (Edward dined out) and by tube to Piccadilly Circus. Great crowds bright street lamps and all cheering singing and laughing.' She was 'home by eleven and the end of the greatest day we shall ever see. Peace and the Huns beaten.'

Parliament was prorogued on 21 November and preparations were put in hand for a general election. Lloyd George and Bonar Law agreed that the coalition would stay together. They issued a joint statement about Ireland. They would explore all practical paths towards a settlement on the basis of self-government, but two paths were to be closed: the severance of Ireland from the Empire; and the forcible submission of the six Ulster counties to a Home Rule Parliament. Would these new promises prove more durable than their many predecessors?

Carson now decided to give up his long-held seat for Trinity College, Dublin and contest the constituency of Duncairn near Belfast. He had differed from the Provost of Trinity, Dr J. P. Mahaffy, over the Irish Convention, and in any case his political centre of gravity had moved north. In view of the new pledges given on Ireland, he could support the coalition.

When the results were known just after Christmas, he had unsurprisingly won a large majority in his new constituency. The Asquith Liberals were destroyed and Ruby was jubilant. 'When it came to the news that Asquith was out we nearly died of excitement. The *Evening Telegraph* kept on telephoning as the returns came in, McKenna out, Simon out, Runciman out, in fact all the old Gang nearly.'[35]

The coalition won an overwhelming majority of 550 seats. But in Ireland there was a different picture. Carson led a party of twenty-six Unionists, all but three in the north. In the south and west Redmond's old party was decimated. The victory belonged to Sinn Fein which won 102 seats; but they refused to recognise the Westminster Parliament and set up their own Dáil at the Mansion House in Dublin.* Carson received a summons to attend this revolutionary assembly.[36] It was said that there was laughter in the Dáil when his name was read out at roll call and answered by silence. The parliamentary map was as plain as the battleground and drawn along the same line. Revolutionaries would contend for Ireland against a small garrison in the north east, which would survive only if it had Britain's support.

Carson was offered a seat in the Cabinet but declined. He had his reasons. He told Lord Reading, his old adversary, that he longed for a whiff of the courts.[37] What was the use, he wrote to Lady Londonderry, of going into government when Ireland was still unsettled and he might have to resign again at any time? He added that he supposed the time must shortly come when he would be asking that a younger man should be the Ulster leader.[38] She had noted in her diary a few days earlier: 'Sir Edward Carson has not been made Lord Chancellor. It shows that if one ever has political principles, as he had about Ulster, he is robbed of his right. FE is brilliant, and self-made ... so he really deserves success, though he has no character.'[39] She had been ill for some time and died shortly afterwards. For all her battle-axe personality she had a shrewd political eye and a lasting warmth for her friends. She was Edward Carson's best friend over more than thirty years, from the days of Dublin Castle until her death. Although he must have irritated her with his continual harping on his suffering, she never ceased to admire his abilities and regret that he had not gained an even higher place.

So Carson went back to the Bar after the 1918 election, as he had after his resignation from the Cabinet in 1915. Again there was no shortage of

---

* The word Dáil originally meant a meeting or tryst, sometimes amatory, sometimes hostile. Only later did it come to mean an assembly or peace conference.

work for him. In their echoing cathedral of a home in the Strand, the courts had the smell of an old, well-loved place. He was reassured to find that he was still trusted and admired by the solicitors on whom he depended for his briefs, and by his contemporaries at the Bar. It was a welcome change from politics. But by refusing to join the government, Carson had in effect handed over the leadership of the Ulster Unionists to James Craig, who continued as Parliamentary and Financial Secretary to the Admiralty in the coalition Government. Craig made good use of his opportunity.

The Treaty of Versailles was signed in June 1919. With it the question of Home Rule rose yet again. Asquith's Act was still in place, waiting to take effect and hanging over the heads of the Ulster Unionists like a sword. In October the Government set up a committee, chaired by Walter Long, to wrestle once more with the government of Ireland.

To reach agreement with the Irish rebels, Lloyd George would have to make them believe that Ireland could be united, with its own Parliament, even if not at once; and at the same time he would have to uphold the pledges given to Ulster. It would call for all his wizardry to reconcile these apparent irreconcileables. It was plain that the scheme would have to involve at least a temporary partition. The Long committee had first to decide whether all nine counties of Ulster, or six only, should be separated from the south.

Craig told the Cabinet that the Ulster leaders were doubtful whether the northern Parliament would be able effectively to govern the Catholic and Nationalist counties of Cavan, Donegal and Monaghan; and would much prefer that the scheme was limited to the six remaining counties. He went so far as to suggest the setting up of a boundary commission to make minor adjustments to the border in order to achieve a more homogeneously Protestant North and Catholic South.[40]

Craig's aims were frankly sectarian – to establish a province governed by Protestants for Protestants. His brother, Charles Craig, made this disarmingly clear in the House in March 1920, when he said no sane man would try to carry on a Parliament with a Protestant majority reduced to a negligible level by Sinn Feiners and Nationalists.[41] Carson now agreed with the Craigs. If he had earlier thought differently, his mind had been changed by the violence and disorder which was everywhere gaining the upper hand. Early in 1920 he attacked the idea of proportional representation (PR) in Northern Ireland, which was bound to be less favourable to the Unionists than the traditional 'first past the post' system. He told Bonar Law that, as he had anticipated, PR 'has increased the difficulties'. 'We opposed it and were never even allowed our views and why it ever was introduced I don't know.' At this time, he was, with Craig, evincing

little or no interest in playing fair with the large Catholic minority within
Northern Ireland.*

Lloyd George unveiled his plan to the House on 22 December 1919. It was
complex and ingenious. Ireland was to be partitioned into the six counties
of the north east and the twenty-six counties of the south and west. There
were to be not one but two Home Rule Parliaments, one in Dublin and one
in Belfast. Both parts of Ireland were to have reduced representation in
Westminster. There was to be a council at which both Irelands would meet,
along the lines devised by Carson in 1917.

On 10 March 1920 the Ulster Unionist Council met to consider the
scheme. Again the question arose of whether partition should be of six or
nine counties in Ulster. In 1916 the Council had accepted a six-county split
in order to help reach a settlement and so advance the war effort. But the
war was over and things were different now. Craig argued, as he had to the
Cabinet, for a division along the sectarian line of the six counties. Carson
agreed. There would, they said, be no security for the Protestants of the
north east if the Nationalist counties were included: the Unionist majority in
a nine-county Parliament would be paper thin. In February, Carson had had
a letter from Fred Crawford, the gun-runner. 'If the nine counties are taken
as they are,' Crawford wrote, 'in ten years time Ulster will declare for being
joined to the rest of Ireland, then God help the Protestants.'[42] After a bitter
debate, the Council decided neither to support nor oppose Lloyd George's
plan. The delegates knew that this meant tacit acceptance. The representatives of the disappointed counties resigned, and the bitterness lingered on.
Carson, as the nominal leader, bore the brunt of the resentment.

The fourth Home Rule Bill was, like its predecessors, called the Govern-
ment of Ireland Bill. It embodied Lloyd George's scheme and passed easily.
Northern Ireland came into being. The results were indeed ironic. The
Dublin Parliament, so long awaited and fought for, never met. Only the

---

* Proportional representation was introduced into Ireland by Lloyd George's Government of Ireland Act of 1920, with the object of more fairly representing
  minority views in the electoral process. Under the PR system, each voter balloted
  for several candidates in order of preference, and candidates were then elected
  under the complicated arrangement known as 'the single transferable vote'. The
  Act also placed electoral law outside the jurisdiction of the Home Rule Parliaments in Dublin and Belfast for three years. PR was abolished in Northern
  Ireland in 1929. The abolition restored the traditional system of deciding elections by a simple majority: 'first past the post'. Bonar Law Papers, 98/6/4, 26
  January 1920.

members for Trinity College turned up for the opening ceremony. The rest were at the Dáil. The six counties were the only part of the island which had not sought Home Rule, but they got it and made it work. The Union was finally ended.

But Lloyd George's Act did not settle the Irish question. It was too late. A rising tide of violence ensured that the scheme would prove irrelevant in the south and west. During the second half of 1919 a campaign of guerilla warfare and murder developed progressively. The insurgents were organised into military units, but after they had done their killing they melted away into the background. Although there were often many witnesses, no one could be found to give evidence. The Sinn Fein leadership neither condemned nor encouraged the outrages. The perpetrators were members of the Irish Republican Army, whose links with Sinn Fein were elusive and shifting. The government responded by proclaiming the suppression of Sinn Fein. The Dáil was raided in December and its leaders were arrested. The military and police were reinforced and began to wreak vengeance by officially sanctioned reprisals which were as brutal as the crimes they were avenging. A special police force was formed from ex-servicemen. They were the 'Black and Tans', so called for their black caps and khaki uniform; and the equally brutal Auxiliaries ('Auxies').

By the summer of 1920 the British authorities had to decide. Either they could apply more repression and, as the military chiefs advised, declare universal martial law throughout the south and west; or they could try to give the Irish what they wanted. They decided on the latter. It took until the end of the following year to achieve agreement.

On 17 February 1920, Ruby gave birth to a son, named Edward after his father and grandfather. Ruby was 35 and her husband 66. The happiness of her home was crowned with the longed for child. On the following day Carson entered the House to a storm of cheering from both sides. He took his place with a flushed face of pleasure. Later that year, the Carsons bought Cleve Court, a small neglected Queen Anne house near Minster in the Isle of Thanet. They spent as much time as they could there. It became the house where Carson was happiest, a refuge of peace from the storm of Ireland. Here he could be in the midst of his two families. His new son, Ned; and Walter's daughters, his only grandchildren, who were at Cleve Court regularly, as were the grandchildren of Bella, Carson's sister with whom he remained on close and affectionate terms all his life.

Meanwhile, the war between Britain and Ireland, for such it was, in spite of the familiar protestations to the contrary by the British Government, spread to the north. The IRA started a coordinated campaign. In the summer of 1920 a wave of sectarian violence swept across the six counties.

Thousands of Catholic workmen were driven from the shipyards in Belfast. Only days earlier, in this highly inflammatory atmosphere, Carson had made a provocative speech on the occasion of the Twelfth of July celebrations to commemorate William III's victory at the Battle of the Boyne. He said:

> These men who come forward as the friends of Labour care no more about Labour than the man in the moon. Their real object and the real insidious nature of their propaganda is that they may mislead and bring about disunity amongst our own people; and in the end, before we know where we are, we may find ourselves in the same bondage and slavery as is the rest of Ireland in the South and West.[43]

Carson's outlook now appeared as openly sectarian as Craig's, and, as leader, he was the one to give it public utterance. The radical press singled him out for attack. According to the *Daily Herald* for 31 August 1920:

> The bloody harvest of Carsonism is being reaped in Belfast. Race hatred, religious hatred, militarism, rebellion have been preached there year after year, and now we see the result ... The gangs who have organised the reign of terror are the very people who protest they are afraid that *they* would, under even partial Home Rule, be persecuted and denied religious liberty!

A year before, Carson had threatened that if any attempt were made to take away 'one jot or tittle' of the Ulstermen's rights as British citizens, he would call out the Ulster Volunteers.[44] The idea of resurrecting a paramilitary force, representing only one side of the religious divide, was irresponsible in the extreme. But Craig seized it. In September 1920, he put forward for the Cabinet's approval a whole series of proposals which would entrench Protestant authority in the six counties. They included the raising of a force of special constables to assist the government in maintaining law and order; and a reserve force raised from 'the loyal population' for cases of emergency. The UVF was to be used to form the reserve, and it was to be armed. A conference of Ministers promptly approved the raising of these forces.[45] The reserve became the much resented 'B' Specials. Within two years, Lloyd George was to describe 'Craig's Specials' as no different from Mussolini's Blackshirts.[46]

In the Spring of 1921 Carson was appointed a Lord of Appeal, and became Lord Carson of Duncairn with a seat in the House of Lords. Lord Beaverbrook described the Upper Chamber unkindly as 'the mausoleum of weary titans' 'There', he wrote, Carson 'carried on sham battles with his former friend Lord Birkenhead over "Home Rule for Ireland". Plenty of fireworks. That was all. Nothing happened.'[47] Carson, however, received his peerage not to debate but to become a judge of the highest court in the land. It is extremely rare for a member of the Bar to be appointed directly to the top layer of appeal. Had it not been for his service as a member of the War Cabinet, it is unlikely that he would have been rewarded with the appointment. For, in spite of his reputation at the Bar, he was far from being an obvious choice. His mind was not of a speculative cast and he was not a jurist. That important side of the work of an appellate tribunal did not attract him. Advocacy was his *métier*. Lord Atkin, himself a great judge and a colleague of Carson's in the Lords, described him as the 'greatest advocate of the lot'.[48] He should have been Lord Chief Justice, thought Lord Blanesburgh, another colleague. Here, in presiding over jury trials and setting the tone of the administration of criminal justice, he might have attained the supremacy which had unquestionably been his at the Bar. 'But unfortunately for us all', Blanesburgh wrote, 'that office never came his way, and the judicial office which did was not really according to his humour.'[49]

Besides, he was not content in the Lords. 'Carson is animated by a desire to get back into the limelight' and 'has not found Lord of Appeal a very exciting job', Lloyd George told Frances Stevenson. The House of Lords, he reported Carson as remarking, is a place 'into which the rays of the sun never penetrate'.[50] Carson confirmed as much in a letter to James Craig in May 1921. 'Of course I feel lonely and depressed at being out of it all ... It is depressing to leave the fight and bear the stern calm of judicial office.'[51]

He had told Lady Londonderry in 1919 that it would soon be right for him to give up his Ulster leadership to a younger man. On 4 February 1921 he announced his retirement to the Ulster Unionist Council and proposed that James Craig should replace him. He told the Council that in the eleven years, during which he had been leader, there had never been a quarrel; and he doubted whether any other leader had had confidence reposed in him for such a long period. The more than forty members of the standing committee had come over to London to beg him to stay. But he had had to refuse. The reason was simply age and insufficient energy. He put aside the sectarianism which had infected his thinking and speaking in the last years, and offered some statesmanlike valedictory advice.

> You will be a Parliament for the whole community. We used to say that we could not trust an Irish Parliament in Dublin to do justice to the Protestant minority. Let us take care that that reproach can no longer be made against your Parliament, and from the outset let them see that the Catholic minority have nothing to fear from a Protestant majority ... Let us take care that we win all that is best amongst those who have been opposed to us in the past in this community ... And so I say: from the start be tolerant to all religions, and, while maintaining to

the last your own traditions and your own citizenship, take care that similar rights are preserved for those who differ from us.[52]

The sentiments have a simple humanity which has echoed uncomfortably down the decades. Their practicality, however, was another matter. It is easy to say that the advice was simply spurned. But time had moved on and mocked such simplicities. There were men in the ascendant in all parts of Ireland who did not want any truck with a separate North or its institutions. Their purpose was to strangle Northern Ireland at birth if they could.

At about the same time as Carson resigned from the leadership, possibly even earlier, a series of furtive approaches to the Irish rebels started. The feelers were productive enough for the Prime Minister on 24 May 1921 to invite Eamon De Valera and James Craig to meet him. Lloyd George told Craig that a settlement with Sinn Fein would be impossible without some arrangement for All-Ireland government. Craig refused to have anything to do with that notion. As far as he was concerned, negotiations with the rebels had to do with the relationship between Britain and southern Ireland, and nothing else. He departed, saying that he would return only if Ulster's interests were affected 'in a practical manner'.[53]

Carson's earlier biographers say that Lloyd George told Carson about the peace moves in August: the Prime Minister said that 'the game was up' and that the government would 'have to give in'; he added that he would have to resign because he could not be responsible for the surrender.[54] There is, however, no documentary support for this highly coloured anecdote. Nor does it seem probable. Lloyd George had no motive for taking Carson into his confidence and every reason to try for peace. He had public opinion to back him. After four years of horrendous war, British people had no stomach for more; and they were appalled by the bestiality of what was being done on both sides. It would not be the last time in Ireland when a campaign of terror was called off because neither the terrorists nor the authorities wanted to go on, and both thought their interests would be better served by talking. Lloyd George did not resign and had no need to. The very idea of talking to the men of violence disgusted Carson. A surrender to them, he thought, would be shameful and disastrous.[55] It was a shock when he discovered that Conservative Ministers were also involved in such disreputable transactions.

The King opened the first session of the Belfast Parliament on 22 June 1921. Although invited, Carson did not attend. He begged leave of absence on the ground of work in the Judicial Committee.[56] Ruby went in his place. At the opening the King made a plea for peace and reconciliation. It spurred the government to act. Lloyd George felt that the royal message was not compatible with renewed repression. Austen Chamberlain, who was acting leader of the Conservatives in Bonar Law's absence due to illness, felt the same, as did Birkenhead. There was therefore unanimity in the coalition for a final effort for peace.

In July a truce was announced. Lloyd George, who had emphasised in the strongest terms that it would be a precondition of a truce that the rebels surrender their arms, found it impolitic to insist. The IRA kept their guns. Taking advantage of the truce, they used them for their campaign of murder in the North. While the editorials and correspondence columns of *The Times* were preoccupied with propaganda statements put out by De Valera, tucked away in a less prominent part of the paper was a sinister report from Belfast dated 6 September. A Mr O'Duffy, describing himself as 'Sinn Fein Liaison Officer for Ulster', had issued an official statement that, during rioting in Belfast, he had placed sentries at vantage points, who had 'made their presence felt'. He had now 'ordered his troops to cease fire'. Then, according to the reporter, he had made an 'amazing statement' at Michael Collins's meeting at Armagh. The statement had been suppressed by the Nationalist Press, but this was what O'Duffy had said:

> These people [Ulstermen] will soon have an opportunity of declaring whether they are for Ireland or the British Empire. If they decide against Ireland we will have to take suitable action. We will have to put on the screw of the boycott, and we will tighten that screw, and if necessary we will have to use the lead against them.[57]

Small wonder the Nationalist papers were not anxious to report it, but it was the shape of things to come.

The talks were difficult and protracted. The Irish delegation was seeking a republic for all Ireland, the British were ready to offer Dominion status with the exclusion of the six counties. The outcome would depend on how far the Irish negotiators would go to reach a compromise. Lloyd George's object was above all to arrive at a settlement, and so remove the question of Ireland from his desk for good. The Act of 1920 had signally failed to do so. The most likely way of reaching agreement with the rebels was to exert pressure on the North. In November Craig was summoned to London to hear the latest British proposal. It was that Northern Ireland would keep its powers, but its representatives would be returned to the Dáil and not to Westminster. Craig was shocked. He turned to Bonar Law – not Carson – for help. Bonar Law was angry at this latest move for selling out Ulster, and he persuaded his Tory colleagues to repel it. Next Lloyd George tried to exert financial pressure on the six counties by threatening to take away the tax concessions granted by the 1920 Act. But again Craig stood firm. Throughout, Bonar Law stood by Ulster. He threatened to return from his convalescence and lead the

Conservatives out of the coalition if there were any weakening of the pledges given to Ulster.

Finally agreement was reached in the small hours of 6 December 1921. Carson, isolated and impotent in the Judicial Committee of the House of Lords, had not been involved. The document which was signed was originally called 'Articles of Agreement', but when the English copy was made the next day, the words 'for a Treaty between Great Britain and Ireland' had been added.[58] The new state was to be designated the 'Irish Free State', and, as a member of the British Commonwealth of Nations, was to have the same constitutional status, and its Parliament and executive the same powers, as the Dominions of Canada, Australia, New Zealand and South Africa. Northern Ireland was to have power to opt out of the Free State – as it speedily did. In that event there was to be a boundary commission to fix the border between the two Irelands 'in accordance with the wishes of the inhabitants'. Members of the Irish Parliament were to swear faithfulness to the King. Defence of the Irish coast and the use of certain Irish ports were reserved to Britain.

The boundary commission was an instrument made to measure for Lloyd George's ingenious, and none too scrupulous, mind. He hinted to the Irish negotiators that it would shave off so much of Northern Ireland that the province would become unworkable and fall into the Free State. Even if the Prime Minister did not intend a swindle, it showed how little he, and probably the rest of Britain as well by now, cared for Ulster. Unionism had become a mere name and it soon fell out of use in Britain. In the event, the commission recommended only a negligible gain to the Free State, and the border was never altered.

When the Irish negotiators brought the treaty home, De Valera, who had stayed in Dublin, at once repudiated it. It provoked immediate dissension and civil war, and to this day Irish political opinion is divided on the treaty. Sinn Fein never accepted the subordination of Ireland to the Crown, and the country eventually became a republic. In a Britain anxious above all things for a settlement that would exorcise the evil spirit of Ireland, the Bill implementing the treaty passed easily.

Unionist opinion in the six counties was shocked by the treaty. There was a well-justified feeling that the small Protestant enclave was in deadly danger. Lilian Spender, whose husband was now the Cabinet Secretary in Belfast, recorded in her diary that a friend had told her that it was the saddest day of her life. 'England *doesn't want* us.'[59] Carson was bitterly discontent. To him the settlement represented abject surrender to the forces of violence. 'No, I think there'd be more decency in a republic than in this humbug', he told Blanche Dugdale, Balfour's niece and biographer, in 1928.

'In fact I'd rather see a republic.' She asked him what plan he would have made. 'I would have left Ulster out of it and given Southern Ireland something like Gladstone's Home Rule Bill. But mind you it isn't *this* settlement I mind so much, as the filthy way it was done, that midnight meeting, and no provisions for the men who had stuck to us.'[60] Elsewhere political opinion was almost unanimously in favour of the treaty, and it was seen as a triumph for the Prime Minister. Even Bonar Law gave it his approval. The fear that Ulster might be coerced into a Dublin Parliament, he said, had proved unjustified, and there was little practical alternative to giving the south and west what was granted by the treaty.[61]

A week after the treaty was signed, Carson made his maiden speech in the Lords.[62] His invective was full of gall. It was aimed first and last at the Unionist Party, whose splendid obsequies, he said, were now being pronounced. He took his former colleagues in the party one by one and flayed them for treachery: Curzon, Austen Chamberlain, Birkenhead. 'Peace!' he said, with justice, as events were to show. 'What is the good of pretence? You are crying peace when there is no peace.' Then he exposed the betrayal which had hurt him.

> What a fool I was. I was only a puppet, and so was Ulster, and so was Ireland, in the political game that was to get the Conservative Party into power. And of all the men in my experience that I think are the most loathsome it is those who will sell their friends for the purpose of conciliating their enemies.

The speech did not increase Carson's credit. Birkenhead, his old colleague and now Lord Chancellor, said, with characteristic extravagance, that it would have been immature on the lips of a hysterical schoolgirl.[63] Carson spoke again afterwards on Ireland, but there was no one in London disposed to listen. His power to influence events was gone. He had broken convention as well. Law Lords take care that what they say in the Chamber is not political. Not so Edward Carson, who was ready to resign if he had done anything wrong. 'What do you think I care', he said, 'about office and my salary, as compared with my honour?' Many did not understand why he was so bitter. They might have realised that it was the pain of failure which had driven him to it. The speech was the last flame of his oratorical fire. After it, he was forced to watch Ireland disintegrate, the border become a battleground, the North riven by sectarian violence, and the South turn into a chaos of civil war, brother against brother. He saw how the treaty had done for 'the little man', as he called Lloyd George, and how in 1922 the Conservatives (for it was now inapt to call the Party 'Unionist') threw him over and installed Carson's old comrade, Bonar Law, as leader and Prime Minister.

With only one possible wavering in 1918 at the darkest point in the war, Bonar Law had remained faithful to Carson and to Ulster. He became ill with cancer, and in 1923 he resigned as Prime Minister. His death followed quickly. Carson was one of the pall bearers at his funeral in Westminster Abbey. The friendship between Bonar Law and Carson had been a long and durable one through times which were never free of anxiety for both men. 'My Dear Bonar,' Carson had written to him when he was ill, begging him to be patient and have a long rest, 'you have been a very kind and considerate friend to me and I have truly missed you since you left.'[64]

Carson resigned from the Judicial Committee of the House of Lords in 1929 without regret, to live among his friends and family at Cleve Court. In 1932 the Prince of Wales opened the new Parliament building at Stormont. In the following year a massive statue of Edward Carson was erected in front of the building, commanding the long downward sweep of the approach. He was present to see it unveiled by James Craig. There he stands, bare-headed in a rumpled suit, his arm raised in a gesture of sombre defiance against the grey Belfast sky. He appeared to his friends as a saviour, and to his enemies as the grim icon of Protestant Ulster intransigence. But he cannot be accounted for so simply. His life was lived in storm. His make-up was a strange mixture of melancholia and decision. The constant need for reassurance and the unhealthy self-pity did not detract anything from his courage and his unfailing power over his followers.

On 22 October 1935, Edward Carson died quietly at the age of eighty-one at Cleve Court, after a life bedevilled by actual or imagined illness. Harry and Gladys had died before him. His body was taken to Belfast where, in the pomp of a state funeral, it was laid in St Anne's Cathedral. The patriot had no nation. Dublin had long gone as a home. London was not his natural resting place. His emotional home was Ulster, with whose Protestant people, although not one of their own, he had formed a unique bond.

He had wanted peace and believed that preparing for war was the way to reach it. It was understandable that among the Loyalists of Ulster, he should be seen as a warrior who had led the province through dark days to the enjoyment of the freedom of which the Union Jack was symbol. 'No man ever gripped and held the affections of a people as did "Sir Edward"', said the *Belfast Telegraph*. 'Of Lord Carson', wrote the editor of the *Belfast News-Letter*, 'it may be said that he was one of those heaven-sent leaders who arise, in times of crisis, to inspire a people with the will, the courage and the faith that can move mountains ... Under Providence he was the chief instrument of the [Ulster Loyalists'] deliverance from a hateful tyranny.'[65]

The assessment of *The Times* was cooler. The editor, Carson's old ally, Geoffrey Dawson, commented: 'His contribution to Irish policy was decisive. According to his critics, it was destructive. Even if that charge were admitted, it would be a defence of his attitude that it was forced upon him.'[66] That approaches the heart of the matter. Edward Carson did more than anyone else to create a divided Ireland. In spite of the rival claims of Andrew Bonar Law and James Craig, he was the Father of Northern Ireland. But he did not will it, or even want it. Necessity created it. Ireland was and is two nations and two races. Those, from Gladstone to De Valera, who felt that Ireland must control its own destiny, could never accept that awkward fact.

Carson devoted his life to the maintenance of the Union of Britain and All-Ireland. That was his passion and he was haunted by an apocalyptic vision of what would follow from its loss. He had no ambition beyond that. He sacrificed everything to it, and lost. When he came to realise that the Union could not stand, it was inevitable that he would keep what he could of it. Only by retreating behind the inner lines of the Protestant north east could he hope that anything of the old Union could be preserved. The bitter problem of Ulster was insoluble. Carson knew it himself. In 1914 he said:

> I know very well that the motto of every government – it is posted outside every department – is 'Peace in our time, O Lord'. But you do not get rid of the difficulty – be it today or tomorrow or a year hence, or be it six years hence. The difficulty will remain, and Ulster will be a physical and geographical fact.

Lilian Spender, the diarist wife of one of Carson's most devoted aides, made a tour of the border in 1923 and saw the tragic division at a different level. She wrote down her impressions.

> The beautiful blue mountains of Donegal stood up in the west, cut off from us, alas, by this tragic state of civil war. It gave one a strange feeling to see a country so unnaturally and so ungeographically divided – like seeing a living creature cut in two.[67]

Notes

1. Sir Richard Temple, *Letters and Sketches from the House of Commons*, (London, 1912).
2. To Sir John Marriott, 6 November 1933, quoted in H. Montgomery Hyde, *Carson* (London, 1953), p. 490.
3. Mina Lenox-Conyngham, *An Old Ulster House and the People who Lived in it* (Dundalk, 1946), p. 146.

Notes to Chapter 1: Dublin

1. *The Builder*, 40 (1881).
2. Edward Marjoribanks, *The Life of Lord Carson* (London, 1932), p. 5.
3. H. Montgomery Hyde, *Carson*, i (London, 1953), p. 5.
4. Marjoribanks, *The Life of Lord Carson*, i, p. 8.
5. Ibid., p. 68.
6. Richard Ellmann, *Oscar Wilde* (London, 1987), p. 18.
7. Quoted in Hyde, *Carson*, p. 11.
8. Trinity College Dublin Historical Society Records, 33, 34.
9. Quoted in Ellmann, *Oscar Wilde*, p. 35.
10. Hyde, *Carson*, p. 13.
11. Ibid., p. 20.
12. Frank Callanan, *T. M. Healy* (Cork, 1996), p. 443.
13. Hyde Papers, D3084/H/3/9, interview with Carson's sister, Mrs St George Robinson, and the second Lady Carson 22 July 1950.
14. Marjoribanks, *The Life of Lord Carson*, i, p. 19.
15. Maurice Healy, *Old Munster Circuit* (London, 1939), p. 45.
16. Hyde, *Carson*, pp. 21, 455.
17. Ibid., p. 22.
18. Healy, *The Old Munster Circuit*, p. 95.
19. Marjoribanks, *The Life of Lord Carson*, i, p. 33.
20. Healy, *The Old Munster Circuit*, p. 72.

21. *Freeman's Journal,* 19 September 1887.
22. Callanan, *T. M. Healy,* pp. 217, 475.

Notes to Chapter 2: Home Rule

1. L. P. Curtis, *Coercion and Conciliation in Ireland, 1880–1892* (Princeton, 1963), p. 103.
2. Michael Collins, *Path to Freedom,* p. 80.
3. 304 Parliamentary Debates, 3rd series, col. 1053, 8 April 1886.
4. Robert Rhodes James, *Lord Randolph Churchill* (London, 1959), p. 223.
5. D. C. Savage, 'The Origins of the Ulster Unionist Party, 1885', *Irish Historical Studies,* 12 (1961), p. 185.
6. *Belfast News-Letter,* 2 February 1886, quoted Savage, 'The Origins of the Ulster Unionist Party, 1885', p. 196.
7. *Belfast News-Letter,* 17, 18 May 1886, quoted Savage, 'The Origins of the Ulster Unionist Party, 1885', p. 202.
8. *Belfast News-Letter,* 3 May 1886, quoted Savage, 'The Origins of the Ulster Unionist Party, 1885', p. 201.
9. Roy Jenkins, *Gladstone* (London, 1995), p. 26.
10. H. Montgomery Hyde, *The Londonderrys* (London, 1979), p. 67.
11. Quoted in Hyde, *The Londonderrys,* p. 137.
12. Quoted in Hyde, *The Londonderrys,* p. 68.
13. Balfour Papers, Add. 49688/9.
14. Balfour Papers, Add. 49688/151.
15. Curtis, *Coercion and Conciliation in Ireland,* p. 193.
16. Balfour Papers, Add. 49808/18.
17. Hyde, *Carson,* p. 72.
18. Balfour Papers, Add. 49709/78–86.
19. Hyde, *Carson,* pp. 71–76.
20. Balfour Papers, Add. 49688/155.
21. Wilfrid Blunt, *The Land War in Ireland* (London, 1912), p. 365.
22. Blanche Dugdale, *Arthur James Balfour* (London, 1936), p. 147.
23. Marjoribanks, *The Life of Lord Carson,* i, p. 93.

Notes to Chapter 3: London

1. L. P. Curtis, *Coercion and Conciliation in Ireland, 1880- 1892* (Princeton, 1963), p. 356.
2. Papal Rescript of 20 April 1888.
3. Balfour Papers, Add. 49808/18, note of Ridgeway annotated by Balfour, 27 November 1887: 'This is for the Pope via Norfolk.'

4. Balfour Papers, Add. 49836/188, notes of interview with Carson, 12 July 1928.

5. Balfour Papers, Add. 49709/89, 9 December 1889.

6. Balfour Papers, Add. 49709/93 12 May 1890.

7. Hyde Papers, D/3084/H/2/38, 13 May 1890.

8. Edward Marjoribanks, *The Life of Lord Carson*, i (London, 1932), p. 137.

9. 7 Parliamentary Debates, 4th series, col. 288, 9 August 1892.

10. 8 Parliamentary Debates, 4th series, col. 267, 2 February 1893.

11. Marjoribanks, *The Life of Lord Carson*, i, p. 148.

12. 8 Parliamentary Debates, 4th series, cols 348, 429, 2 and 3 February 1893.

13. Ibid., col. 446.

14. *Times*, 4 February 1893.

15. 8 Parliamentary Debates, 4th series, col. 1248, 13 February 1893.

16. For instance by Joseph Chamberlain in 1886 (304 Parliamentary Debates, col. 1200, 9 April 1886): 'Sir, it is the difficulty, one of the great difficulties of this problem that Ireland is not a homogeneous community – that it consists of two nations.'

17. 11 Parliamentary Debates, 4th series, col. 837, 20 April 1893.

18. Bonar Law Papers, 24/3/57.

19. 17 Parliamentary Debates, 4th series, col. 640, 8 September 1893.

20. 23 Parliamentary Debates, 4th series, col. 920, 19 April 1894.

21. 27 Parliamentary Debates, 4th series, col. 482, 19 July 1894.

22. Hyde Papers, D/3084/H/3/9, interview with Mrs St George Robinson, 22 July 1950.

Notes to Chapter 4: Oscar Wilde

1. Richard Ellmann, *Oscar Wilde* (London, 1987), p. 414n.

2. Ibid., p. 93.

3. Oscar Wilde, *De Profundis*.

4. Ellmann, *Oscar Wilde*, p. 394.

5. 300 Parliamentary Debates, 3rd series, col. 1397, 6 August 1885.

6. H. Montgomery Hyde, ed., *The Trials of Oscar Wilde* (London, 1948), p. 58.

7. Edward Marjoribanks, *The Life of Lord Carson*, i (London, 1932), p. 198.

8. Ibid., p. 199.

9. Viscount Simon, *Retrospect: The Memoirs of Viscount Simon* (London, 1952), p. 86.

10. Hyde, ed., *The Trials of Oscar Wilde*, p. 40.

11. Marjoribanks, *The Life of Lord Carson*, i, p. 201.

12. Hyde Papers, D/3084/H/2/18, Lord Birkenhead (F. E. Smith's son) to Hyde, 30 June 1950.

13. Hyde, ed., *The Trials of Oscar Wilde*, p. 8.

14. Ellmann, *Oscar Wilde*, p. 416.

15. Hesketh Pearson, *Oscar Wilde*, p. 288.

16. The plea is set out in full in Merlin Holland, *Irish Peacock and Scarlet Marquess: The Real Trial of Oscar Wilde* (London, 2003), p. 286. The indictment contained two counts. The first alleged that Queensberry's card meant that Wilde 'had committed and was in the habit of committing the abominable crime of buggery with mankind'. The second alleged the literal meaning, viz. that Wilde had been posing as a 'somdomite'. In view of the first count and the plea of justification, Queensberry had to lead evidence of actual indecent acts, and not just posing, through his writings or general behaviour.

Merlin Holland's book, *Irish Peacock and Scarlet Marquess*, comprises a complete, verbatim transcript of the libel trial, the first that has been published. The author, a grandson of Oscar Wilde, described in the Introduction how he discovered it in the British Library in 2000. The quotations from the trial in this chapter are from that transcript.

17. Sir Edward Clarke was a former Solicitor-General and had an enviable reputation as an advocate. But he made a number of errors of judgement in the case. See Holland, *Irish Peacock and Scarlet Marquess*, introduction, p. xxvii. He generously offered to represent Wilde without fee in the criminal trial which followed the libel case.

18. Quoted Holland, introduction p. xxviii.

19. Ibid., p. 90.

20. Ibid., p. 166.

21. Ibid., pp. 207–9.

22. Ibid., p. 253.

23. Ibid., p. 273.

24. *The Trials of Oscar Wilde*, introduction, pp. 58–61.

25. Marjoribanks, *The Life of Lord Carson*, i, p. 229.

26. Hyde Papers, D/3084/H/2/18, Birkenhead to Hyde, 30 June 1950.

27. Ellmann, *Oscar Wilde*, p. 435.

28. H. Montgomery Hyde, *Carson* (London, 1953), p. 129.

29. Marjoribanks, *The Life of Lord Carson*, i, p. 231.

Notes to Chapter 5: The End of Unionist Government

1. Andrew Roberts, *Salisbury: Victorian Titan* (London, 1999), p. 651.

2. Edward Marjoribanks, *The Life of Lord Carson*, i (London, 1932), p. 254.

3. [1896] 2 Queen's Bench Reports, p. 425; (1896) 12 Times Law Reports, p. 551.

4. Marjoribanks, *The Life of Lord Carson*, i, p. 163.

5. Reginald Lucas, *Colonel Saunderson MP: A Memoir* (London, 1908), p. 252.

6. *Punch*, 1 August 1896.

7. 43 Parliamentary Debates, 4th series, col. 540, 23 July 1896.

8. Ibid., col. 544.

9. Balfour Papers, Add. 49709.

10. Ibid.

11. Quoted in Blanche Dugdale, *Arthur James Balfour* (London, 1936), p. 245.

12. Quoted in L. P. Curtis, *Coercion and Conciliation in Ireland, 1880–1892: A Study in Conservative Unionism* (Princeton, 1963), p. 417.

13. Marjoribanks, *The Life of Lord Carson*, i, p. 261.

14. 50 Parliamentary Debates, 4th series, col. 1029, 2 July 1897.

15. 53 Parliamentary Debates, 4th series, col. 983, 17 February 1898.

16. 187 Parliamentary Debates, 4th series, col. 400, 31 March 1908.

17. 188 Parliamentary Debates, 4th series, col. 845, 11 May 1908.

18. Quoted in full in Owen Dudley Edwards, 'Carson as Advocate: Marjoribanks and Wilde', in *From the United Irishmen to Twentieth-Century Unionism: A Festschrift for A. T. Q. Stewart* (Dublin, 2004), p. 133.

19. Young, *Arthur James Balfour* (London, 1963), p. 195.

20. Marjoribanks, *The Life of Lord Carson*, i, p. 280.

21. H. Montgomery Hyde, *Carson* (London, 1953), p. 155.

22. *Punch*, 23 May 1900.

23. Marjoribanks, *The Life of Lord Carson*, i, p. 343.

24. Ibid., p. 342.

25. *Times*, 8 February 1905.

26. Marjoribanks, *The Life of Lord Carson*, i, p. 345.

27. Ibid., p. 346.

28. Young, *Arthur James Balfour*, p. 251.

29. Marjoribanks, *The Life of Lord Carson*, i, p. 352.

30. Halsbury Papers, Add. 56374/89.

31. *Times*, 2 January 1906.

32. *Taff Vale Railway Company* v. *Amalgamated Society of Railway Servants* [1901] Appeal Cases 426.

33. 162 Parliamentary Debates, 4th series, col. 1733, 3 August 1906.

Notes to Chapter 6: The Naval Cadet

1. These absurd and illogical distinctions between cases where a petition was available, and those in which it was not, were not swept away until 1948 when actions against the Crown were codified by the Crown Proceedings Act. But they were in full force at the time of the Archer-Shee trial.

2. The full text of the petition is set out in an appendix to Rodney Bennett, *The Archer-Shees against the Admiralty* (London, 1973).

3. McKenna Papers MCKN 3/5, report of Sir Charles Thomas to Reginald McKenna, 27 July 1910.
4. Balfour Papers, Add. 49836/19, 14 August 1910.
5. Edward Marjoribanks, *The Life of Lord Carson*, i (London, 1932), p. 441.
6. Ibid., p. 437.
7. Londonderry Papers, D/2846/1/1, July 1910.

Notes to Chapter 7: The House of Lords

1. Londonderry Papers, D/2846/2/20/72, 20 October 1909.
2. Ibid., D/2846/1/1, 23 December 1909.
3. Ibid., 26 January 1909.
4. Ibid., letter 25, undated, probably 1908.
5. Ibid., 15 January 1910.
6. *Times*, 31 July 1909.
7. Londonderry Papers, D/2846/1/1, 24 February 1910.
8. Denis Gwynn, *The Life of John Redmond* (London, 1932), p. 174.
9. For a full account see Elie Halévy, *A History of the English People in the Nineteenth Century*, vi, *The Rule of Democracy, 1905–1914* (London, 1932), pp. 305ff; also E. L. Woodward, *The Age of Reform, 1815–1870* (Oxford, 1938), p. 81.
10. 16 House of Commons Debates, 5th series. col. 1469, 14 April 1910.
11. Ibid., col. 1478.
12. Londonderry Papers, D/2846/1/1, 17 April 1910.
13. Ibid., 26 April 1908.
14. 16 House of Commons Debates, 5th series, col. 1548, 14 April 1910.
15. Ibid., col. 1551.
16. Londonderry Papers, D/2846/1/1, 17 April 1910.
17. Ibid., 21 May 1910.
18. Ibid., 29 August 1910.
19. Ibid., 27 October. 1910.
20. *Times*, 18 November 1910.
21. Violet Bonham Carter, *Lantern Slides: The Diaries and Letters of Violet Bonham Carter, 1904–1914*, ed. Mark Bonham Carter and Mark Pottle (London, 1996), p. 274.
22. Londonderry Papers, D/2846/1/1, 3 June 1911.
23. Kenneth Young, *Arthur James Balfour* (London, 1963), p. 310.
24. The actual number of renegade peers is in doubt. Carson thought it was twenty, but the biographers of Asquith and Balfour thought thirty-seven voted with the government. Roy Jenkins, *Asquith* (London, 1964), p. 230; Young, *Arthur James Balfour*, p. 312.

25. Londonderry Papers, D/2846/1/1, 30 July 1911.
26. Craig Papers, T/3775/2/1, 29 July 1911.
27. Londonderry Papers, D/2846/1/1, 28 August 1911.
28. Ibid., 16 September 1911.
29. *Belfast News-Letter*, 26 September 1911.
30. Londonderry Papers, D/2846/1/1, 24 September 1911.
31. *Belfast News-Letter*, 27 September 1911.
32. Bonar Law Papers, 24/3/57. The archivist suggests that its date is 18 November 1911, only days after Bonar Law became Conservative Leader. The reference to 'the Craigavon demonstration' suggests that the dating of November 1911 is right. So does 'dissatisfaction in Dublin', as Carson went to Dublin in October; although he told Lady Londonderry that it was 'splendid', he was heckled there. Londonderry Papers, D/2846/1/1, 18 October 1911.

Notes to Chapter 8: The Conservative Leadership

1. Londonderry Papers, D/2846/1/1, 7 October 1911.
2. Kenneth Young, *Arthur James Balfour* (London, 1963), p. 314.
3. Londonderry Papers, D/2846/1/1, 18 October 1911.
4. Young, *Arthur James Balfour*, p. 313.
5. Londonderry Papers, D/2846/2/20/15.
6. Ibid., D/2846/1/1, 23 October 1911.
7. Robert Blake, *The Unknown Prime Minister: The Life and Times of Andrew Bonar Law, 1858–1923* (London, 1955), p. 88.
8. Young, *Arthur James Balfour*, p. 314.
9. Ibid., p. 316.
10. Londonderry Papers, D/2846/1/1, 15 November 1911.
11. Blake, *The Unknown Prime Minister*, p. 86.
12. Londonderry Papers, D/2846/1/1, 15 November 1911.
13. A. T. Q. Stewart, *The Ulster Crisis: Resistance to Home Rule, 1912–1914* (London, 1967), p. 38.
14. 36 House of Commons Debates, 5th series, col. 1425, 11 April 1912.
15. Londonderry Papers, D/2846/1/1, 18 December 1911.
16. Bonar Law Papers, 24/3/56, 18 December 1911.
17. *Times*, 4 October 1911.
18. Londonderry Papers, D/2846/1/1, 19 January 1912.
19. Bonar Law Papers, 25/1/55.
20. Stewart, *The Ulster Crisis*, p. 51. The author quotes a newspaper story that the owner of the Opera House was offered a knighthood as well as a good fee for the use of his theatre.
21. Bonar Law Papers, 25/1/65.

22. Stewart, *The Ulster Crisis*, p. 53. The author gives a vivid account of the whole episode.
23. Londonderry Papers, D/2846/1/1, undated, probably March 1912.
24. Carson was wrong about Asquith's wherewithal. His second marriage to the brewery heiress, Margot Tennant, had insulated him permanently from 'lack of means'.
25. Londonderry Papers, D/2846/1/1, 12 March 1912.
26. Ibid., 27 March 1912.
27. Montgomery Hyde Papers, D/3084/H/3/9, interview with Carson's sister, Mrs St George Robinson, and the second Lady Carson, 22 July 1950.
28. Londonderry Papers, D/2846/1/1, 27 March 1912.
29. Ibid., 14 April 1912.

Notes to Chapter 9: Asquith's Home Rule Bill

1. 36 House of Commons Debates, 5th series, col. 1436, 11 April 1912.
2. *Westminster Gazette*, 15 April 1912, quoting the Vice-President of the International Mercantile Marine.
3. 36 House of Commons Debates, 5th series, col. 1401, 11 April 1912.
4. Ibid., col. 1400.
5. 39 House of Commons Debates, 5th series, col. 771, 11 June 1912.
6. Bonar Law Papers, 26/4/7, 4 June 1912.
7. 39 House of Commons Debates, 5th series, col. 1075, 13 June 1912.
8. *Times*, 25 June 1912.
9. Ibid., 29 July 1912.
10. Elie Halévy, *A History of the English People in the Nineteenth Century*, vi, *The Rule of Democracy, 1905–1914* (London, 1932), p. 551.
11. Albert Venn Dicey, *Fool's Paradise: Being a Constitutionalist's Criticism of the Home Rule Bill of 1912* (London, 1913), p. 127.
12. Strachey Papers, 5/6/5, 7 July 1912.
13. *Pall Mall Gazette*, 24 September 1912.
14. Denis Gwynn: *The Life of John Redmond* (London, 1932), p. 214.
15. Londonderry Papers, D/2846/1/1, 13 August 1912.
16. Ibid., 7 September 1912.
17. Bonar Law Papers, 27/1/49, 22 August 1912 from Homburg.
18. Violet Bonham Carter, *Lantern Slides: The Diaries and Letters of Violet Bonham Carter, 1904–1914*, ed. Mark Bonham Carter and Mark Pottle (London, 1996), p. 328.
19. A. T. Q. Stewart, *The Ulster Crisis: Resistance to Home Rule, 1912–1914* (London, 1967), pp. 59ff.
20. Ibid., p. 61.
21. Ronald McNeill, *Ulster's Stand for Freedom* (London, 1922), p. 103.

22. *Times*, 19 September 1912.
23. *Belfast News-Letter*, 20 September 1912.
24. *Times*, 20 September 1912.
25. *Belfast News-Letter*, 20 September 1912.
26. *Times*, 20 September 1912.
27. Ibid., 28 September 1912.
28. McNeill, *Ulster's Stand for Freedom*, p. 116.
29. Ibid., p. 121.
30. *Times*, 30 September 1912.
31. Londonderry Papers, D/2846/1/1, 5 October 1912.
32. H Montgomery Hyde, *Carson* (London, 1953), p. 323.
33. Alfred M. Gollin, *The Observer and J. L. Garvin, 1908–1914* (Oxford, 1960), p. 404.
34. Elie Halévy, *A History of the English People in the Nineteenth Century*, vi, *The Rule of Democracy, 1905–1914* (London, 1932), p. 550.
35. *Times*, 30 October 1913.
36. McNeill, *Ulster's Stand for Freedom*, p. 48.
37. *Irish Times*, 23 October 1935.

Notes to Chapter 10: Ulster

1. 43 House of Commons Debates, 5th series, col. 1774, 11 November 1912.
2. Ibid., col. 2054, 13 November 1912.
3. 13 House of Lords Debates, 5th series, col. 627, 29 January 1913.
4. Ronald McNeill, *Ulster's Stand for Freedom* (London, 1922), p. 133.
5. 46 House of Commons Debates, 5th series, col. 377, 1 January 1913.
6. Ibid., col. 394.
7. Ibid., col. 464.
8. Ibid., cols 471, 472.
9. A. T. Q. Stewart, *The Ulster Crisis* (London, 1967), p. 226.
10. Londonderry Papers, D/2846/1/1, 18 January 1913.
11. Ibid., 21 February 1913.
12. Ibid., 14 April 1913.
13. Hall Papers, D/1540/3/5.
14. Ibid., D/1540/3/10, 9 August 1913.
15. Ibid., D/1540/3/21, 29 October 1913.
16. McNeill, *Ulster's Stand for Freedom*, p. 161.
17. Richardson was the recipient of a curiously double-edged compliment from Carson's biographer, Ian Colvin. 'Richardson', he wrote, 'was, in fact, very much like Roberts, one of those small, wiry, keen, old soldiers who had learnt to know men and war fighting the Afghans and the Pathans on the North-West Frontier. He found material to his mind in the Ulster Volunteers, with whom

he was as completely at home as with the tribesmen of the Tirah or Zhob Valley,' Ian Colvin, *The Life of Lord Carson*, ii (London, 1934), p. 187.

18. McNeill, *Ulster's Stand for Freedom*, p. 165.
19. PRO, CO 904/27, July 1913.
20. McNeill, *Ulster's Stand for Freedom*, p. 226.
21. *Times*, 27 March 1913.
22. Stewart, *The Ulster Crisis*, p. 132.
23. Speech in Newcastle, 29 October 1913, *Times*, 30 October 1913.

Notes to Chapter 11: Marconi

1. 42 House of Commons Debates, 5th series, col. 667, 11 October 1912.
2. Ibid., col. 718.
3. Frances Donaldson, *The Marconi Scandal* (London, 1962), p. 91.
4. Ibid., p. 92.
5. It may have been Winston Churchill who persuaded the two advocates to represent the Ministers who were their political opponents. Martin Gilbert and Roy Jenkins both say so in their biographies of Churchill but the story cannot be verified. Martin Gilbert, *Winston S. Churchill*, iii (London, 1971), p. 623n.; Roy Jenkins, *Churchill*, p. 225). The idea was canvassed that it was a trap to disable the Opposition by depriving it of its two best qualified and forceful speakers.
6. 54 House of Commons Debates, 5th series, col. 403, 18 June 1913.
7. *Times*, 20 March 1913.
8. 54 House of Commons Debates, 5th series, col. 391, 18 June 1913.
9. Ibid. col. 437.
10. Bonar Law Papers, 29/5/43, 18 June 1913.
11. Ibid., 33/5/37, 21 June 1913.
12. Robert Blake, *The Unknown Prime Minister: The Life and Times of Andrew Bonar Law, 1858–1923* (London, 1955), p. 143.
13. *Times*, 14 June 1913.
14. Bonar Law Papers, 29/4/21, 25 May 1913.
15. *Times*, 17 June 1913.
16. Londonderry Papers, D/2846/1/1, 27 March 1913.
17. Ian Colvin, *The Life of Lord Carson*, ii (London, 1934), p. 183.
18. David Gilmour, *The Long Recessional: The Imperial Life of Rudyard Kipling* (London 2002), p. 231.
19. Londonderry Papers, D/2846/1/1, 26 August 1913.
20. Colvin, *The Life of Lord Carson*, ii, p. 193.
21. Violet Bonham Carter, *Lantern Slides: The Diaries and Letters of Violet Bonham Carter, 1904–1914*, ed. Mark Bonham Carter and Mark Pottle (London, 1996), p. 391, 13 September 1913.

22. Roy Jenkins, *Asquith* (London, 1964), p. 287n.
23. Denis Gwynn, *The Life of John Redmond* (London, 1932), p. 228.
24. Carson Private Papers, September 1913.
25. Londonderry Papers, D/2846/1/1, 21 October 1913.
26. *Times*, 25 January 1913.
27. Harold Nicolson, *King George the Fifth: His Life and Reign* (London, 1952), p. 223.
28. Churchill Papers, CHAR 2/62/56, 12 September 1913.
29. Bonar Law Papers, 33/5/57, Bonar Law to Carson, 18 September 1913.
30. Churchill Papers, CHAR 2/62/59, 19 September 1913.
31. Bonar Law Papers, 33/5/57.
32. Ibid.
33. Ibid., 30/2/15.
34. Ibid., 33/5/58, 24 September 1913.
35. Ibid., 30/2/27, 26 September 1913.
36. Ibid., 30/2/6, 4 September 1913.
37. Ibid., 30/2/21, 23 September 1913.
38. Ibid., 30/2/20, 23 September 1913.
39. Ibid., 33/5/67, 4 October 1913.
40. Ibid., 30/2/37, Lansdowne to Bonar Law, 30 September 1913.
41. Ibid., 33/5/68.
42. Ibid., 30/3/16, Lansdowne to Bonar Law, 10 October 1913.
43. Londonderry Papers, D/2846/1/1, 10 October 1913.
44. Bonar Law Papers, 30/3/23, 10 October 1913.
45. Blake, *The Unknown Prime Minister*, p. 161.
46. Ibid., p. 167.
47. Gwynn, *The Life of John Redmond*, p. 250.
48. Ibid., p. 238.
49. Asquith Papers, 39/70, 27 December 1913.
50. Ibid., 39/72, note of meeting on 2 January 1914.
51. Ibid., 39/79, 7 January 1914.
52. Ibid., 39/117.
53. Gwynn, *The Life of John Redmond*, p. 232.
54. Bonar Law Papers, 33/6/80.
55. Asquith Papers, 39/132, Stamfordham to Asquith, 28 February 1914.
56. Richard English, *Armed Struggle: The History of the IRA* (London, 2003), p. 10.

Notes to Chapter 12: The Curragh

1. Harold Nicolson, *King George the Fifth: His Life and Reign* (London, 1952), p. 226.
2. Ibid., p. 233.
3. Ian Colvin, *The Life of Lord Carson*, ii (London, 1934), p. 237.

4. Ibid., p. 239.

5. *Belfast Telegraph*, 20 September 1913.

6. *Times*, 29 November 1913.

7. Sir C. E. Callwell, *Field Marshal Sir Henry Wilson: His Life and Diaries*, i (London, 1937), p. 130.

8. Bonar Law Papers, 34/1/21.

9. Ibid.

10. Ibid., 34/1/25.

11. Ibid., 31/3/2.

12. Memorandum to the King of September 1913, reproduced in full in Roy Jenkins, *Asquith* (London, 1964), appendix B, p. 547.

13. 58 House of Commons Debates, 5th series, col. 176, 11 February 1914.

14. Colvin, *The Life of Lord Carson*, ii, p. 283.

15. Asquith, *Letters to Venetia Stanley*, ed. Michael and Eleanor Brock (Oxford, 1985), letter 35, 12 February 1914.

16. Asquith Papers, 39/119, Lloyd George memorandum of 16 February 1914.

17. 59 House of Commons Debates, 5th series, col. 934, 9 March 1914.

18. *Wilson Diaries*, i, p. 137.

19. PRO, CO 904/120 and CAB 37/119/36.

20. UUC Papers, D/1327/4/21.

21. Ibid.

22. O'Neill Papers, D/1238/18.

23. PRO, CAB 41/35/18. Asquith to George V, 18 March 1914.

24. PRO, CAB 37/119/44.

25. *Wilson Diaries*, i, p. 138.

26. Asquith Papers, 40/19, note of Seely of meeting on 20 March 1914 with Chief of Imperial General Staff, Attorney-General and Paget; and Sir James Fergusson, *The Curragh Incident* (London, 1949), pp. 51- 59.

27. Asquith Papers, 40/19.

28. Ibid., 40/9 and 40/13, note of Seely of meeting on 18 March 1914, and note of Simon of 19 March 1914.

29. 59 House of Commons Debates, 5th series, col. 2273, 19 March 1914.

30. *Wilson Diaries*, i, p. 139.

31. Hubert Gough, *Soldiering On* (London, 1954), p. 106.

32. Bonar Law Papers, 39/2, first-hand accounts, including one by Brigadier Gough, of the events in General Paget's headquarters in Dublin and at the Curragh.

33. *Wilson Diaries*, i, p. 140, 20 March 1914.

34. Major-General Sir Charles Fergusson, the divisional commander at the Curragh, was the father of Sir James Fergusson, whose history of the Curragh Incident is quoted in this chapter.

35. Asquith Papers, 40/27, 21 March 1914.

36. Fergusson, *The Curragh Incident*, pp. 125, 153.
37. Bonar Law Papers, 34/2/47, 22 March 1914.
38. Ibid., 32/1/50, 23 March 1914.
39. Ibid., 32/1/66.

Notes to Chapter 13: Craigavon

1. Bonar Law Papers, 32/1/36.
2. PRO, CAB 37/119/60.
3. Sir Nevil Macready, *Annals of an Active Life* (London, 1924), p. 181.
4. Ibid., p. 197.
5. Spender Papers, D/1633/2/19.
6. *Daily News and Leader*, 23 March 1914.
7. H. Montgomery Hyde, *Carson* (London, 1953), p. 355.
8. Elie Halévy, *A History of the English People in the Nineteenth Century*, vi, *The Rule of Democracy, 1905–1914* (London, 1932), p. 557.
9. Command. 7318.
10. Command 7329.
11. Sir James Fergusson, *The Curragh Incident* (London, 1949), ch. 16; Robert Blake, *The Unknown Prime Minister: The Life and Times of Andrew Bonar Law, 1858–1923* (London, 1955), p. 205.
12. Carson Papers, D/1507/A/5/3, 14 January 1914.
13. Bonar Law Papers, 32/1/54, 23 March 1914.
14. Ibid., 34/2/51, 26 March 1914.
15. That cautious lawyer, Sir John Simon, Attorney-General, advised the government in February 1914 that the validity of a bar on importation into Ireland, but not affecting the rest of the United Kingdom, was questionable (PRO, CAB 37/119/30), but the point was never tested – although it might have been if the Ulster rebels had been prosecuted, or if a seizure of arms by the Customs had been challenged.
16. Crawford Papers, D/640/22/1, Hacket Pain to Crawford 17 January 1914.
17. UUC Papers, D/1327/4/21, Crawford to Hacket Pain 19 January 1914.
18. A. T. Q. Stewart, *The Ulster Crisis: Resistance to Home Rule, 1912–1914* (London, 1967), pp. 83–85.
19. *Times*, 4 April 1914.
20. Ibid., 6 April 1914.
21. F. H. Crawford, *Guns for Ulster* (Belfast, 1947), p. 29.
22. *Times*, 2 April 1914.
23. Ibid., 3 April 1914.
24. *Unionist*, June 1949.

25. UUC Papers, D/1327/4/21, handwritten copy orders for Major Crawford 6 April 1914.

26. Stewart, *The Ulster Crisis: Resistance to Home Rule, 1912–1914*, p. 187.

27. Crawford, *Guns for Ulster*, p. 47.

28. Ibid., pp. 49, 50.

29. Crawford, *Guns for Ulster*, pp. 74, 5: Agnew's log.

30. PRO, CO 903/18, Chief Secretary's files, intelligence report for 1914.

31. Ibid.

32. Ibid.

33. Ibid.

34. UUC, Papers, D/1327/2/15.

35. Spender Papers, D/1633/2/19, Lady Spender's diary.

36. 61 House of Commons Debates, 5th series, col. 1348, 27 April 1914.

37. Ibid., col. 1747, 29 April 1914.

38. Bonar Law Papers, 107/4/18, 21 December 1921. Professor Jackson believes that Bonar Law and others on the Unionist front bench may have been privy to the gun running, Alvin Jackson, *Home Rule: An Irish History, 1800–2000* (London, 2003), p. 133. It may be so, although some of the evidence rests on the uncertain assertion of Crawford. But in any case, Bonar Law, as he said himself, would have taken responsibility for it.

39. Montgomery Hyde Papers, D/3084/H/3/1, and H. Montgomery Hyde, *Carson* (London, 1953), p. 364n.

40. Asquith Papers, 41/12, telegram of 25 April 1914.

41. Ibid., 41/51, Redmond to Asquith, 27 April 1914.

42. Asquith, *Fifty Years of Parliament*, ii (London, 1926), pp. 139–42.

43. Ronald McNeill, *Ulster's Stand for Freedom* (London, 1922), p. 220.

44. Carson Private Papers,.

45. Asquith, *Letters to Venetia Stanley*, ed. Michael and Eleanor Brock (Oxford, 1985), p. 46, letter 32, 6 February 1914.

46. Alfred M. Gollin, *The Observer and J. L. Garvin, 1908–1914* (Oxford, 1960), p. 425.

Notes to Chapter 14: War and Peace

1. 61 House of Commons Debates, 5th series, col. 1576, 28 April 1914.

2. Ibid., col. 1591. A general federal structure for the United Kingdom had been canvassed for some time as a possible solution the Irish problem. The government had promised to put forward such a scheme on the introduction of Home Rule, and Churchill was a keen advocate.

3. Ibid., col. 1752, 29 April 1914.

4. Bonar Law Papers, 39/4/35, note of Bonar Law 5 May 1914.

5. Churchill Papers, CHAR 2/63/25, annotation dated 30 May 1914.

6. Alfred M. Gollin, *Proconsul in Politics* (London, 1964), pp. 8, 215.

7. McNeill Papers, D/1238/20.

8. 16 House of Lords Debates, 5th series, col. 377.

9. Sir C. E. Callwell, *Field Marshal Sir Henry Wilson: His Life and Diaries*, i (London, 1937), p. 148, 3 July 1914.

10. Bonar Law Papers, 33/1/28.

11. Ronald McNeill, *Ulster's Stand for Freedom* (London, 1922), p. 226.

12. *Times*, 13 July 1914.

13. Asquith, *Letters to Venetia Stanley*, ed. Michael and Eleanor Brock (Oxford, 1985), letter 97, 15 July 1914.

14. Robert Blake, *The Unknown Prime Minister: The Life and Times of Andrew Bonar Law, 1858–1923* (London, 1955), p. 215.

15. Carson Papers, D/1507/A/6/40, 21 July 1914.

16. Bonar Law Papers, 39/4/44.

17. Ibid.

18. Asquith, *Letters to Venetia Stanley*, letter 102, 22 July 1914.

19. Craig Papers, T/3775/10/5, note of James Craig of a private conversation with the King, 24 July 1914.

20. *Wilson Diaries*, i, p. 146.

21. J. W. Gerard, *My Four Years in Germany* (London, 1917), p. 63.

22. Churchill, *The World Crisis*, i (London, 1928), p. 148.

23. Ian Colvin, *The Life of Lord Carson*, ii (London, 1934), p. 422.

24. Asquith, *Letters to Venetia Stanley*, letter 110, 30 July 1914. As a result the amending Bill never came before the House of Commons. In his biography of Bonar Law, Lord Blake says that it would have retained the county option, but without the time limit of six years. Blake, *The Unknown Prime Minister*, p. 217.

25. Churchill Papers, CHAR 2/64/14.

26. 65 House of Commons Debates, 5th series, col. 1829, 3 August 1914.

27. Denis Gwynn, *The Life of John Redmond* (London, 1932), p. 363.

28. Carson Private Papers.

29. Asquith, *Letters to Venetia Stanley*, letter 140, 31 August 1914.

30. 66 House of Commons Debates, 5th series, col. 892.

31. Asquith, *Memories and Reflections, 1852–1927*, ii (London, 1928), p. 33.

32. Alvin Jackson, *Home Rule: An Irish History, 1800–2000* (London, 2003), p. 143 and note 4.

33. Carson Papers, D/1507/A/7/6.

34. Ibid., D/1507/A/7/1, 1 August 1914.

35. McNeill, *Ulster's Stand for Freedom*, p. 231.

36. Londonderry Papers, D/2846/1/1, 13 March 1915.

37. Carson Private Papers.

38. Carson Papers, D/2846/1/1/43, 44, 1910.

39. Redmond Papers, 15261(2).
40. Londonderry Papers, D/2846/1/1/124.
41. Blake, *The Unknown Prime Minister*, p. 245.
42. Gwynn, *The Life of John Redmond*, p. 425.
43. Londonderry Papers, D/2846/1/1/127.
44. Ibid., D/2846/1/1/128, 28 June 1915.
45. Ibid., D/2846/1/1/129.
46. Craig Papers, T/3775/2/12, 9 August 1915.
47. Ian Colvin, *The Life of Lord Carson*, iii (London, 1936), p. 81.
48. Ibid., p. 90.
49. Ibid., p. 89.
50. Reproduced in facsimile in Hyde, *Carson*, p. 393.
51. 75 House of Commons Debates, 5th series, col. 529.
52. *Times*, 3 November 1915.
53. Colvin *The Life of Lord Carson*, iii, p. 118.
54. Churchill Papers, CHAR 2/67/47, 20 October 1915.
55. Lord Beaverbrook, *Politicians and the War, 1914–1916* (London, 1956), p. 156.

Notes to Chapter 15: Opposition

1. *Times*, 21 October 1915.
2. Londonderry Papers, D/2846/1/1/134.
3. Lord Beaverbrook, *Politicians and the War, 1914–1916* (London, 1956), p. 227.
4. Carson Papers, D/1507/C/2/1, Lady Carson's diary, 27 April 1916.
5. Ibid., D/1507/A/15/4, 10 January 1916.
6. 77 House of Commons Debates, 5th series, cols 1474, 1483, 11 January 1916.
7. Lloyd George Papers, F/16/7/29, 11 October 1918.
8. Lady Carson's diary, 25 March 1916.
9. Ian Colvin, *The Life of Lord Carson*, iii (London, 1936), p. 145.
10. Lady Carson's diary, 27 March 1916.
11. Ibid., 31 March 1916.
12. Ibid., 25 January 1916.
13. Hyde Papers, D/3084/H/1A/1, 18 January 1916.
14. Sir Martin Gilbert, *Winston S. Churchill*, iii (London, 1971) p. 688, 19 January 1916.
15. Ibid., p. 697, 1 February 1916.
16. Lady Carson's diary, 13 March 1916.
17. Churchill Papers, CHAR 1/118/89.
18. Churchill Papers, CHAR 2/71/31.
19. Hyde Papers, D/3084/H/1A/3, 26 March 1916.
20. Lady Carson's diary, 24 April 1916.

21. Hyde Papers, D/3084/H/1A/4.

22. Denis Gwynn, *The Life of John Redmond* (London, 1932), p. 466.

23. Spender Papers, D/1295/17/4, 23 March 1916.

24. Robert Kee, *The Green Flag* (London, 1972), p. 549.

25. Casement was tried and hanged as a traitor.

26. Alvin Jackson, *Home Rule: An Irish History, 1800–2000* (London, 2003), p. 153.

27. Gwynn, *The Life of John Redmond*, p. 481.

28. Bonar Law Papers, 63/C/7.

29. Command 8270.

30. Colvin, *The Life of Lord Carson*, iii, p. 162.

31. 82 House of Commons Debates, 5th series, cols 2309, 2311, 25 May 1916.

32. Lady Carson's diary, 16 May 1916.

33. Carson Papers, D/1507/A/17/7, 3 June 1916.

34. John Grigg, *Lloyd George: From Peace to War, 1912–1916* (London, 1985), p. 350.

35. Lloyd George Papers, D/14/2/13, Lloyd George to R. J. Lynn, 5 June 1916.

36. Carson Papers, D/1507/A/17/8, 5 June 1916.

37. Colvin, *The Life of Lord Carson*, iii, p. 166.

38. Carson Papers, D/1507/A/17/1.

39. 84 House of Commons Debates, 5th series, col. 62, 10 July 1916.

40. Ibid., col. 1430, 24 July 1916.

41. Carson Papers, D/1507/A/17/15, Arthur Samuels to Carson, 14 June 1916.

42. Lady Carson's diary, 5 June 1916.

43. Ronald McNeill, *Ulster's Stand for Freedom* (London, 1922), p. 246.

44. Ibid., p. 249.

45. Lloyd George Papers, D/14/2/22, 10 June 1916.

46. Bonar Law Papers, 53/3/1, 14 June 1916.

47. Carson Papers, D/1507/A/17/17, 15 June 1916.

48. Ibid., D/1507/A/18/13 and 23, 11 and 17 July 1916.

49. Jackson, *Home Rule: An Irish History, 1800–2000*, p. 165.

50. Lloyd George Papers, D/14/3/21.

51. Asquith Papers, 16, fol. 207.

52. Bonar Law Papers, 63/C/8.

53. 22 House of Lords Debates, 5th series, col. 507.

54. Lady Carson's diary, 7 July 1916.

55. Carson Papers, D/1507/A/18/7, 8 July 1916.

56. Grigg, *Lloyd George: From Peace to War, 1912–1918*, p. 352.

57. Carson Papers, D/1507/A/17/7, 3 June 1916.

58. A moving account of the battle for Thiepval is given in A. T. Q. Stewart, *The Ulster Crisis: Resistance to Home Rule, 1912–1914* (London, 1967), ch. 19.

59. Carson Papers, 1507/A/18/2, 2 July 1916.

Notes to Chapter 16: The Fall of Asquith

1. John Grigg, *Lloyd George: From Peace to War, 1912–1918* (London, 1985), p. 473n.
2. Lord Beaverbrook, *Politicians and the War, 1914–1916* (London, 1956), p. 320.
3. 84 House of Commons Debates, 5th series, col. 1236, 20 July 1916.
4. 87 House of Commons Debates, 5th series, col. 249.
5. Bonar Law Papers, 85/A/1.
6. Beaverbrook, *Politicians and the War, 1914–1916*, p. 333.
7. Lady Carson's diary, 3 December 1916.
8. Ibid., 4 December 1916.
9. Beaverbrook, *Politicians and the War, 1914–1916*, p. 297.
10. The original, in Aitken's hand, is in the Bonar Law Papers, 63/A/3.
11. Beaverbrook, *Politicians and the War, 1914–1916*, p. 354.
12. Bonar Law Papers, 53/4/24, 26 November 1916.
13. Beaverbrook, *Politicians and the War, 1914–1916*, p. 359.
14. The letter is given in full in Beaverbrook, *Politicians and the War, 1914–1916*, p. 371.
15. Bonar Law Papers, 85/A/1.
16. Bonar Law Papers, 53/4/27 1 December 1916.
17. Beaverbrook, *Politicians and the War, 1914–1916*, original reproduced opposite p. 416.
18. Ibid., p. 408.
19. Bonar Law Papers, 85/A/1.
20. Much ink has been expended on what exactly passed between Asquith and Bonar Law. It seems that Bonar Law did not explain clearly why his Unionist colleagues were advocating resignation. But in the end it did not much matter to the outcome of the crisis whether Asquith was misled or not. Robert Blake, *The Unknown Prime Minister* (London, 1955), pp. 318ff.
21. Beaverbrook, *Politicians and the War, 1914–1916*, p. 435.
22. Dawson, whose name was Robinson until 1917, then confusingly took the name Dawson, by which he is generally known. He worked with Lord Milner in South Africa and became one of Milner's 'Kindergarten'. He was twice editor of *Times*, 1912–19 and 1923–41. Fellow of All Souls College, Oxford, during the 1930s he was a member of the group favouring appeasement known as 'The All Souls Gang'.
23. *History of Times, 1912–1920* (London, 1952), p. 297.
24. Beaverbrook, *Politicians and the War, 1914–1916*, p. 446.
25. *History of Times*, p. 298.
26. There is some uncertainty as to which Unionist Ministers saw Asquith on Monday, but at least Robert Cecil and Austen Chamberlain did. Robert Blake, *The Unknown Prime Minister* (London, 1955), p. 329n.

27. Bonar Law Papers, 85/A/1.

28. The letters are given in full in Beaverbrook, *Politicians and the War, 1914–1916*, pp. 461, 464.

29. Bonar Law Papers, 117/1/31.

30. Lady Carson's diary, 3 December 1916.

31. Blake, *The Unknown Prime Minister*, p. 334.

32. Beaverbrook, *Politicians and the War, 1914–1916*, p. 484; Bonar Law Papers, 85/A/1.

33. Blake, *The Unknown Prime Minister*, p. 335.

34. Spender Papers, D/1295/17/1–4, 8 December 1916.

35. *The History of Times*, p. 246.

36. David Lloyd George, *War Memoirs* (London, 1934), p. 641.

37. Grigg, *Lloyd George: From Peace to War, 1912–1918*, p. 485.

38. Beaverbrook, *Politicians and the War, 1914–1916*, p. 537.

39. Winston Spencer Churchill, *The World Crisis*, iv (London, 1928), p. 1193.

40. Arthur J. Marder, *From the Dreadnought to Scapa Flow, The Royal Navy in the Fisher Era, 1904–1919*, iv (Oxford, 1969), p. 49.

41. Ibid., p. 102.

42. Ibid., p. 64.

43. *The Political Diaries of C. P. Scott, 1911–1928*, p. 276.

44. *Daily Express*, 9 March 1917.

45. Marder, *From the Dreadnought to Scapa Flow, The Royal Navy in the Fisher Era, 1904–1919*, iv, p. 56.

46. For example, Ian Colvin, *The Life of Lord Carson*, iii (London, 1936), ch. 24.

47. There is a full discussion of these issues in Marder, *From the Dreadnought to Scapa Flow, The Royal Navy in the Fisher Era, 1904–1919*, iv, ch. 6.

48. Marder, *From the Dreadnought to Scapa Flow, The Royal Navy in the Fisher Era, 1904–1919*, iv, p. 157.

49. PRO, CAB 23/2 125/1, appendix 1.

50. Ibid., 126/6.

51. David Lloyd George, *War Memoirs*, p. 691.

52. Lord Beaverbrook, *Men and Power, 1917–1918* (London, 1960), p. 154.

53. Ibid., p. 155.

54. Marder, *From the Dreadnought to Scapa Flow, The Royal Navy in the Fisher Era, 1904–1919*, iv, p. 162.

55. Carson Papers, D/1507/B/24/13.

56. Ibid., D/1507/B/27/5.

57. Robert Blake, ed., *The Private Papers of Douglas Haig, 1914–1919* (London, 1952), p. 229, Haig to Lady Haig, 7 May 1916.

58. Beaverbrook, *Men and Power, 1917–1918*, p. 164.

59. Marder, *From the Dreadnought to Scapa Flow, The Royal Navy in the Fisher Era, 1904–1919*, iv, p. 206.
60. Robert Blake, ed., *The Private Papers of Douglas Haig, 1914–1919*, p. 255.
61. Lloyd George Papers, F/6/2/35.
62. Ibid., F/6/2/36.
63. Ibid., F/6/2/37.
64. Beaverbrook, *Men and Power, 1917–1918*, p. 175.
65. Lady Carson's diary, 1 January 1918.
66. Beaverbrook, *Politicians and the War, 1914–1916*, p. 180.
67. H. Montgomery Hyde, *Carson* (London, 1953), p. 489.
68. Alvin Jackson, *Sir Edward Carson*, p. 50.
69. Beaverbrook, *Politicians and the War, 1914–1916*, pp. 538–39.

Notes to Chapter 17: Final Attempt

1. John Grigg, *Lloyd George: War Leader, 1916–1918* (London, 2002), p. 119.
2. Burton J. Hendrick, *The Life and Letters of Walter H. Page* (London, 1922), ii, p. 252.
3. *The Political Diaries of C. P. Scott*, 21 April 1917, p. 277.
4. 91 House of Commons Debates, 5th series, col. 442, 7 March 1917.
5. Ibid., col. 458.
6. Ibid., col. 481.
7. Carson Papers, D/1507/A/22/1.
8. Lloyd George Papers, F/179/6/1, 16 May 1916.
9. A. J. P. Taylor, *English History, 1914–1945* (Oxford, 1965), p. 83.
10. Grigg, *Lloyd George: War Leader, 1916–1918*, p. 120.
11. 93 House of Commons Debates, 5th series, col. 1995.
12. Ronald McNeill, *Ulster's Stand for Union* (London, 1922), p. 257.
13. H. Montgomery Hyde, *Carson* (London, 1953), p. 428.
14. Lloyd George Papers, F/6/3/3.
15. 93 House of Commons Debates, 5th series, col. 2473.
16. Hyde, *Carson*, p. 429.
17. 103 House of Commons Debates, 5th series, col. 1992, 6 March 1918.
18. Bonar Law Papers, 83/2/9.
19. 105 House of Commons Debates, 5th series, col. 318.
20. Ian Colvin, *The Life of Lord Carson*, iii (London, 1936), p. 346.
21. Lloyd George Papers, F/45/9/16, 9 May 1918.
22. 107 House of Commons Debates, 5th series, col. 923, 25 June 1918.
23. Lady Carson's diary, 27 March 1918.
24. Ibid., 1 February 1918.

25. Spender Papers, D/1295/17/1–4, 7 February 1918. Hyde, *Carson*, p. 383, places this incident in 1914, but his source must be Lady Spender's letter.

26. Lloyd George Papers, F/16/7/29, 11 October 1918.

27. 150 House of Commons Debates, 5th series, col. 1270, 16 February 1922.

28. Spender Papers, D/1295/17/1–4, 21 January 1918.

29. Londonderry Papers, D/2846/1/1/151, 13 May 1918.

30. Spender Papers, D/1295/17/1–4, 23 January and 16 May 1918.

31. Ibid., 29 May 1918.

32. Lady Carson's diary, 10 February 1918.

33. Ibid., 23 September 1918.

34. Ibid., 11,12 February 1918.

35. Ibid., 28 December 1918.

36. Carson Papers, D/1507/A/29/37.

37. Hyde, *Carson*, p. 438.

38. Londonderry Papers, D/2846/1/1/155, 22 January 1919.

39. Hyde, *Carson*, p. 438n. F. E. Smith became Lord Chancellor as the Earl of Birkenhead.

40. PRO, CAB 23/18, C14 (19), 15 December 1919.

41. 127 House of Commons Debates, 5th series, col. 990, 29 March 1920.

42. Carson Papers, D/1507/1/A/33/43, February 1920.

43. *Belfast News-Letter*, 13 July 1920.

44. Ibid., 14 July 1919.

45. PRO, CAB 23/22, conclusions of conferences of Ministers, 2 and 8 September 1920.

46. Kevin Matthews, *Fatal Influence: The Impact of Ireland on British Politics, 1920–1925* (Dublin, 2004), p. 80.

47. Beaverbrook, *Men and Power* (London, 1960), p. 184.

48. Hyde, *Carson*, p. 485.

49. Colvin, *The Life of Lord Carson*, iii, p. 436.

50. Frances Stevenson's diary, 14 November 1921, quoted in Beaverbrook, *The Decline and Fall of Lloyd George*, p. 118.

51. Craig Papers, T/3775/2/17, 29 May 1921.

52. *Belfast News-Letter*, 5 February 1921.

53. Matthews, *Fatal Influence: The Impact of Ireland on British Politics, 1920–1925*, p. 34.

54. Colvin, *The Life of Lord Carson*, iii, p. 403; Hyde, *Carson*, p. 459.

55. When Craig met Michael Collins in 1922, Lady Carson recorded in her diary for 20 January 1922 that 'Edward didn't like it much and said he would never have been a party to it, nor would he have met Collins'.

56. Carson to Craig, 16 June 1921, quoted in Hyde, *Carson*, p. 458.

57. *Times*, 7 September 1921.

58. Longford, *Peace by Ordeal*, p. 246. There can have been few precedents for a 'treaty' like this one between a sovereign and his subjects.

59. Spender Papers, D/1633/2/26, Lady Spender's diary, 16 December 1921, quoted Matthews, *Fatal Influence: The Impact of Ireland on British Politics, 1920–1925*, p. 58.

60. Balfour Papers, Add. 49836/188, note of interview with Carson 12 July 1928.

61. 149 House of Commons Debates, 5th series, col. 197, 15 December 1921.

62. 48 House of Lords Debates, 5th series, col. 36, 14 December 1921.

63. Ibid., col. 204, 16 December 1921.

64. Bonar Law Papers, 107/1/33, 1 June 1921.

65. *Belfast News-Letter*, 23 October 1935.

66. *Times*, 23 October 1935.

67. Spender Papers, D/1633/2/26, Lady Spender's diary, 25 June 1923, quoted Matthews, *Fatal Influence*, p. 1.

Bibliography

PRIMARY SOURCES

Belfast, Public Record Office of Northern Ireland

There are large gaps in the Carson papers at the Public Record Office in Belfast. It seems that the missing papers were destroyed in an air raid during the Second World War. Unfortunately, the missing papers include most of the correspondence belonging to Carson (that is, written to him by others) during the Ulster crisis. In many cases, therefore, the correspondence available to researchers is one-sided and consists only of Carson's letters and memoranda to be found in the collections of papers of others.

Carson papers

Craig papers

Crawford papers

Hall papers

Hyde papers

Londonderry papers

O'Neill papers

Spender papers

Ulster Unionist Council papers

Cambridge, Churchill Archives Centre

Churchill papers

McKenna papers

Dublin, National Library of Ireland

Redmond papers

London, British Library

Balfour papers

London, House of Lords Record Office

Bonar Law papers
Lloyd George papers
Strachey papers

London, Public Record Office

As well as the Cabinet minutes and related papers, the PRO houses those of the Chief Secretary's papers from Dublin which survived the Irish Civil War of 1922.

Oxford, Bodleian Library

Asquith papers
Milner papers

SECONDARY SOURCES

There are two substantial biographies: *The Life of Lord Carson* in three volumes, the first by Edward Marjoribanks (1932), and the second and third by Ian Colvin (1934 and 1936) (Victor Gollancz, London); and *Carson* by H. Montgomery Hyde (Heinemann, London, 1953). The authors were all committed Unionists and the books were written in a spirit of uncritical piety. Although valuable sources, neither can really be considered an objective assessment of Carson or his policies. Marjoribanks and, to a lesser extent Colvin derived most of their information from Carson himself, not only from his papers, many of which were destroyed in an air raid in the Second World War, but also from discussion with him. It was an advantage for the writers to be able to hear things at first hand; but their biography must be treated with caution, because much of what is put forward as fact is Carson's recollection many years after the event. Their books have an autobiographical slant, with the risk of self-justification that that implies.

There was a curious footnote to Hyde's book. He was closely identified with Ulster Unionism. The son of a Belfast man, he acted as private secretary to the Marquess of Londonderry in the 1930s, and sat as a Unionist MP for North Belfast between 1950 and 1959. When his book was reissued in 1974, he wrote in a new introduction that unfortunately things had not worked out in Northern Ireland as Carson had hoped. He made a stinging criticism of the Unionist administration of the province. He wrote that Catholics had been treated as second-class citizens according to a gospel of religious apartheid; and he commented, somewhat less than fairly to the report, that the report of the Cameron Commission on the civil rights disturbances of 1968 was a devastating condemnation of the policy of successive Unionist governments at Stormont. But he made no alteration to the text of his book.

There are several shorter books and essays. A. T. Q. Stewart's *Edward Carson* (Gill and Macmillan, Dublin, 1981) is a graceful reworking of earlier writings with some reflections of his own. Alvin Jackson' s brief essay, *Sir Edward Carson*, Historical Association of Ireland (1993), gives a highly original view of aspects of Carson's career; and there are interesting essays by R. B. McDowell, 'Sir Edward Carson', in *The Shaping of Modern Ireland*, ed. Conor Cruise O'Brien (Routledge & Keegan Paul, London, 1960); J. C. Beckett, 'Carson: Unionist and Rebel', in his *Confrontations: Studies in Irish History* (Faber, London, 1972); Andrew Gailey, 'King Carson: An Essay on the Invention of Leadership', Irish Historical Studies (1996); and Owen Dudley Edwards, 'Carson as Advocate: Marjoribanks and Wilde', in *From the United Irishmen to Twentieth-Century Unionism: A Festschrift for A. T. Q. Stewart*, ed. Sabine Wichert (Four Courts Press, Dublin, 2004).

In addition there is a number of celebratory accounts written in Carson's lifetime, designed to be read exclusively by Loyalists. St John Ervine wrote an early and perversely critical portrait in *Sir Edward Carson and the Ulster Movement* (Maunsel, Dublin, 1915) which he forswore in his later and more substantial biography of James Craig.

Other Books and Articles

Adams, R. J. Q., *Bonar Law* (John Murray, London, 1999).

Asquith, H. H., *Fifty Years of Parliament* (Cassell, London, 1926).

—, *Letters to Venetia Stanley*, ed. Michael and Eleanor Brock (Oxford University Press, Oxford, 1985).

—, *Memories and Reflections, 1852–1927* (Cassell, London, 1928).

Beaverbrook, Lord, *Men and Power, 1917–1918* (Collins, London, 1960).

—, *Politicians and the War, 1914–1916* (Hutchinson, London, 1956).

Beckett, J. C., *The Making of Modern Ireland, 1603–1923* (Faber, London, 1966).

Bennett, Rodney, *The Archer-Shees against the Admiralty* (Robert Hale, London, 1973).

Birkenhead, Earl of, *Contemporary Personalities* (Cassell, London, 1924).

Blake, Robert, ed., *The Private Papers of Douglas Haig, 1914–1919* (Eyre & Spottiswoode, London, 1952).

Blake, Robert, *The Unknown Prime Minister: The Life and Times of Andrew Bonar Law, 1858–1923* (Eyre & Spottiswoode, London, 1955).

Blunt, Wilfrid Scawen, *The Land War in Ireland* (Stephen Swift, London, 1912).

Bonham Carter, Violet, *Lantern Slides: The Diaries and Letters of Violet Bonham Carter, 1904–1914*, ed. Mark Bonham Carter and Mark Pottle (Weidenfeld & Nicolson, London, 1996).

Bowman, John, *De Valera and the Ulster Question, 1917–1973* (Oxford University Press, Oxford, 1982).

Buckland, Patrick. *Irish Unionism*, i, *The Anglo-Irish and the New Ireland*; ii, *Ulster Unionism and the Origins of Northern Ireland* (Gill & Macmillan, Dublin, 1972, 1973).

—, *James Craig: Lord Craigavon* (Gill & Macmillan, Dublin, 1980).

Callanan, Frank, *T. M. Healy* (Cork University Press, Cork, 1996).

Callwell, Sir C. E., *Field Marshal Sir Henry Wilson: His Life and Diaries* (Cassell, London, 1927).

Chamberlain, Austen, *Politics from the Inside: an Epistolary Chronicle, 1906–1914* (Cassell, London, 1936).

Churchill, Winston Spencer, *Great Contemporaries* (Thornton Butterworth, London, 1937).

—, *The World Crisis* (Thornton Butterworth, London, 1928).

Cooke, A. B. and Vincent, John, *The Governing Passion: Cabinet Government and Party Politics in Britain, 1885–86* (Harvester Press, Brighton, 1974).

Crawford, F. H., *Guns for Ulster* (Graham & Heslip, Belfast, 1947).

Crozier, F. P., *Ireland for Ever* (Jonathan Cape, London, 1932).

Curtis, Edmund and McDowell, R. B., *Irish Historical Documents, 1172–1922* (Methuen, London, 1943).

Curtis, L. P., *Coercion and Conciliation in Ireland, 1880–1892: A Study in Conservative Unionism* (Princeton University Press, Princeton, 1963).

Dangerfield, George, *The Strange Death of Liberal England* (Harrison Smith and Robert Haas, New York, 1935).

Dicey, Albert Venn, *England's Case against Home Rule* (John Murray, London, 1886).

—, *Fool's Paradise: Being a Constitutionalist's Criticism of the Home Rule Bill of 1912* (John Murray, London, 1913).

—, *Leap in the Dark: A Criticism of the Principles of Home Rule as Illustrated by the Bill of 1893* (John Murray, London, 1911).

Donaldson, Frances, *The Marconi Scandal* (Rupert Hart-Davis, London, 1962).

Dugdale, Blanche, *Arthur James Balfour* (Hutchinson, London, 1936).

Ellman, Richard, *Oscar Wilde* (Hamish Hamilton, London, 1987).

English, Richard, *Armed Struggle: The History of the IRA* (Macmillan, London, 2003).

Ensor, R. C. K., *England, 1870–1914* (Oxford University Press, Oxford, 1936).

Ervine, St John, *Craigavon, Ulsterman* (Allen & Unwin, London, 1949).

Fergusson, Sir James, *The Curragh Incident* (Faber and Faber, London, 1964).

Gerard, James W., *My Four Years in Germany* (Hodder and Stoughton, London, 1917).

Gilbert, Sir Martin, *Winston S. Churchill*, vi (Heinemann, London, 1971).

Gilmour, David, *The Long Recessional: The Imperial Life of Rudyard Kipling* (John Murray, London, 2002).

Gleichen, Lord Edward, *A Guardsman's Memories* (Blackwood, London, 1932).

Gollin, Alfred M., *A Proconsul in Politics* (Anthony Blond, London, 1964).

—, *The Observer and J. L. Garvin, 1908–1914* (Oxford University Press, Oxford, 1960).

Gough, Hubert, *Soldiering On* (Arthur Barker, London, 1954).

Grigg, John, *Lloyd George: From Peace to War, 1912–1916* (Methuen, London, 1985).

—, *Lloyd George: War Leader, 1916–1918* (Allen Lane, London, 2002).

Gwynn, Denis, *The Life of John Redmond* (Harrap, London, 1932).

Halevy, Elie, *A History of the English People in the Nineteenth Century*, vi, *The Rule of Democracy, 1905–1914* (Ernest Benn, London, 1932).

Halperin, Vladimir, *Lord Milner and the Empire* (Odhams Press, London, 1952).

Healy, Maurice, *The Old Munster Circuit* (Michael Joseph, London, 1939).

Hendrick, Burton J., *The Life and Letters of Walter H. Page* (Heinemann, London, 1922).

Holland, Merlin, *Irish Peacock and Scarlet Marquess: The Real Trial of Oscar Wilde* (Fourth Estate, London, 2003).

Hyde, H. Montgomery, *The Londonderrys: A Family Portrait* (Hamish Hamilton, London, 1979).

—, ed. *The Trials of Oscar Wilde:* Notable British Trials (William Hodge, London, 1948).

Jackson, Alvin, *Home Rule: An Irish History, 1800–2000* (Weidenfeld & Nicolson, London, 2003).

Jenkins, Roy. *Asquith* (Collins, London, 1964).

—, *Gladstone* (Macmillan, London, 1995).

Kee, Robert, *The Green Flag* (Weidenfeld & Nicolson, London, 1972).

Laffan, Michael, *The Partition of Ireland, 1911–1925* (Historical Association of Ireland, Dundalgan Press, Dundalk, 1983).

Lee, J. J., *Ireland, 1912–1985* (Cambridge University Press, Cambridge, 1989).

Lenox-Conyngham, Mina, *An Old Ulster House and the People who Lived in it* (W. Tempest, Dundalgan Press, Dundalk, 1946).

Lloyd George, David, *War Memoirs* (Ivor Nicolson & Watson, London, 1934).

Lucas, Reginald, *Colonel Saunderson MP: A Memoir* (John Murray, London, 1908).

Lucy, Henry W., *A Diary of the Home Rule Parliament, 1892–95* (Cassell, London, 1896).

Lyons, F. S. L., *Ireland Since the Famine* (Weidenfeld & Nicolson, London, 1971).

McNeill, Ronald, *Ulster's Stand for Union* (John Murray, London, 1922).

Macready, Sir Nevil, *Annals of an Active Life* (Hutchinson, London, 1924).

Mansergh, Nicholas, *The Government of Northern Ireland* (Allen & Unwin, London, 1936).

—, *The Irish Question, 1840–1921* (Allen & Unwin, London, 1975).

Marder, Arthur J., *From the Dreadnought to Scapa Flow: The Royal Navy in the Fisher Era, 1904–1919*, iii and iv (Oxford University Press 1969).

Matthews, Kevin, *Fatal Influence: The Impact of Ireland on British Politics, 1920–1925* (University College Dublin Press, Dublin, 2004).

Morley, John, *The Life of William Ewart Gladstone* (Macmillan, London, 1904).

Mosley, Nicholas, *Julian Grenfell: His Life and the Times of his Death* (Weidenfeld & Nicolson, London, 1976).

Newbolt, Henry, *The Official History of the War*, v, *Naval Operations* (Longmans, London, 1931).

Nicolson, Harold, *King George the Fifth: His Life and Reign* (Constable, London, 1952).

Pakenham, Frank (Earl of Longford), *Peace by Ordeal* (Jonathan Cape, London, 1935).

Rait, Robert S. ed. *Memorials of Albert Venn Dicey* (Macmillan, London, 1925).

Rhodes James, Robert, *Churchill: A Study in Failure, 1900–1939* (Weidenfeld & Nicolson, London, 1970).

—, *Lord Randolph Churchill* (Weidenfeld & Nicolson, London, 1959).

Roberts, Andrew, *Salisbury: Victorian Titan* (Weidenfeld & Nicolson, London, 1999).

Savage, D. C., 'The Origins of the Ulster Unionist Party, 1885–86' *Irish Historical Studies* 12 (1961).

Simon, Viscount J. A., *Retrospect: The Memoirs of Viscount Simon* (Hutchinson, London, 1952).

Stewart, A. T. Q., *The Narrow Ground: Aspects of Ulster, 1609–1969* (Faber and Faber, London, 1977).

—, *The Ulster Crisis: Resistance to Home Rule, 1912–1914* (Faber and Faber, London, 1967).

Taylor, A. J. P., *English History, 1914–1945* (Oxford University Press, Oxford, 1965).

Temple, Sir Richard, *Letters and Sketches from the House of Commons* (John Murray, London, 1912).

The History of the Times, 1912–1920 (The Times, London, 1952)

Walker-Smith, Derek, *Lord Reading and his Cases* (Chapman & Hall, London, 1934).

Williams, Trevor ed. *The Political Diaries of C. P. Scott, 1911–1928* (Collins, London, 1970).

Woodward, E. L., *The Age of Reform, 1815–1870* (Oxford University Press, Oxford, 1938).

Young, Kenneth, *Arthur James Balfour* (G. Bell, London, 1963).

Index